Glory

By:
Jonathan

Glory
Book Seven of the Series *The Nine*
May 22, 2018, *First Edition*

Copyright © 2018

Cover Photo Credit: Joshua Earle

All rights reserved. This book or any portion thereof may not be reproduced or used in any manner whatsoever without the express written permission of the publisher except for the use of brief quotations in a book review or scholarly journal.

ISBN-13: 978-1-942967-35-4

KreativeMinds Publishing
www.kreativeminds.net

Ordering Information:

Special discounts are available on quantity purchases by corporations, associations, educators, and others. For details, contact the publisher at the email address below.

U.S. trade bookstores and wholesalers: Please use the email address below.
email: publishing@kreativeminds.net

To My Redeemer, through whom all things are possible.

Always,
Jonathan

Introduction

This is the fourth book of my journals, the words of the experiences shown to me by God. This book covers a period of time from September 14, 2014, through February 3, 2015. This was the point along my journey where the Lord would begin speaking to me with directives, rather than just lessons. It would be in these moments where the Lord would begin revealing how the end will come to pass and new beginnings will form. It will be a time of great triumph for His believers, but also a time of great sadness and mourning for the brothers and sisters who have fallen behind. And though it may seem like a tragic ending to an indescribable journey of strength and Love, it is important to see the way the Lord paints the picture of His return. For it is in this manner that hope is imparted, Love is shown, and faith is found. These will be the days of new beginnings, when Heaven and Earth will become one. It will be a time of great awe and splendor. It is said that no one will know the day or hour of Christ's return. This I truly believe. For all that shall be revealed will only be revealed through hindsight. These words are the foresight to know that hindsight will one day be too late. For now, these words must take root: The Messiah is coming.

Always,

Jonathan

Wonders (Part 4)

There is a rubber-band-like effect in the way that God reveals all that He wishes to be known. There is a portion of truth that is offered directly in the moment of His words. But, there is also a moment when the words previously offered unveil a bouquet of knowledge through everything that is eventually foretold. In understanding all that He has shown me and wishes me to see, it has been of utmost importance that I journal all that he has shared so that all He wishes to be revealed will not have been lost. In the beginning, I was not sure why I was being called to write down all that was being shared. It would take just over three years to fully understand the reason – and in that, only partially understand "why me" and where His words were leading.

Throughout the first portions of Wonders – which were divided over the previous three books – it has been revealed how God was sharing with me just how all of the events in my life have fallen upon a Divine timeline – a timeline I would not come to understand until December of 2014. Ultimately, it would take until February 3, 2015, for a robust understanding of the markers to fully fall into view. The markers during my walk on Earth were carefully architected according to His Divine plan, and could only begin to be unveiled to my eyes as the journey ensued and the strength of my Spirit grew.

In the beginning, I was born upon this Earth on May 9, 1981. This was the first date of an earthly celebration – a celebration of God's miraculous Love. At age eight, on December 24, 1989, I was baptized. This was the first date of Spiritual celebration – a formal demonstration of my Love for Him. At age twenty-two, I fell in Love with my soulmate. This was the date that a celebration of Love began. At age twenty-three, the formal celebration of that Love was presented for the world to see on May 25, 2003 – the date of our wedding ceremony. At age twenty-seven, it all came to an end. May 25, 2008, was the date of our last anniversary and the last celebration of Love I would experience before my seven years of earthly Love would come to an end. Just days prior to my thirtieth birthday on May 9, 2011, was the point in time that the lights went out, a dense blackness suffocated my eyes, and my spiritual rebirth began. November 25, 2011, would mark the date I asked the Lord for help. But never did I have reason to ever think about how each of these dates could be part of a greater story being unveiled. There are also at least two more dates that are important – dates that I cannot yet show. For those dates are to be unveiled in Book III – Kingdom, for all of the world to know.

For as it is to be revealed in this book, and forever shall be known, all of the markers placed upon my life are markers of His Divine timeline, a prophecy long foretold. In effect, the events of my life on Earth are a form of a biological key,

Wonders (Part 4)

bound by truth, wrapped up and hidden from everyone's eyes until the day the Lord desired it all to be revealed. The dates surrounding my walk upon this Earth should be seen as a celebration of Love – a Love greater than just Love for mankind. It is a Love of our Father, His daughter, and if so I am deemed worthy, my bride-to-be. It is a Love of our brothers and sisters, the souls trapped in the man. It is a Love eternal, before all others, a Love that travels across the infinite span.

There is a calendar set forth in the Book of Daniel as well as the Book of Revelation, which foretell the events that will one day be revealed through the prophecy of the return of the Messiah and two Sons of Man. The two are the olive branches, the lampstands written about in Revelation 11:4. They are here to proclaim that the Messiah is coming, and rejuvenate the Word. They are to prepare the way for His Grand Return into what has become a spiritually desolate and lonely world. While there has never been a time when more souls on Earth say they proclaim the Word, there has also never been a more spiritually empty time when so many of these souls falsely believe they know all there is to know. For as it will come to pass, few will be chosen, for so many of the lost claim they believe. For there is only one way – through the Messiah – that most will never believe when they see.

On December 9, 2014, I was taken to the heavens where the Angel of the Lord began to reveal His specific timeline in definitive form. The timeline – His timeline – is the calendar set forth in the Book of Daniel as well as in John's Book of Revelation. The markers placed upon my soul were done so in such a way that I would one day come to understand the precise purpose and timing of His plan.

Throughout my life, I never once questioned if God had Divine intentions for me. That was abundantly clear. But the reason and the destination were always unclear. And as His timeline began to be revealed on December 9, 2014, it would take until February 3, 2015, for the gravity of the meaning to be fully unveiled. The divine script, penned by His hand – His story to be told – begins with a man, his first revelation – the beginning – when he learned he was "one of two." For as these words were already written long before I was ever born, I am one of the two foretold, sent here to prepare the way for the Messiah's Grand Return.

At first, it may seem a bit much to take in. Most people believe the period of the End of Days is drawing near, but it will prove difficult for anyone to believe that someone they once knew – or even someone they have never known – could possibly be imparted the words set forth in the books from over two thousand years ago. Even more impossible is that the manner of the revealing will not be seen as the way society expects it might unfold. But, in the midst of mankind's struggles, God's voice shall ring clear. For it was through His Voice two brothers on a spiritual journey would become One, and through the One, reveal Him.

It is certain that God's timing is immaculate, and it would be foolish to think that His timing and messages have been anything short of Divine. His Words have been placed into the mechanics of this generation's machine, delivered in a manner that this generation could understand, through the methods this generation would one day know. There is a reason that I mentioned throughout my writing how everything that has been revealed to me may just be a divinely architected script to help me find my way back home. There is a portion of this experience that has blended my viewpoint of seeing everyone as individuals with everyone as one. And while it is known that this viewpoint has been written about in the Bible, it is humbling more than words can express to experience it first hand. So, if for no other reason, I would ask that the reader see the world through these eyes, see the world as I have been allowed to absorb it, see the ways that God has spoken to me and how He revealed His plan. These Words in the Books of Nine are the 1260 days of prophecy.

The Written (cont'd)

And so it was, on February 3, 2013, "The Written" portion of my journals began. During this time I did not understand anything more than a calling to write while the Lord had taken me by the hand. It would take two years of consistently receiving the specific experiences that God willed for me to write down in order for His messages to begin to take their final form. Though the experiences have taken over three years to write, the breadth of "The Written" preface sections in books IV, V, VI, and VII were written on February 3rd.

Over the preceding weeks, I had been working on the drafts of the sections of "Wonders" and "The Written" as time allowed. Barring the occasional message from God that I of course had to journal, everything else in Books IV – VII was complete. And though it may be difficult for the reader to accept how His grand revelations continue to occur, this final entry in "The Written" is one great and final example.

This portion of "The Written" draws the conclusion to the four divisions of the experiences that God has shared with me over the last three-plus years. As I write this final section of "The Written" – the last section of the experiences He has intended for me to write down as this book takes its final form –

Glory

it is important to note that today is February 3, 2015, specifically two years to the day the journal entries to "The Written" began, and a day that marks the conclusion of this portion of His intended words. But not until just moments ago did I realize that today would be the final installment of the words He desired to be revealed through me.

For many reasons, today has been extremely special in my personal relationship with God. Today holds another divine marker in the greater story being told. But it was not until earlier this evening that I opened up the first section of "The Written" from Book IV – Rebirth I, that I understood the significance of today's grand conclusion. When I flipped over to the first entry of "The Written," my intention was to read how each of the sections was worded in order to see how best to form this final section. As I read through the very first introduction of "The Written" and reached its end, I saw the date of the very first entry that began the part of the journey – the portion where I knew – I was specifically called to write. It was only then that I noticed that the entry was exactly two years ago today.

The recognition of the two-year mark was more than just interesting. For in one of my most recent experiences in the heavens – the last extremely detailed experience I have had leading up to today – I was instructed by an angel to tell an elder angel that "I was ready to climb the mountain." The angel responded to me, "Very good. Your next step is for two years…" I lost harmony in the moment due to my excitement of hearing a precise directive. Unfortunately, I had zero un-

The Written (cont'd)

derstanding of what the two years were in reference to other than it was my "next step." Up until moments ago, I had thought that the "next step" must be referring to the duration of the next portion of the upcoming journey…and, truthfully, it still may be. But, in communion and receipt of the messages that God has shared with me today, the divine significance I could never have predicted, the spiritual events that will be revealed near the conclusion of Book III – Kingdom, and most importantly, the final entry and revelation that appears in this book, the directive could not be any clearer.

For two years, I have diligently carried His specific message through for this generation and generations to come. And though mankind will face the end of a harvest cycle in the time forthcoming, these words must be completed and compiled for those left behind when the time has come. So, as I had no reason to know February 3rd was the date "The Written" began until moments ago, it is easy to see now how he always desired for it to draw to an end.

For the reader, this is just one example of how His words are Living. His message is in constant motion. His words mean many things for different reasons at different points along the journey. They are not to be translated or modernized in any way. These words are meant to be as they are, so that they shall be. So as this portion of the "The Written" began in written form on September 14, 2014, this section is being introduced through these words on the very same day that the last entry draws the journal entries to an end. Thus, this is the circle, a demonstration of how the snake eats its tail, a divine

Glory

explanation of how the beginning and the end are always One, as they always were, and as they always will be. Glory be unto Him.

...

September 14, 2014

In this morning's experience in the heavens, Bryan appeared to me. The setting was a close proximity of my apartment in Fort Lauderdale. Bryan began talking to me about having a family stay at my house when he came over. I thought about his words and was confused. At this point, I was still unclear of the heaven and Earth divide in the moment. I was still trying to identify my surroundings.

As I thought about Bryan's words, I realized I did not even recall him coming over to my house and felt extremely confident that even if he did manage to arrive without me being aware, there was no possibility there were others with him. But as he spoke, I realized he was telling the truth. I went ahead and cleaned up and got dressed. I walked into the living room all chipper. Indeed Bryan had told me the truth. In my living room were two female angels that had arrived with him. I asked them if they needed anything. One of the angels wanted to take a shower, so I led her to my bathroom. We each made a couple of suggestive jokes about showering and then I left her alone. I came back with a towel, careful to avert my eyes and respect her privacy when I handed it to her. While

The Written (cont'd)

we made playful jokes earlier, we each were very comfortable and trusting in each other. The jokes should be seen more as a playful recognition of the divide of body and spirit. After she dried off, we went outside on the patio and talked for a bit. The other angel with her mentioned how none of the other residents leave pillows out on their furniture because of the wind. Though she had a point, I remained headstrong in keeping my furniture nicely appointed. While we were sitting outside, I noticed a hat that did not resemble anything earthly and decided to put it on. Eventually I lost harmony and returned to my body.

September 15, 2014

During meditation today I heard a voice say, "Let's take a trip – just you and me – to New Zealand." Then I awoke.

September 16, 2014

This morning's experience was one of my most memorable to date. After a seemingly disjointed spiritual encounter while my soul found balance, I stood before a man that resembled Enoch. I thought for sure it was Enoch, but I did not ask him. There were shadows all around me, light was cast only upon him. He said, "Now consider this: your Father [equals/is...there was no word, only what was implied] the universe." He then shared with me a vision that was comprised of "the local planetary system," which is what is classified on Earth as a solar system,. I understood the image to be a visual illustration of the word "universe." That was all that was said. Seven words. But they were powerful. He essentially said, "Your Father is the universe, which birthed you." It sounds so simple in words, but it is drenched in meaning. The weight of being told my Father is everything further expands my perspective in understanding just how much God Is everything. It was emphasized that "My Father" was the universe meaning my direct line of communication to Him is through everyone and everything.

September 18, 2014

Today I was awakened in the night at 4:00 a.m. to my heart pumping with such huge force. It was not anything unnatural, or anything that I had not experienced before. It was not even biological. What I was experiencing was the pulsing of the energy of the moon upon my soul. The body is in full alignment between the hours of 2:00 a.m. and 4:00 a.m. This is when communication with God is the easiest. There are other nuances, like the phases of the moon (half moon is best), but for the most part, these are the times the most intimate times with our creator can occur.

As I felt my body finding alignment, I concentrated on being able to interact with Lisa's spirit (a girl I had met a few days prior). I wanted to share with her spirit "the way" while

The Written (cont'd)

her earthly body was at rest. During this time, my soul did find communion with hers. I am not sure how much she will know happened when she awakes – and I will not ask her when I see her again – but I wanted to let her soul know that God was protecting her.

September 21, 2014

Today on Earth I met my daughter where her mother lives and took her to see my alma mater's football team play. When we returned to the hotel, we each got in separate beds, said our prayers, and went to sleep. Midway though the night I was awakened by a clicking on the wall in front of me. I noticed that the tapping was something that was not audible, but rather a spiritual tapping. As I stared at the wall in front of me, a demon came racing through the wall and tackled my soul on my bed.

I wrestled with it as it fought me as hard as it could. The demon identified itself as Abbadon (pronounced ABAYDUN). It wanted to strangle me and take my soul. I was initially caught off guard and therefore did not have the reaction to call upon God's strength to free me. Abbadon forced a vision upon me of the Georgia Guide Stones. I had never been to the stones, but they were only a little over an hour away from the hotel I was in. I saw the stones and lines of text in the vision. Abbadon cut me off from my daughter as well.

Glory

I kept trying to tell Georgia to wake up because I knew she was being attacked while in the vision with me. I kept saying, "Georgia!" but she could not hear me. I tried willing her to wake up from my soul as well. Abbadon forced me to read the lines on the guide stones. As I read the words, it revealed that math was the language being used – the only real language that exists. Every line contained a code that only those with knowledge of sacred geometry could unravel. And though I was not shown the meaning, there was something specific to how "fifteen degrees" was represented by specific words or combinations of letters. I eventually was able to will my soul back into my body and out of the grasp of Abbadon. I turned to see my daughter who was still sound asleep. She was none-the-wiser to all that I had just experienced.

Before I fell back asleep, I prayed to God, and then spoke directly to the evil spirit and let it know that I would invoke the hand of God if it did not leave me alone. There was a click that came from the wall – a tapping like I heard before the demon appeared. I understood it to be a submissive acknowledgement of my warning. Before I was able to fall back asleep, Abbadon shared with me the name "George Eval [something that I could not understand that began with the letter T]" as part of the spirit I saw. There was an emphasis on Eval (pronounced EVAHL). Perhaps it was saying that the spirit was "evil" or maybe it was revealing more of the mysteries to the guide stones. Regardless, it understood my warning and never returned.

The Written (cont'd)

Following that terrible encounter, I was taken to the heavens where an angel and I spoke about a financial decision I needed advice with. After we talked about the circumstances, I was taken in the company of three other angels to a restaurant. One angel was male, the other two female. The male angel wanted to treat everyone to the dinner and had already made reservations at the restaurant for us. Another male angel appeared while we were having dinner and paid me a couple of compliments on my spiritual journey so far.

September 22, 2014

This morning's travels to the heavens were not as clear as I would have hoped for. The first experience began with me receiving a punch card for grief counseling. It had three holes punched in it for different services I was supposed to receive.

Another experience involved an angel telling me something about being able to save two hundred thousand out of three hundred thousand. When I journaled the experience, I first wrote it down indicating money, but I can now see that the numbers may relate to something broader – like in the experience when the angels helped me understand the numbers involving 1% of the population.

When I returned to the heavens, I was hanging out with a male angel. We talked about all of his success and stories about women. He had still not settled down. He seemed more pressed to talk about how he could help me. We hiked through the mountains and later went to a football game. The hiking we did together. The football game just happened out of coincidence. I was meeting other angels at the game and since we were both heading there, we just went from our hike straight to the game.

Returning once again to the heavens, I found myself in the company of the souls of many people I knew from Nashville. They were all grieving over the loss of a friend. I did not know Rob all that well, but his death on Earth was an unexpected and tragic accident. I spent a while in the heavens consoling their souls. I eventually returned to my body.

On my final trip to the heavens this morning, I stood before a television. On the news was a picture of Lindsey and Chris (the guy she was dating at the end of Gravity Calling). A news anchor was reporting a headline about a situation regarding the two of them. And while the incident was clearly detailed in the experience, I think it is best that the details are not mentioned here, for they are unimportant to this story. The importance was that a message was shared. The content was specific to helping me understand the journey I am on. But in the moment, I wanted to know more, though I was not allowed to hear anything else.

As it would turn out, weeks later I would talk to an old friend from Nashville. We were catching up and talking about how to help one of our mutual friends going through a tough time in his life. In the midst of the conversation, this friend brought up – completely unprompted and on his own – the details of a situation that Chris had been going through and

The Written (cont'd)

the tough times that had followed. That is when I learned that the details of the news report were actually true – in all of its specificity and all of its clarity. The details of the headline were as clearly spelled out as a news headline of current events today. I do not know if Lindsey was involved or not – only the incident from Chris's experience. It is possible she was there so I would recognize Chris in the picture. Either way, it was another case of forewarning about earthly events while in the heavens.

September 24, 2014

In the heavens, a brunette angel was telling me how much her male counterpart would be excited in how "overvalued" a particular piece of property was in a shopping center before us. I pondered the thought, trying to understand her logic since it seemed backwards to me. Meanwhile, a blonde angel decided to invite me to Turkey for their "regular trip." I asked my angelic guide if he thought I could travel to fifty countries in two years. I told him I wanted to accept a new challenge for myself. I did not receive a response…just a glare. His austere gaze caused me to lose harmony and return to my body.

When I returned to the heavens, I was in a tall, cylindrical building that represented something similar to a "publisher" in the music industry. I was either a worker or a helper to the processes that were occurring inside. Nothing was unusual. It seemed like a normal work environment. The angel that reminds me of a girl I know named Marissa was accompanying me (blond hair, blue eyes, svelte, pretty). As we were being led to a different part of the building by a male angel, I was asked a question. Somewhere in the dialogue with the male angel, I was shown a phrase that I had written on a white sheet of paper. This short phrase somehow represented all I had ever written, summed up in a few short words. I looked at the paper and acknowledged that I had written it.

The female angel became nervous for me when I acknowledged my writing. Immediately, the male angel led us away from everyone and called "his boss." He asked that she come down immediately. I was unsure what was going on. The angel seemed to notice my confusion so he began giving me praises for my writing. I was a little timid because I did not want anyone else to read it. Everything I had written was personal, and I thought having others read it would demonstrate ego. To him though, it did not matter. All I was seeming to understand in the moment was that I was in a "publisher's house" and I was suddenly being viewed as a "producer" versus "a nameless contributor."

Suddenly, the great female angel appeared. It was "the girl." All of the angels had a more human element to them rather than the untouchable blinding Love that generally permeates these experiences. The boss angel was stark. She took all three of us downstairs. She called for her assistant to start "lining things up for us." I heard as she called and spoke to "her boss" which I can only think could be one of the archangels or God Himself.

The Written (cont'd)

To her boss she said, "We need to meet. When can you? Let's do it today. Can you do it now? It is important that it is now." The person on the other end of the call agreed. I realized that whatever was going on was centered around me, but I was still confused. I knew I always wanted to be a successful writer (in the heavens... never was that a thought on Earth), but I assumed it would just be me working among others who had already become successful since it is such a controlled landscape. The woman looked at me and said, "I'm not sure if you know what is about to happen, but you have [arrived], and you are about to have our full support on the road to success. You will likely be placed in the spotlight from the fame, but do not let that bother you. Get excited."

She then led us in to meet with her boss – an angel of the Lord. Right before we reached the door, I excused myself to go to the restroom. I noticed the angel that reminded me of Marissa was following me (trying to be sneaky about it though). Eventually, I managed to flip roles and follow her as she tried to be stealthy about her actions. I eventually managed to pin her back in the back of a bathroom so she would have to reveal herself. She tried to hide in a stall thinking that it was a bad set of circumstances that caused me to catch her.

I opened the door she was hiding behind as she tried to play coy. I asked her why she was trying to sabotage the meeting. She said, "I'm sorry. I've worked so hard, I really want to be the one. You landed there without intention, almost on accident." I looked at her and said, "You know I've been doing this for my sister. I had no intentions of being chosen, but if they chose me there must be a reason. But I don't want the fame that will come with it. You know me. But in the end, either you, me, or my sister will make it. And in any case, it will cause us to succeed. So it doesn't really matter who makes it as long as someone does." The angel looked saddened but accepted it. She headed back to the group. I lost harmony in the heavens before I was able to continue into the meeting.

September 25, 2014

    This morning I traveled to and from the heavens many times, but could not seem to bring back any relevant information until the last of my travels. In one of my final voyages of the morning, I found myself standing in the middle of a series of glass windows. I noticed there was also a piece of artwork by Pervis Brown upon the glass. My attention fell upon an etched message from heaven he had placed into the glass. This message made this particular piece of art very valuable.

    I returned to my body and journaled the experience. As I began to find my opportune alignment, I felt knocking beneath my bed. It was an earthly manifestation of the spirit. As I lay there, unmoved by the knocking, I was taken to the heavens and shown an oval, dark stone with letters and words all over it. I could not discern the language or the words. It appeared to be Sanskrit, but I could not focus on the letters well enough

The Written (cont'd)

to be sure. While I was trying to read the words, I was shared very broken communication regarding a hat again.

September 27, 2014

In this morning's vision, I called to speak to my cousin Matt on the phone. God had tasked me to speak with him because he was smart enough to understand everything Bryan and I have been going through. I heard the voice of Julianna (his wife) telling me "he isn't here" and that "he has been out for a while." It seemed she was preventing him from talking to me, so I told her that he really needed to chat with me about everything. She and I had a brief spiritual conversation and the experience ended.

September 28, 2014

This morning's experience began with me playing football again. I continue to struggle with throwing the ball accurately. Apparently the angels sensed my frustration and asked me if I kicked the ball well. They seemed to think I was more of a kicker. A ball came hurdling toward me which I caught. It was thrown by the elder angel who was my guide for this experience. I caught the ball cleanly with my two hands. The ball traveled so fast that it made a sound like a small explosion when I caught it. The noise caused my senses to come into view. I looked above at the stars overhead. The angel said,

Glory

"When you kick the ball, don't you see the stars above?" I had to think about it for a minute because it was difficult to understand how high I would have to kick it to see the stars above. When I returned to my body, I could understand it was all metaphorical. But, in the moment, I took the words literally. It must have been humorous (or frustrating) to the angels. Hopefully they had a good laugh at my naiveté.

September 29, 2014

This morning, the experience in the heavens carried a theme of a heist. There were two angels that wanted my help in acquiring something. They wondered where the "V" hotel was, looking to me for answers – an answer I did not know. We all wandered in search of the V. After returning to my room, I decided to go down to the garage to retrieve something from my car. Unbeknownst to me, the elevator I stepped into arrived on the rooftop instead of taking me to the parking garage down below. I stepped off, curious about my surroundings.

The sky above was not exposed, though I understood this to be the roof level. I could see "workers" who were filthy and tired cast about the room. Old newspapers and magazine covers were strewn about. It looked like a place of degenerates who were all riding out some type of chemical high. The carpet beneath my feet was red, and the area was marked as a construction zone. As I walked through the room, heading to

The Written (cont'd)

the other side, I apologized to the people I passed. I did not speak much, but I said enough to let them know I had taken the wrong elevator. Everyone looked at me as if I was not supposed to be there. Their eyes of judgment were heavy.

I started to realize that I was not on the 39th floor of the building. Rather, I had arrived at the 1st floor of the V. The hallway opened up into a large atrium with black marble floors. The building had towering ceilings made of glass. The building was like a grand art hall. I walked forward to an escalator that would take me down to the floor below. It was perhaps a three-story ride down the escalator, which was made of an impossible shape. It contained no stairs and only artsy bends in its structure.

I walked around the hall and located a male angel that the female angels were looking for. I knew the female angels thought I would never find the place, much less find the destination before they did. I wanted to return to tell them, but when I stepped outside of the front door of the building I was chased by a man with blonde hair and sunglasses. I ran as quickly as I could and eventually lost him. But no sooner than I thought I was safe as I reached a red car on the street, than I heard footsteps behind me. The windows of the car were partially down. I jumped into the front seat and attempted to speed away from the scene, but the man was too quick. He jumped into the backseat. He had a gun and a silencer. At this point I lost harmony and returned to my body.

Glory

September 30, 2014

There were several experiences in the heavens this morning, but the one I could return with had to do with dolphins. I found myself standing in a building in the heavens. I walked outside. There was a wrap-around balcony. When I walked out, I saw red in the bay of water. It was the first of May (no year was given,) and I was staring at two dolphins in the bay. There are never dolphins in the bay, so it caused me to pay close attention. I turned my gaze to the left, and there I saw several killer whales.

As I continued looking left I saw there was a dead killer whale that was producing all of the blood I saw in the water. It was on its side in the shallow water. I could not tell what had killed it. I walked down the steps and was met by a female angel. I tried to tell her about all I had seen but she acted as if she did not believe me. In front of her was a small fish that looked like a puppy dog. I watched it play in the shallow water. I looked up and looked back down to see it too was about to die – just like the killer whale I saw.

In just those few seconds when I took my eyes off of it, something had happened. I eventually picked it up and pushed it into deeper water hoping to heal it. I knew it required oxygen and was fearful the wounds would cause it to sink and drown. I watched it take a breath and then go under water. It would then rise up and breathe. I was not sure, but it seemed

The Written (cont'd)

as if the water was going to heal it. I was still fearful it would die though.

October 1, 2014

I arrived in the heavens and found myself standing in a house that was abandoned. Stacey (my ex wife) was standing there with me. The house was grown over and had fallen apart. We reminisced about how we once thought we would buy this particular house as a fixer-upper, but we could each now see how it went to ruins. We walked around through the house. I found three coats left in one room. These were coats left from the last time we visited there. One coat had an impossible texture. It was black, had a furry collar, a poufy body, and a vinyl sheen. My "father" was with us.

The roof started leaking at one point, and Stacey went to see what caused of the leak. I spoke with other angels who were also in the house with us. Near the end of the experience, I saw my old friend Jason. He was sitting in the backseat of a car which was parked in the garage under the house. When I walked up to him, he was crying. He asked if there was any "club" or "group" he could join with me. He mentioned Mensa which caused my heart to break for him. I could see he held every bit of guilt inside of him for his actions to me in the past. I could also see his soul longed to understand the truth of the spirit, even though he usually just dismissed religious topics in earthly conversation. I held no ill feelings toward him and had forgiven him long ago. I said, "Of course," and began to tell him about the spiritual group that another one of our mutual friends (ironically with initials J.C.) was joining with me (as well as others).

October 3, 2014

Tonight's experience was brief. I was in the heavens, in a room filled with light. An angel stood before me in a white robe. The angel seemed to be Enoch again, but I did not get a great look at his face. In his hands was a sign he was using as a flashcard. He was showing me numbers. I began to try to remember the first number, but as I was reciting it, he flashed another number at me. I decided I would have an easier time trying to remember one number instead of two, so I committed the number to memory. I recited it over and over until I forced myself to return to my body to write it down – all the while reciting it over and over. The number was 802292177. I have no idea what it means. It was written in black ink upon a brownish scroll-textured sign in the angel's hands.

October 4, 2014

This morning's experience was a little hazy. It began with me standing in front of a counter. There was a girl on the other side facing me. She was shorter than I and proceeded to sit down in front of me on a stool. She pulled out a drawer as she

The Written (cont'd)

searched for something. As she did, I noticed a shelf above my head that held glasses inverted underneath it – much like a wine glass rack. As she pulled out her drawer, the shelf extended closer to my face and away from her. I could now see the shelf held bottles and glasses. One of the bottles began to fall off, but I managed to catch it. It seemed more like a B-line story while the primary storyline was held in the conversation between the girl and me. But even though I thought the conversation was the focus, the only thing we seemed to talk about was her height. We talked about how she was so much shorter than I was. I eventually returned to my body, jotted down the notes and returned back to the heavens.

In the next experience, I was standing in a diamond mine. This was not a stereotypical tunnel-like mine. This was more like an excavation site in a rocky/sandy area. The mining company was hard at work looking for any diamonds they could find. While I observed the heavy machinery, I seemed befuddled at why they used so much effort to seek out the diamonds. As I mulled over this troubling thought, I walked along an edge of where a portion of the Earth had been mined. All I had to do was run my hand along the edge where the vertical wall of Earth met the horizontal wall and I would dislodge pebble after pebble. Within the pebbles I was finding diamonds larger than anything the miners had been able to find. I was not sure if I wanted to tell them how they had been missing the most important part of their efforts. I continued to run my finger along the joint in the Earth as pebble after pebble fell out revealing an unending supply of diamonds.

Glory

    I then decided to walk to the edge of the mining site where a lake or stream gently lapped against the disheveled Earth from the mining effort. The water was clear, and I could see that it was only a few inches deep along the shoreline. There was a fine edge of shallow water before it dropped off. Again, I took notice of the number of diamonds in the water. I reached my hand in and pulled out what I realized to be the largest diamond ever discovered on Earth. I did not revel at its worth. I was more intrigued at how the mining company had missed everything it was looking for. I continued to stick my hand in the water. It was cold – icy cold. I would pull out chunks of ice, break them open and find large diamonds within the ice. Eventually, one of the mining owners came over to me and asked me what I was doing. When he saw the large diamond I held, he became really excited and wanted to know how I did it. I told him it was simple, but they were missing where to look.

    The experience ended, and I wrote down the notes from the experience. I immediately returned to the heavens where I found myself to be formless in the void, observing a message. In this message I was told that I would be receiving a check for a million dollars. It was brief, and I returned to my body. Honestly, I have no idea what it means. I am not led or driven by money, so I do not think it has anything to do with something to come in my life – perhaps, but probably not. I think it was most likely a representation of the value of knowing where to look for the "diamonds."

The Written (cont'd)

October 6, 2014

This morning brought forth two separate experiences. In the first experience, I was standing upon the beach. I looked out upon the ocean and saw a fire burning. In earthly descriptors, the smoke funneled up from the horizon in a dark cloud, getting wider at the top. It looked much like a gasoline fire – as if a boat with a full tank of gas had caught fire and was burning uncontrollably. However, in heavenly descriptors, I would have to say that the smoke was not coming from a boat. In fact, I think the smoke was meant to offer guidance to an upcoming sign that will appear on the Earth.

As I stared at the fire, it was as if I was being told there is a fire upon the waters, whereby the waters represented the spirit, but the fire represented a duality. In one interpretation, it could be seen that the divine radiance of God was on fire – burning out upon this Earth. Or, it could mean that the divine radiance of God was sending a sign that He was about to appear – like a form of Indian smoke signals. Or, it could be that the dark smokiness of the fire represented an ill-founded radiance – as in the coming of an anti-Christ. In whatever message that was shared, I know that it was much more than the idea of a boat burning upon the water. As I gazed across the ocean at the fire billowing up, I felt sadness.

I returned from the experience and made a few notes before closing my eyes and finding myself in a much different heavenly setting. For quite some time the usage of coats within my experiences has been critical in understanding my spiritual walk. The coat has almost always been a reference to the story of "the coat of many colors." If one were to dig into that particular biblical story, it becomes easy to see that the coat is archetypal to God placing a garment of recognition upon a soul, so that others may see its blessing. I could write books on this subject alone, but for now, I need to at least reference the spiritual significance of the coat because this trip to the heavens involved an even grander moment of clothing metaphors.

I was being escorted around the heavens by an angel. The angel was male and one that I see often. He was talking to me about my coat and jeans. I looked at the coat I was wearing and the coat that he was wearing, and they were similar, each about mid-thigh in length. Each coat was well-worn, but had a very distinctive marking. The coats were darker in color to blend in to the night, but the distinctive markings upon the coats were in the form of a colored bead of trim that went from the base of the coat around the collar and back down to the other side of the coat. The bead on my coat was red. The bead on the angel's coat was blue. I wondered which color I liked better. I also wondered if the colors represented "levels" similar to a martial arts belt system. While the conversation with the angel was muddy in interpretation at best for me, my soul understood what was being said. My earthly mind wondered if the angel was telling me I needed a blue-trimmed coat. Whatever the case, I understood I was supposed to look at the coats and the jeans in the store he was taking me to.

The Written (cont'd)

We arrived in the store. It was small, but had all of the necessities I was looking for. I was escorted to a red table that seemed to stand out among all of the other displays. Upon the table were stacks of jeans with big labels describing the brand of the jeans. The jeans themselves did not have any labels or markings. The labels I saw were to help me understand more about each pair of jeans. I glanced at the jeans and decided I wanted to walk around the whole store before I began trying to read the labels of everything.

I walked over to a rack of coats. I thought that I may be looking for a replacement liner on my coat since it was obviously well worn, and my angel guide was trying to tell me something about the coats. I shuffled through an oval-shaped rack of coats looking for my size and brand. To my surprise, the "brand" I was wearing was unavailable at the store. I cannot recall specifically the brand that was available, but I wish I could. The brand consisted of two words that almost certainly held a significance to explore. In the moment, I read the labels, and understood the meaning to be something along the line of "Land's End or Those Of The Earth's End." Undeterred, I wondered if another liner would fit in my jacket. I eventually found the portion of the rack that held my size and saw that this particular portion of the rack was empty. I was very confused, but the confusion began to subside as I understood the meaning.

I began to realize that the coat I was wearing was special – it was made for me by God. In the heavens, it is easy for the human mind to forget the archetypal significance of every symbol and recall the history of the journey. It was clear that the coat I was wearing was not a typical "off the rack" coat that just anyone could find. And while I did not quite understand why the angel was telling me so much about my coat in this particular moment, my mind ran in circles about the words potentially indicating the wear-and-tear my coat was beginning to show.

With those thoughts running through my head, I was ushered over to the table with blue jeans again. The angel found it important that I see the jeans and get a pair. I now knew that spiritually, I was being provided pants. I stared at the table with the jeans. There were three distinct stacks of jeans, each with a label describing its style. The first pair I picked up was from a stack on the right. I read the label. It had two words that I again struggle to recall. I know that the words had a very spiritual feeling about them. One of the words seemed to be "blue" or something like that. At the time, the words were clear. I repeated them over and over in my head so I would be able to recall them, but the upcoming moments would cause this moment to fade from my mind before I returned from the heavens. If I could make my best guess without the accuracy of knowing for sure, the label read something like "Lone _____" or something of a similar feeling.

The angel touched my arm, and I put that pair of jeans back down. I picked up the next pair and read the words on the label as clearly as I have ever read anything in my life, "Messiah." I stood there dumbfounded at the words on the label. I knew even before picking up the jeans that I was going

The Written (cont'd)

to choose a pair from that stack (it was the center stack). But now I was left staring at a name deciding if it would be sacrilegious to wear a pair of jeans that was called "Messiah." I looked at the angel who just kept looking down at me – smiling even. I began to put them down, and the angel instructed me to hold on to them – that I needed to receive a pair of jeans today. We began to walk to the exit with the jeans in my hand, and I could not help but continue to re-read the label. The thoughts caused me to return to my body where I wrote down all of my notes.

As I am typing this, there are obviously many potential meanings that the label could hold. But before even digging into the meaning of the label, I have to explore the thoughts of the archetypal meaning of "pants." So far, I cannot find another meaning that holds more significance than saying that the pants represent "growing up." Another way of saying it is, "put your big boy pants on" or "he/she wears the pants in the family." All of these thoughts lead me to believe that the pants represent the next step for me. If a coat represented warmth and Love of my Father around me, pants must represent the clothing of the vehicle of man. Legs get a person from point A to point B. Legs are the very definition of how movement and motion occur in human form. So to see pants in an archetypal sense, would be pointing to the motion – the mover of the body in earthly form. With that said, I would have to understand being given any pair of pants by an angel must mean that it was time I was called to go into motion for the Spirit.

Glory

The tougher part of understanding is in the choice of materials. Blue is most certainly a color of spiritual significance. It is representative of water and Earth as well. The fabric of the pants was denim, which must represent a casual nature to the effort. Jeans can be worn in most any informal situation, so I would have to think that the call to action in a casual sense means to "keep it real" and "keep it unassuming." Basically, this means that I should not attempt to make a big splash of being given this direction. My direction is to move unassumingly.

The final portion of understanding comes down to the label. Anything I write here holds the potential of misinterpretation by anyone who may one day read this, so I must say everything delicately and with great care so that these words are not misinterpreted as giving false testimony or allowing ego to be involved. If this experience in the heavens was a movie and someone was watching it for the first time, I think the first impression is potentially the most correct and also the most likely to be misinterpreted.

Essentially, from a third person point of view, a soul who wears a coat from God was given a pair of pants that was essentially a set of instructions: "Here, you are being asked to continue being a vehicle for the Spirit, but now you must understand your role has increased. You are to be a leader among the peoples, a messenger of the Word, all the while remaining unassuming in nature, effort, task, and gesture." And, if that is the interpretation, the first thing someone would interpret this as would be, "It is the second coming." But that must not be the interpretation, for each of us has the potential to find Christ within ourselves. If we are each a vessel that houses a doorway to God, it is our task to become carpenters, build the house, find the door, and open it. This is Christ. Christ is not "accepting God." That is the definition of a Christian. Finding Christ is surrendering as a vessel, architecting a house for God through His Grace within the body, building the House inside as a great spiritual ark that bridges two destinations, with every bit of care that could possibly go into building it, recognizing the body as a temple – a holy sanctuary that holds within it a house, and eventually, building the door that God will one day knock upon from the other side. Once that door has been built, and once He has knocked, that door will open, and an embrace of the grandest gesture of unfathomable Love will occur. It is then that Christ has been found within. And once Christ is within, and God has given instructions, then others may find Christ through the vessel – for it is a window, a direct doorway into God's eyes.

October 7, 2014

I found myself sitting in a grand hall with classmates in the heavens. The "hall" was a grand semicircle (possibly a full circle, but it was so big the horizon caused the edges to fade from definition) surrounding a teacher. There were three rows, with each row slightly more elevated that the row in front of it. I sat on the first row. The teacher stood up to talk.

Glory

While the teacher was speaking, a group of guys to my left continued giving me a hard time. In the moment, everything was clear. But, upon returning to my body I was unable to write it all down. Essentially, they were ridiculing me for excelling in the class. As the class progressed, the group of guys became increasingly more like hecklers. I eventually stood up in the middle of a silent classroom and shouted at one of the hecklers in front of the class. It was the only thing I knew I could do that would bring embarrassment to him. I sat down feeling frustrated that I had to stoop to that level.

Eventually a second class began. This time there was a brunette speaker. She was the same brunette angel I see frequently. This was a much harder class, but another class I was successful in. As the class went on, the same group of guys began heckling me again. This time, they kept trying to grab my penis through my clothes. The amount of frustration was driving me crazy, but I tried to just push their hand away more forcefully each time. Eventually, the guys became more relentless, and I stood up in the middle of the class again and shouted at them.

The teacher stopped mid-sentence to witness my outburst. I shouted at the guy saying something along the lines of, "How hard is it for you to keep your hands to yourself? Why do you have to continually try to touch me over and over when I clearly want nothing to do with it? There is something called sexual assault and that is what you are doing right now. If you continue, I will file a sexual assault suit against you, and you will not get away with it." I turned to look at the teacher and

The Written (cont'd)

shrugged. I apologized, and she nodded at me to let me know it was okay. I sat back down.

At the end of class, I walked up to the teacher and apologized again. She said that it was okay and that she understood. I told her that was the second class in a row in which that had happened to me. She looked at me bewildered – as if it was either surprising I was in two classes, or that something so bizarre could happen twice. I eventually parted ways with her and went home.

My house was in a forest, set off from the road. When I arrived home, I realized I was being hunted. Men with guns appeared at my house and tried to come in through the garage/basement. There were five or six of them. They cornered me against cinder-block walls planning to do their worst. But in the blink of an eye, I slipped out and then had them all cornered instead. I looked at my hand and saw that one of them had managed to cut me between my thumb and first finger on my left hand. It hurt, but it was a small cut. It was one of the few times I have felt pain in the heavens. And when I say heavens, this was clearly another event in the heavens, but it was part of the war between spirits.

As I recognized that I had the upper hand, I decided to run out of the house so as not to inflict harm on them. As I ran, I picked up four playing cards and tried to throw them like ninja-stars. I failed at that…miserably. But, I was able to get out of the situation. Outside of the garage, there was a metal gun and a stainless steel axe lying on the ground. I picked up both and began to run away with them. As I ran through the woods, I looked back to see another group of men had arrived and were fighting against the group that was in my basement. They had all moved to a spot in the woods behind my house though. I could tell it was evil versus evil.

I looked down the barrel of the gun and thought about pulling the trigger. But as I did, I heard a voice call my name. I knew it was God telling me to let it all go and not harm them. I looked at the gun and threw it to the ground. I looked at the axe, which was an interesting shape – something I had never seen before. I decided to hold onto it, even though I knew I would likely be told to discard of it by an angel or God at some point in the future. I ran through the woods to the street. I awoke.

October 8, 2014

Since I have arrived down in Fort Lauderdale, I have not attempted to ask anyone out. I figured that my first priority was to get moved, finish the contract that helped me get here financially as "strongly" as I could, until finally I could begin to find my writing groove. With the first two tasks completed and the third on the short-list of my to-do's, I have begun to look around at the landscape surrounding me. Honestly, I have had no idea where to start. I still hold strong to the belief that God will place the right girl along my path when it is right in His eyes. Over the last few weeks I entertained the notion of dating websites, but with much hesitation. At this point, I can

The Written (cont'd)

say I have joined every popular website that exists, paid for the subscription (3 months, 6 months, etc.) and have subsequently deleted my account the following day – all except for one which I still deleted after letting it run its course for a little over a week. Anyway, the point is that I think something is lost in those sites – that feeling, the essence of another that cannot be summed up in two-hundred and fifty characters or less. With each site registration, I immediately felt a gash applied to my soul. It was painful to endure that one site for the seven-plus days. It has nothing to do with the women, replies, likes, favorites, winks. Instead, it has everything to do with the sinking feeling that I was defying God's personal playbook for me. So, with each attempt to gain control of my dating life, I subsequently relinquished it upon a good night's sleep.

So I say all of this to say – at dinner a week or so ago I met a beautiful woman named Tracy. It was very obvious that we were each entertained at the notion of each other, but I did not ask for her number. Tracy worked at the establishment I had dinner, and I figured that if she was interested, I would know more. In every situation past, the woman has given me her number or asked for mine – all without me having to take action. It is one of those "divine signs" that I am sure will change one day. I am not married to the idea that it has to happen this way for me – but it is fun to watch.

The second time I had dinner at this restaurant, it was obvious that Tracy was extremely entertained at the notion of her and me having something more. She had that look in her eye that I have only seen a handful of times in my life. It is the abundance of her soul gushing from the whites of her eyes, creating a glassy encasement over those windows to her soul. It was as if the soul said, "Hey, let me clean off these windows and add just a little sparkle so that someone will want to peer deep inside." It was a moment that most certainly caused me to pause and take notice as the world became a blur around that particular moment. But our conversations were always held short due to her working and the one crazy event I did not see coming.

And while I will likely write about this incident in much more detail in one of the chapters of Book III, the important point to take note of here is that a man walked in, sat down beside me, and began sharing a story about his life...all unprompted by me as Tracy and I carried on our conversation. It became readily apparent that God placed this man in my life for me to help. Merely conversation and coffees over the upcoming week (as it would prove to play out) was what this man needed to help him find his way through a storm of his mother passing, losing his job, placing faith in another employer who had not paid him for his labors, etc. For a moment, I was looking in a mirror at myself during my darkest times. Albeit, the details were slightly different, the overall story was the same. I knew this man needed help. So for three hours we talked, and at the end, I left the restaurant without pursuing Tracy any further. For whatever reason, God placed that on pause in my life.

Over the week, I wrestled with when I should return to the restaurant to talk to her – or even if I should. Could it be

The Written (cont'd)

that God was asking me to be patient? Could it be that God was saying, "Not now?" Or perhaps He was saying, "Not her." I have not been in this situation before, so I decided to tread carefully and ask God for guidance. For a few days I wrestled with whether it was my decision to explore on my own. Eventually I came to reason that nothing else is "mine" so why would this be different? In the early morning hours of October 8th, I prayed for help in understanding. In the early morning hours of October 8th, He spoke.

As I meditated, I found myself standing in the heavens. I was sitting down in a booth with red leather bench seats. It was a luxurious setting for a table. The room surrounding faded from view. This was a lesson – but for what I did not yet know. The setting was unfamiliar to me. As I sat at the table, Tracy came into view to wait on me. She asked me about dinner, where I placed an order. She left, and in a few minutes, she returned from the blackness. This time she sat down in front of me – eager to talk and commune rather than wait on me. As we talked, it was obvious that she was interested in knowing me. Her actions, her words, her smile... Another server came to our table and saw Tracy sitting down and said, "Oh! Are you going to have dinner?" She seemed puzzled but was really happy for Tracy. Nothing else had to be said other than those words for me to see a story unravel about her life, the server's care for her friend, the role I played in that situation, etc.

Tracy stood up as if concerned she would get in trouble for spending too much time with me. I immediately blurted out in a strong and confident manner, "Yes. Stay. That's a great idea." I did not want to give her time to think, or for the server to offer doubt. The server smiled and walked away. Tracy walked over to a door that was now in my field of vision – nothing else – just a door and the booth in the darkness. She shut the door, and the room fell into view. I saw that the booth I was sitting in seemed to be placed obscurely in a hotel room. If a hotel room could be viewed as three or four times as wide as it was long, the door would be located in the top right (from an overhead view), along the widest wall. The booth would be in the place the first of two beds would be for a double occupancy room. I could not help but find amusement and confusion in the moment. I watched Tracy's actions intently now. It would seem that the server was voicing her satisfaction in Tracy and me getting to know each other.

Tracy and I made small talk, and eventually she said something along the lines about a guy that was trying to ask her out. I immediately picked up on her coy and playful way she intertwined it into the conversation. I knew she was talking to me and giving me the green light if I wanted to take her out on a date. I laughed and role-played it with her, toyingly letting her know I saw through the charade and was going to have fun in the moment. I said, "Oh, you do? And how is that going to go when he gets up the courage to ask?" She smiled and said, "Terrible. It always goes terribly."

She began to explain to me something about tattoos. At this point I realized I was not wearing a shirt and said, "Well, I guess you can see I don't have any tattoos." I walked over to

The Written (cont'd)

the bed and lay down on it to continue casual conversation – nothing sexual about my actions of moving over to the bed. She smiled and said, "I know. I already noticed." At that point, there was a knock at the door. She became really nervous, and I told her it was okay. For some reason, fear and panic set in for her. It was as if she knew she was doing something she should not be doing – defying some cosmic order placed either upon her or me. Her reaction spoke volumes to me, but I wanted to make her feel safe. I thought it was the server coming back to take her order for dinner, or maybe to bring me mine.

    I walked over to the door, still shirtless, and opened it. I immediately realized how this was going to appear from someone on the outside. They would see a shirtless man with a beautiful girl behind a closed door, with the comforter of the bed ruffled from where she and I had been sitting/lying and talking. The girl stormed in. She started asking me questions in rapid-fire succession. I said, "Whoa. I'm just a guy trying to figure out how to ask out this girl." The server stopped in her tracks. She was dumbfounded by my response. She looked extremely disappointed, and confused. The moment a girl looks at you and "you know you've done something to hurt her but aren't sure what" was the feeling that overcame me. As I stood in the doorway, she walked away, and I stood there, staring out into nothing.

    I was left with the overwhelming feeling that interaction with Tracy is okay, but to try to date her was not planned for me on my course. In fact, I believe that the "server" (obviously an angel as should be apparent in how these experiences are presented to me) knew when and where I should meet the right girl. So, as hard as it is for me to stomach, I know that I cannot take Tracy out. We can get to know each other from afar, but nothing more. Her soul knew that as well – as if I was forbidden at this time. I know that sounds bizarre, but I asked for guidance, and this is the answer I received. It does not have to make sense to others – just to me.

October 11, 2014

This experience began with a vision of a person whom I have not spoken to in quite a while. I once really liked a girl named Sam. She and I connected in a way only two souls could do. She was dating another guy at the time and so, if for no other reason, I knew the timing was off. The night before I was to move to Fort Lauderdale I received a text from her telling me that she and her boyfriend were breaking up. Unless she was making a blanket announcement to everyone in her life, the text was ripe with possibility. She had been in a relationship with a guy named Jason for at least the better part of two years. She knew I liked her, and we shared a great friendship when we worked together.

She often told me that if we had met at different times it would be different, but she would not step out of her relationship – and I never asked her to do so. This was just part of idle conversations we shared about our past relationships, seeing

The Written (cont'd)

each other as old souls reconnecting, etc. Often it was unprompted by me – I just let her talk. It was as if her getting that off of her chest was therapy enough for her own soul. I am not going to say it was not hard. But I made a friendship work without her becoming the wiser. Often I think that the manner in which I usually present myself defies all logic in everything that is going on operationally inside of me. But that is part of the walk. Others should see strength, happiness, resolve, and kindness. Anything else should be a conversation between God and me regardless of how hard it is for me to comprehend – or even to function without resolve. On the outside, others should only sense peace.

So, the day before I left for Fort Lauderdale – with her not knowing when I was moving, only that I was moving at some point in the future – I received a text saying that she had broken up with Jason and they were moving their separate ways. How is a person supposed to respond to this type of text? I have no idea – and ultimately I decided nothing was better than me jumping at a possibility. I saw the potential written in the stars, but realistically every action would be wrong – especially on the heels of a break-up. So, I decided to sit on my thoughts and respond in time.

Eventually, after I had arrived in Fort Lauderdale, I responded about being there for her anytime she needed – a face of consolation in the time of loss. In the end, I thought that perhaps this could have been a test to get me to remain in Nashville, and I wanted to demonstrate my resolve in following God's plan for me. In truth, the two people that could have been used to dissuade me were Lindsey and Sam. But even with Lindsey, I was moving before anything transpired – which was all part of the plan. If she chose to open the box, then there could have been potential for something, at some point, to be determined upon God's will. The only other person that could be used as a pawn to prevent me from going was Sam. So, if the man in rose-colored glasses was in action, his only two puppets could have been Sam or Lindsey. If God was in play, testing me with His plan against a woman in my life, His only two puppets that could have held strength were Sam and Lindsey. So either way – good or bad, temptation of Love or test of faith – I was resolved in moving to Ft. Lauderdale and allowing the pieces to fall where they may. First and foremost, it was important to follow God's plan for me.

So this morning, as the vision began, I saw Sam standing before me. She walked up to me and asked why I never replied to her text about breaking up. My heart broke for her because I saw the truth in her action of letting me know about her breaking up. I cried. I wept in sadness not for what I did, but rather because what was done had to be done in order for God's plan to fall into place. It broke my heart to see her so sad because I did not want to hurt her, and knew she did not understand my situation – or even her own situation. As we spoke, I explained to her that she knew how I felt and why I could not respond – not right after she had broken up and while I was leaving. I told her, "I knew I wouldn't make it here," that it could all go in wrong ways, and that she "deserved right." It seemed that because of my lack of action that

The Written (cont'd)

she was either back with Jason or in another relationship that she had not planned on. I could see her unresolve – how she was confused at everything. We talked a lot about it.

Eventually the conversation turned into a soccer game – a recurring theme as of late. At another point it became hockey and then returned back to soccer. Lately in the heavens, soccer seems to be the new hockey for me. We were on a large open field with trees surrounding us in the distance. The field was encased in an ochre light. There were no goalies. The goal seemed to be to just kick the ball past the other team. I made one good pass that was kicked by another and we scored. There was another ball that was hurtled to me, but went over my head and into the woods. I went off to find the ball. While I searched in the thick brush before the woods, one of the players – another angel – came up to me and began talking. The experience faded out.

There were at least two other experiences that occurred at this point, but I tried to keep pressing through to each scenario instead of returning to my body to journal the experiences. However, in typical fashion, it worked against me, and I was unable to recall these two other experiences. I eventually called myself back to my body to journal the experience which is where I was left with only remembering the experiences above.

When I returned to the heavens, I was on a plane. There was a redheaded female with milky white skin. She was beautiful. Her hair was long, full of body, and a shade of red that defies the best attempts at Earth to replicate the perfect red hair color. She sat next to an older man. She was happy and in Love with him. The plane landed, everyone went their separate ways.

Somewhere along our different paths I saw the redheaded girl's mother. I had noticed her on the plane, but did not think much about it at the time. Her mother had red hair as well. She and her daughter looked a lot alike. As I walked down the street, I saw her mother ambushed by a group of men and taken down an alley and into an underground bunker. I followed the attackers and watched her as she was dragged out of a tunnel. I could not do anything to help. I could only watch.

Later, I arrived at my destination for the evening. I was staying in a two story hotel that was along an ocean's edge. The hotel was ochre with a wooden, white-picket railing. I was standing on the second floor looking out. It was nightfall. As I gazed out upon the moonlight reflecting off the ocean, I took notice of the redheaded mother dragging a cardboard coffin down a dirt path on her way out to the beach. After she reached the beach, she dragged the coffin into the ocean and began jumping up and down on it, attempting to sink it.

I had the impression she was trying to kill her daughter, but at the same time I knew that – for whatever reason – the manner in which her daughter was encased in the coffin would prohibit her from drowning. I knew I had a few moments to decide my best approach at saving the girl. I watched on when one of the hotel staff arrived. He was a familiar angel that I called "Rob," but I think that was my earthly mind placing an identity on an angel I did not know the name to. I most cer-

The Written (cont'd)

tainly do not think the angels name is Rob. But as the angel walked up to me, I explained what was happening and felt I now had support if needed. I darted out to save the girl knowing this other angel had my back if needed. I swam out in the surf of the ocean and dragged the coffin back to shore. At this point, the mother was still standing on top of the coffin. When I reached the shore, I cut a hole into the cardboard where the girl's face would be. When I made it through the cardboard I realized that the girl was wrapped in plastic. I cut through the plastic and saw the girl's pale face. Her stunning locks of red hair were wrapped around the edges of her face.

I ripped open the hole in the coffin to make it bigger. I slapped her face a couple of times to get her to revive. She eventually awakened and immediately stuck her arms through the hole in the cardboard, wrapping them around my neck. I told her briefly what had almost happened to her, and she tightened her embrace – leaning in to kiss me. Her lips were flushed red – plump with the passion of the moment racing within her. I observed her lips as if it was a slow motion pitch of Love thrown from the Hand of God. It was a kiss for the ages – one that I had never experienced anything similar to in my earthly walk.

I did not have much time to enjoy the moment because I knew that it would be perceived to be awkward from the outside. I saved a girl from dying who immediately kissed me – a girl who was happy in Love just earlier in the day. But somehow, I also knew that the man that she was in Love with had deceived her in order to try to kill her – the same man had deceived her mother as well. I felt safe that her Love could be pure, but I did not want to be perceived badly. However, I knew this was the girl I was intended to be with.

Somehow in all of the moments of meeting souls and angels in the heavens – there was a lock that ensured me that this was what I was looking for. Maybe it was the feeling. Maybe it was her soul. Maybe it was everything. But in all of the possibilities, the truth remained that this experience would transcend into the Love I would one day find. Perhaps I had just found it in the heavens, and it was God letting my soul know that a Love for the ages will happen for me, if not in this earthly life, then here in the heavens. Or perhaps it was God saying, "Here she is." And quite possibly, that is enough for me to know at this point. As I stood there with her arms wrapped around me, I became aware that her body was unclothed, though it did not seem to matter to anyone around.

The angel I called Rob came down and apprehended the mother for me. The redheaded girl continued to pull herself into me, kissing me in the most intimate way – soft, slow, hovering just close enough to feel the tingle between our lips without touching. The hovering is what made the biggest impression. It was wrapped up in a timeless moment where the image of her lips almost touching mine is as picturesque as anything could ever be. Once we "established our bond" I had to leave her to go after the men that came after her and her mother. "Established our bond" is the only way I can describe that moment because it was as if that one moment was sealed

The Written (cont'd)

in eternity forever, and somehow is, and always was, my destiny.

The experience ended and I was able to return to my body to take these notes. Immediately afterwards, I found myself in the heavens again. I was, again, aboard a plane. This time it was landing, and I was with two male angel guides. They took me on an adventure, but with purpose. It is possible it was in pursuit of the men who attempted to harm this new girl that I can only call "my destiny." The angels led me to a rope bridge/ladder. They were in front of me. At one point, the ladder split in half where I was to continue onward across the impossible shape of the remaining half of the ladder/bridge to ascend. I was told not to look down. I knew we were high above everything. I also could not see where we were going. We were in a cerulean sky where the rope ladder ascended at such an incline that it vanished into the horizon. But it is important to note the rope had slack in it to create a slight curve. There were no straight lines – they were all curved. As we climbed, the angels kept looking back upon me – checking to see if I was okay. When we reached the top, it was a nearly impossible end. The ropes just vanished into nothingness – only blue sky. The angels jumped in front of me. But as they jumped they held onto the rope bridge. So, I did the same.

When I jumped, the only way I can describe what happened was as if the downward force of gravity began to invert the world around me as I swung down into a cavern. But, it seemed as if I passed through a dimension, where everything

Glory

inverted itself. The cavern was a small tube in darkness. I realized the two angels in front of me were either killed or had vanished for the lesson. I saw a grenade thrown into the tube. It was thrown up into the tube as if I was standing in the tunnel of an enclosed slide about to let gravity pull me down. I was not fearful of the grenade. I picked it up and threw it back down the tube. I slid down and dismounted into the dirt. I held my arms above my head in celebration of an Olympic-like dismount. It was an action in jest of the situation. I found it funny – I was almost arrogant of my skill in making the passage. The grenade went off several yards in front of me. I was safely outside of the blast radius, which made the dismount that much more entertaining to me. I smiled at the absurdity of my James Bond-like style and timing.

As I walked through the cave, the angels ahead of me appeared. They were not killed after all. I saw a picture on the wall. I understood it to be 12" x 12". The frame was silver. The paint held a sparkle within it. It shimmered like the important markings I have seen previously in the heavens. The picture held several symbols upon it and was crafted with a glaze-like paint style that emulated rain and glitter. They seemed to be important symbols that I have come to understand as the language of the heavens. I think some people refer to it as Enochian, but I have not had any reason to call it that specifically. However, it may be easier to refer to the symbol as Enochian just to maintain fluidity in the context of my writing.

The Written (cont'd)

I took the picture from the wall and held onto it. The angels looked at me, intrigued that I would want that particular piece of artwork. My intent was to study it at a later time.

I eventually made it through an escape hatch into a jail yard. There was chain-link fence surrounding the compound and a tower in the middle of the yard. The power had been turned off. I had been in this location in the heavens before. I am not sure when though. In the past I had been unable to escape. But, this time was different. I ran around the yard and found three pipes protruding vertically from the ground. They were located near a work-shed. I immediately ran across the tops of the pipes and up the wall of the shed parkour-style. The top of the shed let me have a greater view of the surroundings. I saw workers in the yard tending crops and some vehicles on the horizon. I knew those vehicles held soldiers within them to help keep prisoners inside. I ran over to where the workers were tending the crops and impersonated one of the workers to hide my identity for when the soldiers arrived. They did not know any better, and I was able to escape out of the gate that they opened for their entry into the jail yard.

October 12, 2014
Early Morning

This experience began with me in the company of two angels. They seemed to be twins – two women who continued to do the exact same thing. As one moved, so did the other. I

Glory

was fascinated by all that I was witnessing, and words cannot properly put it into context because there is no framework in the earthly mind to rationalize the abstract essence of the experience. Eventually, one of the twins asked me to participate in a play. I was taken to a large auditorium. The stage and floor were black. The seats were mauve. The lighting was a bath of light blue. When I walked up to the stage with the angel, she introduced me to the group (who was obviously the cast for the play). Apparently there was a performance about to occur.

I was asked to be a rock. My role consisted of crouching in front of the group and not moving. As the play went on, it became increasingly boring, but I was intent on holding my ground as this "rock." Partway through the play, one of the female cast members whispered to me, "You haven't done this before, have you?" I shook my head in a subtle "no" movement. She then began telling me everything I was doing wrong. A couple of the other cast members became involved in the conversation. This was all while the performance was in motion before an audience. I could sense that we were in a place that the audience was not focused on, which gave the cast the leeway to make small talk without being heard.

I eventually was told to roll under the stage and out the back because of my poor performance of "not moving." I could sense the audience was disappointed in my performance too. I could not understand how "not moving" could be taken as a "poor performance" when that is specifically what I was supposed to do. It was as if I did not understand how to stay

The Written (cont'd)

still even though I thought I was doing a great job. Immediately my mind filled with the possibility that I was doing a poor job in Fort Lauderdale with "learning to be." Possibly "learning to be" meant "staying still." And, if I was to stay still, then I clearly did not know how to because I would not be receiving this lesson.

Once I rolled to the backstage area, I was told to follow a line of people that ended with a stagehand "checking" those same people. He was clearly the boss or supervisor backstage. I already knew he was an angel – as was everyone I interacted with. I walked through the line and took notice that everyone was being scanned with a handheld device. Upon the device a three digit reading appeared. It looked sort of like an infrared thermometer – but I am sure that is what I needed to see in order to understand what was being communicated to me. I felt there was a necessity to have a reading of 82 when I was scanned. I was concerned that I was "sick" and would not have the right reading. When I reached the stagehand, he assured me that I should not be nervous, but I could not help but worry about what it would mean if my reading did not show 82.

When I was scanned, the device beeped and three numbers appeared. I understood them to read "81.7." I immediately panicked because it did not read 82. It is important to understand that I also began to realize that 81.7 was almost 82. And though it would not make sense in an earthly sense, it seemed that 817 was really close to 820 – which was the appropriate way to understand the meaning. The angel

Glory

looked at me and smiled. He said, "See? I told you that you'd be okay." I was still confused in the meaning of 817 and did not quite understand what to make of it. I returned to my body where I took notes of the experience.

A short while later, I began to do my research on "817." I learned that 817 in the Strong Concordance is the Hebrew word "ASHAM" which means "guilt, to have fault, to sin." I immediately became saddened at the meaning. I thought that the angel's message must mean that I was still harboring guilt over a sin – or maybe that I was just "sinning." I struggled with this thought because I had no idea where in my life I was sinning. But as I did further research, I came across another website. It was a blog by a lady named Joanne out of Australia. She offered definitions to numbers given to people by angels. This intrigued me for a number of reasons – the first of which was that I said nothing about the word angel in my Google search.

When I arrived on her page, I began reading the definition. I looked to the left and saw the month that she made this particular blog entry contained seventy-seven entries. This was a divine stamp from God letting me know there was significance to be found within her words. I came to understand that each of the numbers held important meaning – and in combination, they held a greater meaning together. Essentially, I learned that the number 8 represented the lessons of manifesting wealth, future, and security. Suddenly, making it to the "8th floor" now made sense – as did part of my purpose in Ft. Lauderdale. In the end, Joanne said that 817 was affirmation

The Written (cont'd)

that the angels saw my actions and understood my intent – that they wanted to make an acknowledgement to me that I was moving in the right direction and to keep moving forward. Obviously more comparisons can be made between the definition of ASHAM (aleph-shin-mem) and the definition that Joanne offered. As different as they seem, they also seem to be bound together in truth.

October 12, 2014
Afternoon

During a meditation around 4:00 p.m. today, I found myself in a deep relaxation. My soul was whisked away to the heavens. When I arrived, I was sitting in the middle of four others at a bar table. To my left and right were two couples. I was sitting between the women – who were each larger in size than their male counterparts. There seemed to be one more angel in front of us, but he seemed somewhat hazy for my recognition. I was the only "single" person in the group, and most definitely the only human. The other four around me were angels. I immediately felt that I was surrounded by at least one of the archangels – quite possibly all four.

I have not had an experience where I interacted with the four archangels together, so everything I was experiencing seemed new. My perspective of the entire situation was "out of body." I viewed myself – and the entire scene – in third person from behind my soul. As I looked to my left, the woman turned and looked at me. She was beautiful – blonde. For a moment I questioned if she was "the girl." At this point, my familiarity with the angels and the heavens seemed to have strengthened my clarity in vision of these situations. I suppose that makes sense as the soul is like a muscle, learning to grow. How can you observe all of the detail without clarity in eyesight? When babies are born they see shapes and colors, eventually giving way to definition and understanding of their surroundings. My learning should be viewed no differently.

In the beginning, "the girl" was so immensely beautiful that I could offer no explanation as to her description other than "blonde and blue eyes." So, as I sat there, I wondered if I was sitting next to the girl. As the thought ran through my mind, I sensed she understood though she acknowledged without words.

I was also in this experience with an unsettled question about whether I would find Love in this lifetime. I did not plan on taking this question with me to the heavens, but that was nonetheless how I understood the basis of this scenario. The angels on either side of me seemed to tell me without words that they were biding their time on introducing the Love of my life to me to make sure I was ready. It did not seem to have anything to do with whether she was ready. It seemed to have everything to do with whether I was ready. They both seemed to want to shield "their children" from hurt, and keep them protected. Think of this transference of understanding as a father protecting his daughter from the man she dates.

The Written (cont'd)

We sat a little longer, and I turned to ask the angel on my left more questions. I was inquisitive. It is not everyday you sit between the holiest of angels and have the strength in the soul to understand the scenario. No words were spoken, which made it that much harder. It was an unspoken conversation. So as I turned to my left, I was met with the face of this great angel. It literally – not metaphorically – caused everything around me to disappear from view where only the face was in my field of view. It looked like the face from the Statue of David. The face had such strong and stern features. The hair was blond and fell in loose curls around the left ear. The eyes were a blue of indescribable color. As I gazed into the eyes, they opened up into what I can only describe as images of the Earth spinning around. It was as if the eyes of the angel held the Earth.

I knew I had seen this angel before. She was not a she – but rather a "he." This was Michael. In the one other time Michael let me know who he was when I stood before him, the same austere, imposing gaze was given to me. He was stoic. His hair was the lightest shade of blonde possible. His face was square with pronounced cheekbones. As I stared I tried to process how I could mistake him for "the girl." Or perhaps I had mistaken him for "the girl" all along. While he carried an heir of femininity, he was most definitely masculine...quite possibly the most masculine definition of masculine I have ever observed. He had such strength and – as a straight man it is difficult to describe him this way – but every bit as beautiful in the way I would describe a woman. But it was the austere strength in his gaze that set him apart. As I soaked in the image of his face, I was taken to different locales. An airport was one – sitting on a plane; the others I cannot recall.

As we returned from the mind-bender of a trip that defies every bit of earthly description, I realized my original perception of sitting between four angels, two male and two female, was not completely accurate. It could be possible that I saw myself sitting between two archangels represented by their male and female states in order to bring me comfort in understanding. The angel ahead of me was a haze, but could have been the third archangel. My viewpoint could have been through the eyes of the fourth. So that is one possibility.

The other thought that ran through my mind was that I could be sitting between the four archangels – each displaying their role with me; on my right and on my left – the two closest to me in my experiences. But as I soaked it all in and tried to understand, the angels must have sensed my desire to understand. I was continually impressed the concept of a mirror. I began to wonder if my viewpoint from behind was as if I was seeing it in a mirror – so my right would be my left, my left my right and so on. Most certainly there was something really important about the mirror, and I do believe that it had to do with my understanding of directions – which would make sense because traditionally Michael is documented as appearing on a person's right, Uriel on the left. And Uriel is most certainly the other angel I have interacted with the most (Anael as well).

The Written (cont'd)

As I began to lose harmony in the moment, I decided it was important to understand more about my desire for Love in an earthly sense. I was shown an image (in motion) of a woman carrying two other women in her arms. Each was holding the other so that no one was carrying all of the weight. They were all naked. I could not see their faces or their private areas as they were all connected in some intertwined sexual bond. I was told that this image represented the carnal bonding of mind, body, and soul through the expression of Love. Unlike most experiences that take a little hindsight or reflection to understand, the angels helped me understand this meaning in that moment. In fact, all of the meanings were made clear to me instantly. In all of the meanings, I understood it to represent "what was to come."

October 13, 2014

I arrived in the heavens and stood before a female angel who had not revealed herself to me before. It was very clear that she was new in my experiences and wanted me to understand that part of the moment. We played soccer together and got to know each other. Eventually, we were forced to spend thirty days together on a trip. I could not understand if this was a spiritual thirty days or part of my next thirty earthly days. It seemed this angel will be my guide during my experiences in the heavens over the next thirty days... but the meaning was hard to understand.

Glory

As we talked and got to know each other I found out that she was the daughter of someone I knew – but I was offered no more clarity. There was a lot more I learned. We must have spent hours getting to know each other. She eventually began to become fond of me, but it was a hard road to win over her affection. At one point I was shared something about a plane flight and a girl wanting to kiss me – or perhaps I wanted to kiss her. I do not know if it happened or not. This was just one of the snippets I could recall. After I returned to my body and began to journal the experience, the details faded from clear recollection. Perhaps over the next thirty days there will be more clarity.

October 14, 2014

I had a really long experience in the heavens this morning. My angel – my guide – seemed to want to spend the majority of the time just talking. We talked while we kicked a ball between us. This was another motif with soccer involved. I thought for sure I would remember all of our conversation when I returned to my body, and in fact, I did. But, each time I returned I became more intent on returning to the heavens than on writing it down. I (as usual) felt overly confident in being able to retain the conversation to journal at a later time. Unfortunately, after several back-and-forth attempts at traveling, I could not recall any of the details of any experience to journal.

The Written (cont'd)

October 15, 2014
Early Morning

There were quite a lot of experiences in the heavens for me this morning. And, as it turned out, Bryan also had a powerful experience of his own. It is interesting to note that the date adds up to 7:7 (the year reduce sums to seven while the month and day reduce sum to seven). I have taken notice that in addition to the half moon visions, there is also an interesting correlation with dates that sum to seven before the year (which makes them seven-and-seven days) as well as days that sum in totality to seven (including the year). Today was another example of this phenomenon.

Before I write about the large, detailed experience, I think it is important to first mention a portion of one of the motifs that I cannot recall in much detail. In this experience, I found myself being spoken to by a male angel. He was asking me my thoughts on what would be perceived to be "everyday scenery" in the world around us. In one question, we stood outside of a farmer's house. To the left of the simple one-story whitewashed house with a wrap-around porch was a large bale of hay. It was the type of bale that is seen on large farms. But, it was evident that there was only enough acreage for one bale of hay to be rolled. The angel asked me about it to which I blurted out something negative regarding the commercialization of farms and how large companies seem to make the money while the land-owners are taken advantage of. The angel passively scolded me as he explained that seeing a bale of hay in a farmers yard was good because it meant that the farmer was doing whatever he could to make money. It also was not a sign of commercialization because the farmer likely got out and rolled the hay himself, doing anything he could to find a revenue stream for his farm.

There were other scenarios the angel asked me about that I can no longer recall, Those scenarios were simple – like asking me about a coffee cup, etc. This portion of the experience went on for a long time. I am sure my soul retained the knowledge while my feeble human mind failed to return the lessons in complete detail. Sometimes that is just how it works.

The primary experience I want to write about began with me standing before the angel that reminds me of Carrie Underwood. She essentially has the most perfect features. Every time I see her I am in awe. I saw her from a distance and walked up to her where she seemed glad to see me. I could sense that something else was bothering her unrelated to our encounter – something that was stressful for her. When I approached she said, "Good. You are here." She then grabbed my right arm and said, "Let's go." She was sneaky as if she did not want anyone to see us together so I played along.

After grabbing our coats from a wall, we walked out the back door of the room we were in. She seemed drunk or tipsy. This was a first for me in witnessing an angel in an imperfect state. Or maybe it was I who was not focused which made her motions seem off kilter. After we left the building, she began telling me how much she liked me, but did so in a coy way. I

The Written (cont'd)

am not sure if I asked or if she brought it up, but there was clearly something going on in a relationship she was in. She said something about how she liked me because I "didn't know John, Luke, or any of his friends."

At that moment I tried to rationalize if she was talking about the two biblical characters from the New Testament. Apparently she was in a relationship with one of them – which makes sense seeing as she appears in similar times that I am imparted knowledge from Luke. Anyway, we went into the next building where the waiter and staff recognized us. It was obvious to them that our time together was "out of place" or would be closely scrutinized by others. There was a sense, though, that we were in a safe establishment – away from anyone who would talk, including the wait staff.

The angel was not overly touchy – we did not hold hands – but she occasionally held onto my right arm with both hands. We walked down some steps and sat down at a table and talked. It was like a fine French restaurant. The tables were donned in bright white table cloths with red roses in clear vases on the tables. Our coats were black and in stark contrast to the tablecloths. She told me how she Loved our time together and really needed to figure out how to "be with me" but it did not seem lustful or wrong. She eventually looked at me and leaned in to kiss me. It was like a slow motion kiss that ignited my periphery in white. Her lips were a soft blush-red. Everything about it consumed me. Even more importantly, I did not lose harmony. I held strong. This is when I felt her Love for me.

Glory

We ended up going back to the original mansion we walked from and had to discreetly go our separate ways. She seemed drunk again and one of John or Luke's friends took her when he saw her stumbling with me. He did not have any suspicion though. He knew we were friends and that she was playing a specific angelic role in my life. At this point even I did not know we were anything more than friends. It is like reading a book for the first time where you are the main character.

I eventually walked to a small bar. I did not want to drink, but I wanted to fit in. I decided to order a glass of Pinot Grigio. The bartender looked at me like she knew me really well. I had a sense she knew I could be the life of a party or quiet and standoffish. It seemed she was unsure which direction I would go. She asked if I wanted a flute or a glass. I did not understand her, so she clarified, "Champagne flute or glass?" I replied that she should choose whichever she wanted to use. After all I did not plan on drinking whatever she brought me. It was just for appearance.

I eventually saw an extremely wealthy man and was curious how much he thought was reasonable to pay for an obscure book. Was it one million dollars? When I walked over to him and asked the question, he said he had spent two million dollars on a book before. It was then I realized that on Earth, some of the wealthiest individuals hold prized religious books no one is even aware exist. I began to ask him where I could find someone who had spent that type of money on books or art. I knew it sounded like I was being superficial to him, and I feared he thought so, so I tried to clarify my intentions about coming across obscure religious texts. He said he knew, but he avoided answering the question. He did not seem like he wanted to share those sources with me. He wandered off down a hallway.

I walked down the hallway some time later and saw the blonde angel in a hot tub surrounded by several male Angels. I think they were trying to sober her up. I walked by and said, "Hello," to the group as I headed to my car. This area had a bluish green aura about it. When I got to the entrance the valet went to pick up my car. To my right, in a perpendicular part of this large mansion, was a balcony several floors up. I saw the man who I had chatted with earlier. I shouted out to him, "Thanks," and again tried to downplay my intentions. He did not seem amused. I sat in the car and realized that nothing was familiar about the interior of the vehicle. I began to back up and then pulled away.

October 15, 2014
Afternoon

During meditation today, I fell into a formless state for most of the duration. Near the end, I heard a child's voice that said, "My dad claimed he wasn't – although he may be. After all he was 33." As I heard these words, I saw a small ship in the ocean. The seas were choppy and a man was climbing in from the ocean onto the boat.

Glory

October 16, 2014

The experiences in the heavens were, again, long and detailed. However, this time when I retuned to my body, I could not shake the swirly feeling that causes me to lose recollection of the event. All that I can recall is that I was in a house that was "for sale" according to a for sale sign in the front yard. My angel guide walked me through the house and was teaching me anything that I could learn. This was just one of the motifs of the journey. Eventually, we walked down a hallway, and she pointed out a painting on the wall. She did not focus on it too much, but I blurted out that it was an Akiana portrait. She looked at me surprised and said, "Yes. Yes it is." She then went on to explain the importance of the painting and in Akiana as a chosen messenger. She told me how her artwork was important.

October 17, 2014

This morning was filled with numerous experiences. I did my best to write them down as they occurred. The first experience was right when I began to meditate. As my soul began to waft between the heavens and Earth, a park came into view. I was standing on a path. I heard a voice originate from behind me, and then appear before me. There was a man running North along the path, and he began to speak while he approached. He said, "I'd rather hear you talk than any of these

The Written (cont'd)

others." He never quit jogging. He only turned around enough mid-stride so that I could see his whole appearance.

He was well tanned, middle aged with dark, brown eyes and dark, brown curly hair. He was wearing a thin, white headband and a white smock or tunic. I am not exactly sure what his garment is called, but it is the same garment I have seen in the Greek scenarios adorning the angels when speaking to the other spiritual children. It is also the same white garment that many of the elder angels have worn, as well as Enoch and Jesus. This particular man reminded me of Richard from the television series, Lost. I knew it was not him, rather the dark eyes, hair, and facial features were what caused me to take notice of the similarities.

When I heard his words, my earthly body lighted in a big smile. It was my own smile that caused me to return to my body. I do not think my spirit had completely left my body, so it reacted in kind to the words. My smile is what startled me out of my meditation where I immediately wrote down the words. And though I do not think I have mentioned it before, this earthly reaction to something in the beginning of meditation is common with me and helps me balance long enough to write down the experience. This was the first of many to occur during the morning hours.

The second experience took me to a similar setting as the first. And while part of what I am going to say will sound disjointed, sometimes this is due to knowing (or flashing into and out from) a backstory to the characters involved. In this setting, I was involved in some type of media coverage of a group bicycling across America. They wore yellow jerseys. The woman that I was speaking with had joined because she had a master plan about how to meet another man that was in the biking group. He was unaware of her existence, much less her intentions. But what I came to understand was that spiritually, they were soul mates (in some sense of the word). They were both single, and the woman just had to create a scenario that the man would feel was coincidence in how they met. The rest would happen as spiritually intended.

The third and fifth experiences related to my ex-wife, Stacey. In all of my years after my divorce, I cannot think of one time I have had a grand dream, vision, or heavenly experience regarding Stacey. It may be possible there was something minor, but definitely nothing as overwhelming as the experience I just had. To set the scenario, it is important for me to point out that this upcoming weekend, Stacey is flying with my daughter down to Ft. Lauderdale. Overall, the options would be for me to fly back and forth in order to fly with Georgia each way, or for Stacey to fly and stay somewhere in Ft Lauderdale while Georgia visits with me. We chose the latter option this week just for scheduling purposes. Regardless, that must be said because the experience centered around that scenario.

In the experience, I picked them up at the airport and dropped Stacey off at her hotel. I took Georgia back to my place. We went to bed and woke up for the next day of activities. When morning broke, we were ready to spend a day at the beach. We went out and spent some time on the beach in

The Written (cont'd)

the morning hours and came back in to have lunch. Around this time, I had a call from Stacey. While I do not recall specifically what she asked, it prompted me to take Georgia and go to her hotel. While there, Stacey became very flirty – in a way that I had apparently repressed. This was Stacey from the first year we were together – young, flirty, in Love. She seemed intent on getting me back. In that moment, I recognized her intentions and fought an internal battle over nostalgic emotions and practical logistics. Much of what I arrived at in my mind focused on why she would suddenly want to be with me after hating me for so long.

Georgia went to play in another room, and Stacey continued to flirt with me. I inquired about her boyfriend. She casually threw him under the bus as she explained he did not get her anything of significance for Christmas. I thought long and hard about it and came to the realization that she wanted to be married to him, although she did not Love him. My mind raced at that meaning. Likely, it meant that she never Loved me either, and I was being manipulated in this present moment because she knew I could provide for her. She told me about how her now ex-boyfriend bought himself and his mother extravagant items, but he would not spend the money on her. I never let the flirting go any farther. I tried to figure out a way that we could stay amicable, but the old feelings I had for her had now been dug up from the depths of my soul. I suppose it is safe to say that she was my one true Love – however, it was one where I never felt it was reciprocated.

Glory

While we continued to talk, she told me that she had already booked a dinner for her, Georgia and me at a nice restaurant – one that had entertainment for children as well. It was not a familiar place in the earthly world. I became a little disgusted that I was not spending the weekend with Georgia alone since I could see through her plans. When dinner time arrived, I came back by the hotel to pick them up. However, only Stacey appeared when I arrived. She told me that Georgia had a baby sitter, and that it would be just her and me – that we needed to talk.

I was filled with sadness, intrigue, happiness, and more sadness. The cycle was a jambalaya of mixed emotions. The dominant emotions were the desire for Love and the awareness that this was a game of charades and not true Love. When we sat down at the table Stacey told me how excited she was that I would have dinner with her. She told me that she did not think I could ever forgive her for the way she had acted in our past. I suppose if she was going to pull on all of my heartstrings, this was what was transpiring. I tried to divert the conversation back to Georgia, but she kept reassuring me it was good that we were talking – just her and me.

The conversation led through dinner and into a long walk afterwards. Internally, I remained conflicted. The single greatest question I had was, "Could I be the provider if she was willing to Love openly?" And if she could truly Love now, would she Love me physically, ferociously, and unconditionally as well? Finally, the last question was whether we would be open with each other or just let each other be closed off, where

The Written (cont'd)

we would live among each other, flirt and feel a passionate fire, but be far enough apart that neither were bothered by distance. All of these feelings were confusing, and I dreaded the entire experience. I could not understand why I would have this vision – especially now after all of these years. I once Loved Stacey, but she became a different person. Today, I am an entirely different person – and I suppose she could be as well. Maybe that is what is important in all of this. I do not think it had anything to do with feelings. Maybe, if anything, it was our spiritual selves having a moment of forgiveness in the heavens. What if that was truly what took place? What if Stacey just said, "I'm sorry," to me in spiritual form – in a manner in which she has not been able to do on Earth? And, by her expressing how she was glad that I finally gave her the opportunity to speak to me, that she received resolve to her own spiritual questions in whatever context the spiritual timeline took place.

At a cursory glance, it would be easy to interpret this experience as a dream – wishful, lustful, longing for resolve at a surface level. In a spiritual sense, it should best be interpreted as a parallel timeline wherein the actions of what happens here on Earth should best be observed as the context from which the spiritual experience was instantiated. Could it mean that the experiences are separate and discreet? Absolutely. Could it mean that they could manifest in reality? Absolutely. And as perplexing as that may seem, it should best be understood that through the spiritual experience, I have been imparted understanding of truths hidden beneath the actions of earthly manifestations. Regardless of how far the truth is buried, it is still there. The most important thing is knowing, because in knowing, all action is irrelevant and reaction becomes the gateway to redemption.

The fourth experience occurred in the midst of the scenarios involving Stacey. In the wee hours of the morning I had to use the bathroom (earthly body). I awoke briefly, urinated, and returned to bed. As soon as I began to meditate, I appeared in a shower setting. I knew it was not earthly. As my soul began to surmise the setting, I heard the words, "Get off!" shouted out in a demonic-like voice. I turned to see an apparition with no defined features pushing through the shower curtain and then vanish. I was not scared of the apparition, but I was left wondering the intention of the words.

I initially thought the words related to Stacey and were a warning to stop thinking about her. Maybe the words were a reference to my celibacy vow I have made with God. The voice and appearance were not angelic, so I have to place that under consideration. I am still not sure, but regardless, I awakened, jotted down the notes of the experience and returned to the continuation of events with Stacey.

October 18, 2014

Of all of my experiences in the heavens, I have never had one quite as vivid and alive as this one was. In the past I have explained some amazingly realistic experiences — so I do not

The Written (cont'd)

want these words to lessen the gravity of those prior experiences. In fact, when they have happened, they are as mind-blowing and fantastical as they seem when I write about them. But this time was different. I cannot put my finger on precisely why, but this experience was more hyper-real than any I have ever had.

This experience began with me sitting on a balcony staring out at a setting that looked similar to my condo's setting, but this one was distinctly different. I was sitting in a chair on what I would guess is the eighth floor of the building. As I stared out, I kept repeating to myself, "Something isn't right." I looked out over the edge of the balcony and saw a pool that was at least an acre in size, if not more. There were kids and parents in the pool – everyone enjoying the company of the others around. I sat back down trying to understand why something felt off.

I looked to my left and saw two large broken mirrors that extended from the floor to the ceiling of the patio. They were at least eight feet tall. In the mirrors I saw reflections of what I can only describe as "everything – the past, the present, and the future." As I stared at the mirrors to my left, I said, "Wait! Something isn't right." I immediately recognized my soul was in another location. I had no idea whose body was my vessel. It did not seem like a typical experience where I am in the company of angels, for this one had mortal characteristics. In the grandest experiences I have had in the heavens – the ones where I have seen the face of God, spoken to Jesus, the archangels, and Enoch – they all have a certain hyper real feeling, but anything that corresponds to a flare of mortality is not involved. The feelings can be the same, but there is a special understanding of spiritual form versus mortal form.

Perhaps as I grow, the two will become one. But for now, the experiences are all slightly different. Maybe it has to do with my mental awareness in the moment – like I am more acutely aware of the experience. The point is that this one was so real that I was immediately aware my soul was not on Earth and was in the form of something tangible, something that felt mortal.

I looked around and stood up. My rapid movement caused the world to begin to spin, and I began to lose harmony. I instinctively reached down to ground myself and regain my balance. When everything came back into balance, I walked to the mirrors and turned to the left to look into the glass windows of the suites that attached to the patio. I could see people inside. I began banging on the windows to try to get someone's attention before I lost harmony.

In the first suite, no one paid me any attention. I continued working my way left, down the suites. I banged on the window of another, again with no response. The third window had blinds that were open. I peered inside. It felt like I was in a child's body which did not have full control over its bodily movements. When I banged on the glass, it felt weak and broken in movement. As I focused on the action, I finally banged enough for an older lady to get up off of a chair and come to the door.

The Written (cont'd)

She was very slender and well aged. She had brown hair that was permed in a way that old ladies do. She wore glasses and her chin was pointed. She seemed in earthly years to be in her late eighties or early nineties. She walked to the door and opened it up slightly. As she did, she said, "Hey Ale[ph/x]." I put the name in brackets because I was unable to clearly decipher the word. In context, it sounded like Alex, but in reflection (and after a conversation with Bryan) I feel extremely confident she said Aleph – the first letter of the Hebrew alphabet.

When I heard her words, I was startled. This was the first time I had not been referred to as "Jonathan" in the heavens. And, because I knew this setting was very different than experiences past, it prompted even more questions. I replied with a question, "Alex is my name?" She responded, "Yes." I apologized for being forgetful and tried to quickly explain I was having to collect my bearings. I decided to press further. I asked, "How old am I?" She responded quickly, "Just a few months. You have not been here six months yet."

My mind raced at the possibilities. I was in the form of another with a name I had never heard. I was only a few months old – an impossibility in earthly terms. I felt like a child, but there is no way I was only a few months old and walking around. The lady was much taller than I. Everything seemed in proportion to her size, not mine. This led me to believe I was definitely a child in some context. I decided to ask the big question next. "What part of the world are we in?" I phrased it like this because I knew I was not in Florida, or likely even Earth. I was quick enough in thought to ask it in a manner that would not give me away. But before she answered, the anticipation caused me to lose harmony and I returned to my body.

I journaled the experience and managed to return to the same setting, albeit with a little less clarity. During my time in this location I went down to the pool level. There was a series of unfortunate mishaps that continued to happen to me along the way. I kept telling people the bizarre story. The first two involved something along the lines of a conversation on my "wings" and not realizing they were there. Something comical transpired which prompted the story. Eventually, I headed toward a grand entrance adjacent to the pool. The entrance was made of alabaster walls and gray stone walkways. On either side of the door there was a raised terrace. On the right, there was a female angel with a hose. As I was sharing my comical stories with my angel guide, the angel with the hose somehow managed to soak me in water. This made the stories even funnier because whatever had happened prior had made me change clothes. So even with a new change of clothes, I became soaked with this water.

The only other real details I can remember is how one angel told me he was initially unaware his wings were growing too. He actually managed to singe the wingtips, which caused the wings to temporarily have stunted growth. Others shared stories with me about their wings. My impression was my wings were beginning to grow – that an earthly experience I had with a jellyfish stinging either shoulder blade while I was

The Written (cont'd)

caught in a riptide and praying to God for help was the beginning of their noticeable growth in earthly form.

October 19, 2014

This morning in the heavens, I walked into a room and headed to a safe in the wall. I heard, "He's here to take the lawyer test." The voice was male, booming and deep. At that time, I heard a female chime in. She responded to the male voice and said, "Don't do that and save my forty-two thousand dollars." I never saw where the voice originated, and the experience subsequently ended before I opened the safe.

I jotted down the notes of the conversation and returned to a deep meditation. Almost immediately I felt a strong tug at my core from underneath. At that moment my body became spiritually aligned. It was as if the tug caused my soul to spiritually snap into alignment for travel. Immediately I found myself over a large body of water facing a shoreline. My angelic guide continued to reiterate, "Remember, this is the nineties." I saw a formless lady trying to pick up a row of something formless in the water. I was supposed to watch and help the lady… according to my guide. But to describe how formless the experience was and how I was supposed to find understanding would be tantamount to a blind person seeing the most basic shapes for the first time. I lost harmony, returned to my body and wrote down the experience.

Glory

I returned immediately. This time, I was in the water. Again, I was formless, and I was aware of the presence of a line (that is the best way I can describe it) along my right side. On my left side was a dock. I became aware that the line represented a lady. A man at the dock with blonde hair and a white coat kept telling me, "Watch out Jonathan." I was still trying to gather my bearings, but I was able to understand that my position between the dock and the "line/lady" was what the man was referring to. He was trying to reach out from the dock and pull this lady to the dock. I was not sure why he was trying to reach out to her, but as he worked he offered for me to "dock against his dock" while he worked. I assumed I must be in a boat myself, but everything was formless, except for the man, so it was hard for me to understand. As the man worked he exclaimed, "I don't have to like you Jonathan, but you need to watch out." He seemed to have an evil vibe. If he was wearing something other than white, I might have assumed he was the man in rose-colored glasses impersonating an angel. He was flashy and wore sunglasses which I never see among the angels of light.

I lost harmony and returned. After writing down the seemingly impossible description of a formless adventure I had returned from, I returned to another almost impossible to describe moment. This time, while I was formless, I was in the shape of a line. I was helping people. Below me, there was a twenty-five-year-old girl who needed help. However, it was reiterated to me that she was a two-year-old child. The girl that I was helping was represented by two lines beneath me

The Written (cont'd)

that were closer together at the top than they were at the bottom. If perspective existed, it would be as if I was staring up the rails of a ladder extending to the horizon. However, I could not decide if the layout was due to perspective or design. I was shared the word "Chelsea" – not as a name, but rather as a concept of the action.

My guide was instructing me to move this girl up a path that led back to my home. At the time, my understanding was that "home" was in relation to where I reside in Fort Lauderdale... not as a specific point, but rather a general region. But in retrospect, "home" could have been "heaven." There were others in addition to the girl I had to help as well. I could see the action with the motion. In the background, I heard the lyrics to a song I had never heard before repeating over and over. The words being sung were, "She is so beautiful." Overall, this may be the most abstract experience I have ever had, but it made sense spiritually. I eventually lost harmony and returned to my body.

I again wrote down the experience and returned once again. This time the context of the experience pertained to me wearing a t-shirt under a shirt. I apparently was wearing a V-neck white t-shirt under a button-down collared shirt. It was not like other t-shirts I had ever worn. I walked around asking the angels around me if I looked okay (as in dressed appropriately), to which they all responded that I looked great. But, for some reason, my undershirt was bothering me. I pulled aside one angel I felt closest to and took off my top shirt. When I showed him how baggy the shirt was he said, "Oh, you shouldn't wear a V-neck..." That was the confirmation I needed that seemed to support my thought that it was overly baggy and made me look clumsily dressed. When I put my shirt back on over the white V-neck, everyone was happy. Similar episodes continued, but I was unable to retain all of the information.

After the experiences ended, I researched the word Chelsea. I learned that it is an old-English word used to describe a harbor. I definitely think that I was being shared the word to help me understand the context of my journey. As for the white V-neck, it took me nearly a week before I realized that what I was wearing was the white smock-like garment that I have seen many angelic teachers wear in my visions. It is not really a t-shirt, but rather a complete garment. The context of my experience was demonstrating to me that I was a spiritual teacher growing into my role (hence how baggy the garment was). The button down shirt was demonstrating my earthly role – the facade I have to live as I grow spiritually.

October 22, 2014

I found myself this morning in a dark and foreboding landscape. It was nighttime and had an eerie atmosphere. There were two houses divided by a wall. One house was a structure like one would find on Earth. The other structure was more like a strip-mall. On the strip-mall side, there were zombie-like individuals roaming around. They were not evil,

The Written (cont'd)

but rather lost or unawakened souls. On the far end of the strip mall I rented a unit. For some reason it felt purposed for me. I left the grounds of my residence and proceeded across the wall to the other end.

The journey to my rented unit could be made for a variety of reasons. This particular time, it was to throw trash away in a receptacle near the door. I explored the inside of the residential house pretty well. From the outside it appeared to have three or four stories, depending on which side it was viewed from. It needed a new coat of paint. Its current coat of paint was peeling and in pretty poor condition. The people on this side of the wall were very knowledgeable of the heavens, but I could tell that this was not a great place. It was more like a halfway house between heaven and hell.

On my final trip to the zombie side, I ran across a black man in a yellow rain coat. He appeared near the end of the strip mall. When he appeared, I was startled. He was tall and had more life than the rest of the zombies. I immediately became nervous. I threw away the trash in my hands and decided to take a different path back to the house so I was not in his line-of-sight. I passed a few other zombies. When I had almost made it back to the wall, I neared a garden where the gate was. At the exact moment I reached the green garden, the man in the yellow jacket appeared around the corner. Linearly, it did not make sense how he could have beaten me to this place, but that did not matter. Instead of acting scared, I just continued onward to the gate. When I reached it, I remained calm and collected. I never ran. I opened it up and held the gate open for the man. I said, "After you." He nodded his head in acknowledgement and entered through the gate.

After he took a few steps, he approached me to speak. I played it off and said, "Well, hello sir. And what made you want to speak to me? Was it my dashing good looks that you must have noticed across the way?" My reply was entirely out of place because I am never arrogant or sarcastic in my visions. But, this was strong with both. He motioned to the house before us. We were facing the backside. He said, "Every ninth floor – you heard me – I know what I am talking about..." His voice trailed off. It was as if he was about to tell me something spiritual in the architecture he had discovered, but when I looked at the house, I only saw four stories. It puzzled me for a brief second which he must have picked up on. My puzzled expression must have been why he continued on with his justification in "knowing what he was talking about." It caused me to lose harmony, but I did not return to my body.

When I regained my bearings, I was no longer with the man behind the house. Instead, I was in a room with a letter before me. I tried to read the letter. The words were poorly written, but I knew the poorly written words represented the transmission method and the context represented how well I was able to receive and how well the information was being sent. The letter seemed to be from someone else. I thought it was from Wilson or about the earthly job I was doing for Wilson's company. About midway through the jumbled words, I understood that the author was saying he had solved his dilemma about investors – at least partially. The words said

The Written (cont'd)

something about "1244" and "I collect on square." There were some other words, but the gibberish prevented me from repeating it back and memorizing it easily enough to bring it back with me to Earth. My impression was that I was being told to have faith in my current employment, but the context of the house and atmosphere makes the communication and interpretation seem questionable.

I returned to my body, journaled, and once again returned to the heavens. I heard a voice that sounded like the voice that came from Leia's bounty hunter mask in the opening scenes of the movie, Return of the Jedi. The voice instructed me to "follow." I was in a square tube ascending. The voice said, "You are on the eighth floor and ascending." I thought I was heading to the ninth floor. There was something pleasing – as if I had been given a purple coat in that moment. It was archetypal, but the symbolism must be understood during this moment of ascension.

There was an East-West guide-harness put on me (something that helped me manage my motions only in those directions). I asked for a North-South guide to be placed on me as well so that I could make sure I was not "being touched along the way." I was not sure it I was being tricked into following a bad path, or following a way out of the area through this tube. I also was not given any more info other than the ninth floor represented the completion of a cycle.

As it all began to fade, a voice rang out from above, "You're repeating what you said you have to do." This phrase was repeated many times from a female angelic voice. That was the last thing I remember as I returned to my body.

October 23, 2014

I was standing with two teenage girls who were trying to sneak off to their first "race" together. I assumed it pertained to NASCAR, but I honestly have no idea why. They bought their tickets and were supposed to have parental supervision. They chose to go without supervision. They sneaked off and boarded a plane. The plane had a red tail and a white body. Both girls ended up being murdered. One was killed in the cargo hold near a crate.

When the plane landed, the parents found out about the news. The news reporters found out as well. The parents of the two girls had recently experienced another loss, which made this one that much more severe. The girl's friends – one couple where the guy was a songwriter – wrote a song for her to be performed at her funeral. It was emphasized to me that the song was a potential chart-topper.

I was also shown a scenic view from the girl's hometown. There was a large lake that reminded me of the lake just north of Chattanooga. In the water near the shore there was a letter. At first I thought it was the letter "P" but after I stared at it, it is possible it could have been an "R." The friends of hers saw it and asked if one of them had put it there, but no one had. Though there was not much more context, it was shown to me

The Written (cont'd)

that the mechanic/baggage guy was the murderer. He had been on the plane.

I returned to my body, journaled the experience and returned to the heavens. In this experience, I received a mass text of pictures from the life of a model (who enjoyed showing off her pictures). I thought it was from a girl I knew in Nashville, but then again, I think it was more archetypal than specific in identity. In the experience I was with my "sister" – who I understood to be my angelic sister. She looked disappointed when she saw me receive them and saw who they were from. Though there must have been thousands of pictures that scrolled at an incomprehensible rate, the last text said something along the lines of her being drunk and wanting me to have everything from her. My angelic guides did not seem thrilled at the situation. And while I continued scrolling through her lifetime of pictures, I had no recognition of anyone in the pictures – including whoever sent them to me.

October 25, 2014

In this experience, my earthly sister was wanting to visit. She was somewhere within the state of Louisiana. She was on a bridge that intersected with a road to Fort Lauderdale. As I observed this motif, a beautiful girl roller-skated by us in a white bikini and white skates. There was an emphasis on God wanting us to learn all that we can without His direct help. Part of it was just in the concept of healing.

Glory

There was a girl named Sarah in the motif. She reminded me of one of my sister's friends from middle school. She wanted to speak to me about life. She answered some question on a piece of paper on which I was writing.

October 26, 2014

Though I forgot to write down the experience upon returning, the most I can remember was something about the motion of moving "down and around" a building.

October 28, 2014

Bryan's vision he texted me about (word-for-word and unedited from his text):

I was standing in my front yard at the dawn of the morning; there were faces I have never seen. As I look to the sky to see the moon taking its last glimpse at the Earth, a man I've never seen before stood beside me and pointed to the sky exclaiming, " what the hell was that right there just in front of that moon there's 2 more in a triangle, and 2 more beyond that. They were a total of five moons in the sky. I found myself walking in a distant city and looked down at my Citizen™ wrist watch, which was unexpectedly rusted. Hay bellowing voice from the sky said to me, "just as stainless should not, but does rust, time does, and will, move forward. All is temporal in this place, beset by space, which is not. This too shall

The Written (cont'd)

pass." I felt saddened, but realized the futility of my walk, and thusly returned to my car. Elders sat in the streets of this broken down town discussing the significance of the "Morning of The Five Moons". I then awoke. The girl was there, but she was different: short hair, svelte & tall, beautifully androgynous. (No homo). Her jawlines were sharp & defined, high cheek bones, brilliant blue eyes, and wearing a gray pants-suit.

Fourth Revelation

There are times when a person must stand trial for his sins. During this journey, there have been continual efforts by the angels to help me seek forgiveness for my earthly sins. The first experience of this Fourth Revelation begins with that very same theme. And though a soul may be chosen to do work for God if that soul so chooses Him, it does not mean that past sins are forgotten, or that forgiveness must not be sought. This was the lesson of how the Fourth Revelation was initially presented, though the reason for its inclusion as the Fourth Revelation is due to the way it ended.

As the experience began, I found myself in a courtroom. After standing trial in the heavens during the most uncomfortable of situations, I came to understand the meaning of it all to be that this was a moment of judgment in God's eyes. The judgment was not just about past sins, but rather His impending decision of whether I had sought true forgiveness and had proven worthy enough to carry the weight of His upcoming directives. This is how the Fourth Revelation began. It would end with an answer to weeks of prayer and questions I had where I found myself pleading to God for clarity in His great plan.

Glory

During the previous weeks, I have questioned how I was supposed to be a leader for His chosen people, how/why they would listen to me, or even if I understood His directive clearly. With every question regarding hearing His directive, I was continually met with confirmation after confirmation. But the motion of how I was supposed to move, how I was supposed to lead, was absent of direction.

I am strongly cautious – especially in anything of this magnitude – for in every movement forward, history will forever be written and remembered. I could not wrap my mind around how I could be tasked to be a leader on Earth when it seemed to be such a struggle to help my own family see beyond their own beliefs. And, even though the questions may seem out-of-place in the context of this writing, I questioned how I was supposed to build an ark as Noah was tasked to do. And what would that even mean if that was truly one of His directives?

It was in direct response to this question that God answered in the most miraculous of ways. This was the Fourth Revelation. Though it took a little research after His answer was spoken, I came to understand that my questions to God were no different than the questions Moses asked Him when he was asked to lead His people to the Promised Land. So I should not have been surprised that His response would have occurred in the same way He spoke to Moses – though crafted for modern times. The story of Moses seeking confirmation from God has stood the test of time – thousands of years. But the way His answer was presented to Moses was in such a way

Fourth Revelation

that I did not quite understand the complete meaning of the grand architecture in His response until I experienced this Fourth Revelation in the heavens. This was the day I saw the Ineffable Name of God and understood why it cannot be spoken or written.

...

October 29, 2014

The experience began with me being called in to a legal proceeding to review how a previous court case was handled. I was talking to two "officers" that were angels. At the time, the conversation seemed very fluid. However, I recognized one of the "officers" as the male angel that reminds me of Richard from the television show Lost. The other one had blonde hair. I joked with them about the evidence, and they seemed amused at the misfortune, though I was careful to say that it was all in the past, etc. Throughout the conversation, I wanted them to know I accepted my wrongs, but I was still frustrated over the court case being handled unjustly.

Eventually, I was asked to show up in a courtroom where I was asked to stand up and testify. The judge was reviewing why I was convicted in order to reassess if it was just. I was asked to sit at a table by the judge, though I chose to stand up during the proceeding. The jury was to my right. There was not a table for the prosecution. There was only a large table for the defendant and the section for the jury who all appeared to be very rigid, cold, and stern.

As I stood there, the jury was asked to read how they arrived at my original conviction. As they searched for the page of paper in the packet, it became apparent something was wrong – as if the packet was incomplete or misfiled. As I stood there, I noticed two male angels standing along the left hand wall. They were there in my support, but would not waiver in appearance to their opinions. The courtroom was also full of witnesses. The judge pressed on to the jury while they feverishly searched through their packets. "And?" he asked. "Somebody needs to read what happened."

The lead juror said, "Your honor, it isn't here. I remember the testimony but it seems to be misfiled." The judge looked at me as if asking me to chime in. I said, "Your honor, this is what I've been saying. From the very beginning this case hasn't been about guilt or innocence. It has been about technicalities of opinion." I then recited my testimony and recited word-for-word the judges prior conviction. The courtroom was entertained at the humor and my sarcasm.

In truth, the events coupled with my style of oration was meant to demonstrate how absurd my previous judgment actually transpired. At the end, the judge said, "Good. It sounds like the judge ruled correctly." He was obviously not entertained by my delivery or style of oration. I replied, "Your honor, with all due respect, while the judge ruled this, I asked for a blood test...repeatedly. And though I know it sounds absurd, I was laughed at and told that I was going to jail. It does

Fourth Revelation

not matter whether I was right or wrong. I have since learned there are both good and evil forces working underneath everything that seems real. Actually, there is no evil, only hard redirects of goodness. So as absurd as this all seems, that is the story."

The two angels spoke up and said something I could not decipher to the courtroom. I thought they were calling out the technical challenges my case had as well as how even the current case was not filed correctly. The judge seemed to waiver at whatever the angels said. The judge said, "I have to have paperwork. I have to have it all right here. Somebody get me the paperwork. Are you going to tell me this was misfiled after everything else that went on with this man?" He seemed angered at having a technicality change a conviction when he and I both knew the truth of the action that took place.

I was stared at coldly until he said the words, "You can go until I receive my paperwork." I walked to the door on my right. The jury was to my right and the left was the audience. There were a couple of rows of people in front of the jury as well a group of angels on my right that were smiling at me. A couple of female angels smiled and congratulated me. It seemed as if the judge admitted to the legal technicalities being wrought with problems which led to my dismissal. And though he never said it was officially dismissed, the reaction by the female angels helped me understand that it was almost definitely going to be tossed out. The two male angels told me congratulations as well – even more confirmation in everything working in my favor.

Glory

As I walked out, one of the male angels (the one that looked like Richard from Lost) said something along the lines of, "See, eventually everything works out." Someone else said, "It must be a great birthday present." As I heard that, I realized it was May 2nd – seven days prior to my birthday, though no year was given. Also, I recognized that 5/2 sums to seven. It was at this moment I knew with certainty that the case was being tossed out.

In another experience during this morning, I received a direct answer to my prayers before going to sleep. I spent a long time on the beach on Earth just speaking with my Lord, my King this evening. During that conversation, I acknowledged all of the events that had transpired throughout the day and what I thought they meant. I had a challenging conversation with my earthly father earlier in the evening. During that conversation I could not get him to understand a specific message that God was trying to share with him, and that had been shared with me. My dad remained headstrong in his thoughts. It was during the conversation with my dad that I realized I could not yet begin to share with him my relationship with our True Father and the marvels that He has shared with me. I realized that if it is truly God's intention for me to lead people, then I have a long road ahead of me because I cannot even convince my own parents of important things that God is sharing with me. I was overcome with sadness.

As I prayed aloud to God, I realized that I also was unable earlier in the day to get Bryan – my spiritual brother and believer in all that has been shared with us – to take one specific

Fourth Revelation

afternoon acknowledging God's plan that included him. I have never tried to press the points to any of my family members or even Bryan because pressing is a force of opposition to thought. In the conversation with Bryan, I only set up questions so that he could willfully follow the call. But even the most artful approach wherein my father and Bryan could each shape their own opinions on the subject matter of each conversation still managed to fall upon deaf ears. And while I have included this example with Bryan in this journal entry, it should be noted that this was an extremely rare moment with him where there seemed to be some force at work preventing the message from being revealed. Good or bad, lesson or test... I do not know. But, it was rare.

During my prayer, I reflected on this simple fact: if God intends for me to lead a people, and/or build an "ark," then how would I ever be able to demonstrate to them that I was not crazy, or falsely interpreting His plans for me? I began to question my own interpretation of God's communication to me. I was at a breaking point. I asked for Him to help me understand if, somehow, after all of the confirmations upon confirmations, I had managed to misinterpret His intention. I asked Him to help me understand if I was truly being tasked with leading His chosen people and possibly even to build an ark.

As for the reason the question came up with the ark, for over a year and a half, Bryan and I have both received instructions to build an "ark" but the specifications have remained unclear. The directive was most clearly defined when I asked

Glory

God during a prayer, "Am I really supposed to build an ark?" to which God's voice boomed out from the silence, "I asked Noah to build an ark, didn't I?" But all we have understood to this point is that an ark is a concept that bridges two points. These two points could be between spirit and God (as in Ark of the Covenant), a vessel (such as Noah's ark), and even a concept such as books (that bridge God's words to the minds of those who cannot or will not hear His voice).

There are even more potential interpretations, which is why Bryan and I have understood the directive, but have sought further clarity on His direction. It has been more akin to knowing we were going to college to seek a major that would support a directive in Ark building. But as the journey has continued, over the last month or two I have come to a much more complete understanding of this "ark" and what it is that I believe God intends. My understanding has arrived through prayer, responses, and reflection on all that I have been able to write over the last several years of these heavenly experiences.

Over the last few months I have not said anything in prayer to my Father regarding my understanding of this newly refined ark concept. Instead, I have chosen to further explore my understanding through His daily lessons. I wanted to return to Him once I thought I understood His intentions and have a more matter-of-fact conversation about what I believed I had learned thus far. Up unto this point, all I knew was that Bryan and I had a directive to build an ark...as crazy as that sounds... and yes, we both know it sounds crazy. Could the

Fourth Revelation

biblical stories we have read about from childhood also be taking place with him and me? That seemed impossible until there was confirmation after confirmation... However, in all honesty, I am not sure if Bryan will move in action, or choose to stay inactive and merely temporal, as was demonstrated when I tried to get him to come down to Fort Lauderdale for an afternoon (I was paying all expenses as well), and he could not make time with his schedule. It was not my request, but rather God's request...and he chose to ignore it. In this moment, earthly challenges in life consumed his attention.

So, during my prayer, I asked my Father for understanding and clarity in His directives for me. There have obviously been numerous questions bubbling up for me, but I have held back on the big questions until I had a better grasp on what He has been attempting to communicate to me. How could I lead a people if I could not even guide my own family? Why would Bryan not even acknowledge the calling – and he is my very own spiritual brother? And if I had somehow misinterpreted my own personal growth with a calling, then what was the purpose and intention of the ark? Also, there was another more personal question I had about a way to understand His word. More than anything, I just sought my Father to help me understand these questions in no particular order, with no defined timeline. In fact, I asked for Him to share with me when the time was appropriate, but that He should know at the very minimum, these are the questions that I have no answer for.

So this leads me to the next heavenly experience of the night. The backstory had to be set so the gravity of the experience could best be illustrated. Hot off the heels of the courtroom saga, I returned to the heavens. In a room, Bryan appeared in the distance holding a single piece of parchment paper/scroll paper/canvas/or something of a similar texture. He was holding it outward from his body, facing me. He walked to me from the dimly lighted surroundings into the room of light.

As he approached me, he said, "I have been given a Hebrew word, and I now know the answer you seek is in the Hebrew word." As he approached, the piece of parchment became the only thing in focus. Bryan disappeared from the vision. Another angel appeared beside me to help me understand what it was that I was seeing. If I had to interpret Bryan's presence, I would say that the angel initially presented himself as Bryan to help me understand that Bryan was as integral to what I was seeing as I was in receiving the message. I did not understand there to be two different entities in the vision, but rather one that transitioned from Bryan to one of the angels I see regularly.

As I attempted to read the word on the page, it shifted before my eyes. I thought I was seeing four distinct Hebrew letters. In fact, I felt confident there were only four letters. But, whenever I tried to read the four letters as a word, I saw two words, one consisting of two letters, the other of three letters, each word bound by a common letter – Aleph. It was as if the four-character word transfigured upon itself to form the words that had to remain in motion. The first several attempts at reading the word continued to be Aleph-Beyt (read traditional-

Fourth Revelation

ly right-to-left). This word means "father" and I understood that it was talking about my Father, whom I have recently expressed a will to call Him Father and King rather than just "God" during our conversations. I desire for my conversations with my Father to be intimate, which is why I have felt led to use those terms rather than the generic "God" or "Lord." Those two words seem more akin to saying "sir" or "ma'am" rather than an intimate name...but then again, I also do not think that using the term Father or King can be used with the same meaning without finding that intimacy with Him.

So as I read the word, I could only focus on Aleph-Beyt, but when trying to see the whole word, it transformed into Aleph-Shin-Resh. As I understood the three-letter word, Shin and Resh would lose focus and Aleph-Beyt would refocus. I knew the word was three letters, but carried a deeper meaning than the three-letter word itself through the addition of the fourth letter. It was as if the word Aleph-Shin-Resh was stamped on either side by the word "Aleph-Beyt." I was not sure of the context, but I knew that it was important. I recognized that it was undoubtedly related to my prayer earlier in the evening, but I was unsure of the word that I was being shown. At the time, I was not sure if it was a four-letter word, or some type of phrase that was being shared with me for guidance. After I committed the experience to memory I returned to my body.

I took notes and returned to the heavens. Later, after I had one more experience in the heavens, I turned to researching the word I was shown. My first and only search on Google

Glory

consisted of "four letter name for God Hebrew." I had the impression the word was the name of God, though I have no context as to why that feeling was impressed to me. I assumed it was just another, lesser-known name. Of course YHVH appeared and I clicked on the first link to see what all it had to say. But after clicking the link, my world stood still for just a moment. The page I arrived on shared that in Exodus, when Moses believed he was being called to lead people, he asked God to give Him his name to know he was hearing the true voice of God and not being mislead. God replied (in the English translation), "I am who I am." And while I have never paid much attention to this verse (it always just seemed like backstory), the page I was on broke down the original Hebrew phrase in which Exodus was written.

The phrase for "I am who I am" was written in Hebrew pronunciation as "ey-yah asher ey-yah." The word for "who" was Asher, which is spelled Aleph-Shin-Resh (one of the words I was given). On either side of Asher was the word for "I am" – "ey-yah." For me, without even comparing the message I received, this expresses two important facts. The first is that it confirms Bryan's previous vision that a person should never identify with the phrase "I am" nor are we to identify as a "who" – but rather we are to identify as vessels, which is a "what." The word "who" is reserved for God – and only God. According to Bryan's divine message, "We are the sum of our choices, not of our mistakes." Our identities should never be viewed as "who" which leaves the only spiritual claim to that identity as God Himself.

Fourth Revelation

This is why the message that God delivered to Moses was so important to have been written down for generations to see. It was not because God said, "Because I said I am." The divinity in the message was in God referring to Himself as a "who" bookended with the one phrase that represents identity – a phrase that we, as vessels, are not. This is something I wrote about in Book I – Gravity Calling. So, the entire phrase Moses received was obviously what he needed to hear in his question to God, but it also confirms all that Bryan and I have been receiving. The fact that we speak English and not Hebrew, makes bridging the language of the Divine to our minds much more challenging.

It is also important to note that the word I have felt best expresses my relationship with God is "Father." This is the way that God and I commune. It could best be seen as how a child will stick with a name for each of his parents and rarely (if ever) deviate from the words. Mother is always mother, and not mom. Mama is likely never going to be changed to Mommy. So for me, when I received God's message in written form, it was viewed as His divine signature to a word that cannot be spoken but was communicated in a way that is intimate between the two people communicating. For me, God replied to my firestorm of questions by showing me His name: "Father, Who, Father." It is essentially the same response Moses received...where the word Asher was the word used to describe Our Great Creator.

And while I would be stepping out on a limb to express what Moses likely received in His direct communication with

Glory

God, in understanding that the Ineffable Name of God is ineffable which therein lies a paradox, it stands to reason that Moses saw the same letters as presented to me. And, it also stands to reason that if Hebrew was the only spoken language today, and I had to explain how God confirmed to me that He was truly calling me to action (knowing that my spiritual understandings of concepts like "who," "what," and "I am" are far deeper than the general student would understand without further study), I would explain the Ineffable Name of God in the way it was communicated to me archetypally: "The Father Who Is The Father," which would be further simplified into, "I am who I am."

So, in understanding the message delivered to me in this context, it is to be understood that I was shared the same message as Moses, in response to essentially the same question. I had never read the Hebrew translation of Exodus. I was only familiar with the English – and the storyline at best...not the intricate details that support the story such as this phrase's Hebrew meaning. In retrospect, this newfound understanding also caused me to recognize that the Torah contains the story of Moses's life, summed up in just a few sentences. Who knows how quickly the story transpired, or how long Moses took to receive His messages. Single verses could take days, weeks, months, years... after all, he lived hundreds of years of a divine life. All of those years are summed up in a short story. These journal experiences are written as they occur... and all of these experiences have transpired over three years for me so far.

Fourth Revelation

At this point, I have written nearly three-hundred-thousand words in my journals alone spanning approximately three years. This does not even include the application of the experiences to action in life. So it is important that a modern perspective and relative understanding to historical texts are observed in how the words of the Books of Nine are communicated. It is not as if scrolls and ink were in endless supply back in ancient days. It was a labor to even make a scroll or find the pigments to create ink. In modern times, we have computers, spellcheck, laser printers, and printing presses. Writing was pretty much an extreme effort in ancient times versus today.

So, after journaling the Asher experience, I returned to the heavens once more. And I suppose it is important to emphasize why I call this location "the heavens" and not "Heaven" proper due to the events that occurred next. I found myself standing in my apartment that I currently live in. I walked into the living room and noticed my patio door was open. On my patio, I have two chairs, a rocking chair, and a table with two more chairs. As I peered outside of my door, I noticed a dark figure sitting in the lounge chair closest to the door. It was Lucifer. He was wearing a black suit and sitting in a power-metro-GQ-legs-crossed pose.

I did not feel fear. Instead, it was like a casual run-in with an opponent. Neither of us was there with an agenda. Clearly there are no feelings of hate toward each other. Hate doesn't exist in spiritual form. It was a curious feeling. It was as if Lucifer admitted that he would not be able to conquer or sway me with his best efforts, and now he was just there on a casual visit. Either way, I did not want to socialize with him, so I walked outside and told him that he needed to leave.

He was unmoved by my desire for him to leave. He just sat there calm and collected. I asked him why he was there. He looked at me and said, "I'm just curious more than anything. I'm interested in why you are being shown God's favor." In that moment, I understood. He once was God's most Loved child and due to his own actions, was cast out from God's favor...left to run amuck in the darkness. He was sad – hurt even. He would not admit it though. He hid it behind the flashy appearance of his black suit, his sharp and edgy appearance, his GQ approach to style, and the women he paraded around to lure the lost with desires of the flesh (which I now see is why sex is viewed as such a spiritual influence). My unyielding faith in God and His continued nurturing of my soul was something that caught the attention of Lucifer. More than anything, I could see Lucifer wanted someone to talk to – honestly, as if he was in need of a friend, knowing full well he would never have one.

Unfortunately, that is not something I can, nor will I ever offer. I told Lucifer one more time that he needed to leave – that we were not friends or buddies. He seemed saddened, but accepted that fact. He turned and, as he flew off my patio, he vaporized into a black cloud swirling off into the distance. In the end, I know he was aware of the events that God shared with me during my travels tonight. In fact, he could just as easily have been playing the "sad child card" to see if it would lure me away from God, but I really think it was the first time

Fourth Revelation

I saw his hurt rather than his facade. He truly wanted to see what I had or was doing differently than other souls.

It actually served as another affirmation for my own journey and the events that had transpired over the evening. How much more of a confirmation of God saying, "Yes, you are going to lead the people," in the same manner he confirmed to Moses, than also having Lucifer show up at your doorstep (literally) to try to see why God was showing me favor. It is also important to note that I had not yet understood the Hebrew word Asher. I had to research that afterwards, which is when all of this experience fell into place that much more precisely. Time is linear, but the understanding of all that is communicated cannot always occur linearly.

The Written (cont'd)

October 30, 2014

Though I do not have anything very intriguing to journal, I spent the majority of my time in the heavens playing football this morning. I really do not know why these sports motifs continue to occur unless it is like "PE" for the soul... as if the body, soul, and mind need to stay in good practice with understanding how they are yoked together. It is just a thought, but rationally makes sense. Maybe there was not much need for a new lesson, but rather to maintain spiritual fitness.

October 31, 2014

On the day the world celebrates costumes, masks, and evil spirits (Halloween), I cannot be surprised I received my Day of Judgment from my Father. Honestly, this was not a day I could ever have imagined. Nor did it come with fanfare or understanding of the gravity of the moment until after I awoke and journaled the experience. If I were to say that I have experienced some of the grandest experiences I could never have imagined, it would still be an understatement. Standing before

Glory

God, the archangels, Enoch, Jesus, and the heavenly wonders is beyond imagination. Every experience is rife with grandeur, pregnant with meaning. And yes, each experience could have stood alone for all the remainder of my days, and I would have felt more humbled and blessed than is conceivable. So, as I begin to explain this next experience, understand it is the end, not the beginning that holds all of the meaning.

The experience began at a concert event. One of the angels that I could best compare to Taylor Swift in features was on stage. I never gathered if she was singing or speaking. All I knew was that I was standing on the front row, my daughter was on my left – an angel separated her and me. The angel on stage continued to show me attention (flirty) as she was on stage. It was as if I was the only person in the audience. I could tell she was trying to grab my attention and bring me into the heavenly experience. In retrospect, this was a celebration of sorts – one that this particular angel was intended to bring me into the experience.

At one point, she forced me to try on the shoes she was wearing. I played it off well because they were women's shoes. I just joked with her about it. Later, she asked me, "Do you like these shoes?" I was puzzled about how to respond. I said, "I do, but remember I'm a guy." She laughed. She knew what she was doing. She tossed them to me and said, "They're yours." After I caught them, I showed them to my daughter and let her have them.

After the concert, I exited the arena and later re-entered. There was a large football field in the atrium. I lifted it up as if

The Written (cont'd)

the entire field was a piece of carpet only to reveal another football field beneath it. It was as if the field was layered on top of itself. I rode a giant railing down to the bottom of a great staircase and headed down a long corridor. As I began to walk down the long tunnel (hoping to find the entrance to the hockey game), I was stopped by an angel that was wearing a thick cloak. The angel's face was not visible, nor was anything else. The cloak was a reddish hue.

I knew the angel was a woman. She said, "Here – let me mark you." She lifted up my right hand with her left hand. Her skin was light and delicate. I could tell she was likely the angel I had seen earlier on stage – but this time cloaked. She pulled out a marker with her right hand and quickly drew a large circle over the top of my right hand. She then dotted an X pattern with 5 dots above it. The entire marking was large enough that the dots were over the top of my wrist. She emphasized the marking by making sure I had heightened sensation with the sensation of the marker to my skin – especially as she drew the five dot pattern. When she finished the marking she said, "Good. Now you can go." At that moment, I understood the marking to be a divine marking that allowed me to come and go from wherever the hallway led, sort of akin to being marked for re-entry of a club or venue.

At the end of the hallway was a dark room – similar to an old movie theatre. There were reddish drapes along the walls and a balcony in the rear. I entered in the balcony section. I observed only a handful of people in there. These people were

Glory

mostly children and seemed to be dark-skinned. I realized it was not the hockey game and turned to walk out.

When I exited, I became hung on a piece of denim hanging from the rear of the door. I did not panic, but I felt a sense of urgency in trying to leave without anyone asking questions. As I tried to free myself from the denim, it ripped in half. My foot was still hung. As I looked down, I noticed I was wearing a brand new white pair of sneakers with a price tag still attached. The tag became hung on the denim and ripped off. I immediately grabbed the price tag because I did not want to leave evidence of my departure. I went back up the hallway and down another in search of the hockey game.

After I lost harmony, I realized the significance. Hockey game aside, this was a moment I saw the Mark of God for those who will be saved in the End of Days. An angel marked my right hand with the seal of God to allow me to pass. It is even more interesting because the only references to a mark upon the right hand are made in Deuteronomy and in Revelation. In Revelation, the right hand is mentioned as containing the mark of the beast. In Deuteronomy (to which I have paralleled my life) it references God's mark for his stewards. Later in Revelation, it is revealed that the angels must mark the 144,000 of God's people before those with the mark of the beast are judged. If anything should become apparent right now, it is that the end of days is near and that the marks are happening at this present time.

The Written (cont'd)

November 1, 2014

While I cannot explain how this was communicated to me, I do know that the mark I received was the seal of God rather than the mark of the beast. And, even though that is what I initially thought, yesterday I had a lot of time to dwell upon the possibility that I could have been marked by the beast. Though I live my life as pure and Christ-like as possible, having this thought enter into my mind must be viewed as how important it is to scrutinize every detail of the journey. The fact that this level of scrutiny would even arise in light of the amazing experiences that have been revealed to me should be seen as how delicate the grace on either side of the defining line for the mark of God or mark of the Beast remains. But now I know without a doubt that I received the seal from God. Most importantly, the circle on my hand represented "the whole, the truth, the light." The rest will be revealed in time.

Also, just in an effort to document everything, I had an experience this morning that is uncomfortable to write about. I want to emphasize the difficulty in writing about this particular type of experience, but transparency in these writings is of utmost importance. So with that said, in the experience, there was a very quick motif of a beautiful woman attempting to milk my body of my seed, but I told her to stop when I realized what was happening. In the end, it was too late and I ended up spilling forth all over her face...so much...so, so much. I do not like to write about this, but I just want to make sure I capture everything from these experiences. After it happened, I made a joke about the volume of the seed. The girl seemed pleased at her effort even though I was disappointed in mine. I returned to Earth, but only to discover that the experience was purely spiritual with no earthly repercussions.

In earthly terms, I am committed to a celibate lifestyle until God says otherwise. But even in the commitment to Him, I have felt I have been sexually blocked for some reason... or perhaps this feeling has been His intention with this aspect of my life all along. I am not really sure, but I have prayed for guidance about the recognition to the changes in my body. It has been as if there has been a hormonal shift in that chakra point. So, I suppose it is possible that the experience was a spiritual effort to resolve biological issues within my body.

In earthly terms, I have felt that my sexual drive has been spiritually blocked and not blocked due to earthly reasons. But after the event took place, I assumed I must have mirrored the experience in my physical body (which I did not). And, as unexpected as it sounds, when I tried to jettison back to my body, it was as if God wanted to make sure he still communicated to me while my soul was in the heavens.

Before I was able to return, I was shown the face of Barack Obama. It was as if I was being told that he would be the last President, or a vine to the root of evil that is being brought upon the Earth. In reality, I am unopposed to Obama as I have recognized he is just a puppet for a greater initiative. I really do not have an opinion for any politician and definitely do not place any judgment or higher level of cause-effect upon

The Written (cont'd)

any of them. So, with that said, I want it to be clear that I have no agenda with Obama, nor have I ever really thought anything of him being the final puppet in the greater spiritual battle. In fact, he perhaps is not even an active player. However, the symbolism I was shown was his face as a sign of the end of times, as the usher to the end of days (however aware or unaware he may be). It does not mean that Obama should be viewed in a negative light, for many will never know the marker their spiritual journey played upon the divine timeline until after the time has passed. For everything and everyone should be viewed with open eyes.

And, while at first blush what I am about to say will sound impossible to hold truth, it could very well be seen that the emphasis on "Abomination of Desolation" that is referenced throughout the Bible in regard to the end of days carries with it a transcended meaning. Much like the words "atom," "Adam," and "adon" all carry the same archetypal meaning beneath the modern translation, many modern homophones can be understood to share the same root archetypal meaning. So, there is a high probability that "Abomination" could also be heard as "Obamanation," and in that, a homophone that transcends millennia of linguistic deterioration is revealed.

I know – most people will say I am reaching. And in truth, I cannot say I do not empathize with their viewpoints from the foundation of earthly eyes and mind. But those who dismiss any option of this possibility have already missed the most important part of the calling, which is "learning to see." We are all students in His divine schoolyard. Some will hear the lessons. Others will say much later in life, "I wish I had paid attention in [insert class of choice here]."

So it is important to understand, if the language of the Divine is understood at its root archetypal level, then it can be seen how language has transcended generations of regional changes, dialects, translations, etc. Again, at the base, explore the three words I listed initially as they can also be seen as the first example of divine architecture to the spoken language. There is a reason that in the beginning, God created Adam. There is a reason why the fundamental basis of science is the "atom." There is a reason that one of the many names of God, is "Adonai" which is rooted on the word "adon."

Read how the words for "abomination of desolation" are written in the Bible. Most specifically, Daniel 12:11 refers to the "abomination of desolation" being "set up." Studying this particular combination of words will open the eyes to possibility. I am not saying all of this to say "it is," but rather to say, "it could be." Unfortunately, the greatest conundrum of all for those who seek reason through hindsight is that in this case, hindsight will be too late. For generations will be left behind, as those chosen will be taken by His holy angels. The timelines are not specifically clear – and God has not yet shown any specific days – but it is safe to assume that in light of the possibility of a visual queue being revealed upon his divine timeline, that the strongest exploration of this possibility should occur without bias or egoic dismissal.

In the end, I was shown the face of Barack Obama just as I have been shown many other great signs and wonders. I was

The Written (cont'd)

impressed that his role is a visual queue revealed upon the divine timeline – the specifics to be revealed at a later time. Or, perhaps, this is all that will ever need to be known as other events unfold.

November 3, 2014

This morning's experience began with me being patted on the top of my right shoulder by someone walking by. At that moment I heard a laugh. Those two events triggered all of my spiritual senses to fall into view. Though I recognized I was in human form, it was as if I was the size of a cell in biology and the other souls were represented by faces upon abstract shapes. If I could compare it to an earthly example, it would be sort of like how SpongeBob is animated as a face upon a sponge. The facial features are very pronounced upon an abstract shape.

After spending a significant amount of time in this abstract scenario, I walked outside from the building I was in. It was now apparent I was in a hotel. I walked through the hotel and into a parking deck. Inside, I twice saw a group of Japanese men ushered into the building. The angel ushering in the people was named Salome. When I walked outside of the building the colors were muted. The sky was a pale gray. I was standing in front of a large expanse of concrete. A black helicopter was parked in the middle of the expanse before me. There was no pilot. I saw a man who reminded me of an old

Glory

childhood friend named Jon. He wanted to get into the helicopter.

As I walked up to him, I became aware of the others being ushered into the building. The only way I can describe my understanding of the scenario was that the people being ushered into the building were "lost souls with the potential to understand all that I have been privy to thus far." The man who reminded me of Jon resisted the idea. I laughed at his childish reaction to going inside. I patted the ground, laughing at how awesome this experience is. I decided to leave Jon on his own. I turned to walk away and head down the street, but lost my sense of sight. Behind me, I heard someone with a crackly voice trying to catch up to me. The crackly sound was a lot like distortion to a signal transmission.

November 5, 2014

This morning's travels to the heavens were fairly hazy today. My experience was hampered by a late night watching the movie, Interstellar, on its opening night. Earlier in the day I had been led to watch it even though it was a movie I had planned to see at a later point. Regardless of the scenario that led me there, the late finish to the movie caused my body to be off-center when I travelled to the heavens. All I can really recall (though it was extremely vivid during the whole experience) was a big group of people surfing in a wave pool. I also was excited to try this out. I have never surfed before, so

The Written (cont'd)

there was not a real baseline for me to experience this motif. I recognized it was metaphorical in meaning, but could not tie it all together very well.

There was also a re-emphasis on "Hercules" throughout the experience. This has seemed to be a theme for a while for me, though I cannot quite figure out why. I suppose there could be a theme in the movie that was just released that I need to see, so I will plan on doing that. At the same time, the Hercules constellation is above the Earth exactly where I sit on the beach during my meditations. I would not have known anything about the constellation if I had not researched Hercules after it had been emphasized to me.

November 6, 2014

This morning's experience has left me with a lot to understand. It began with me standing in a mailroom. There was a mother with a boy child who doesn't speak. She wanted to make sure I "got my mail." Her first words to me were, "304, right?" She was referencing my current apartment number on Earth. We were standing in front of cubbies that had mail folded up inside of them. My box was overflowing. I began to pull out the stacks of mail. I seemed to be looking for something in particular, but I am not sure what it was.

My second handful of mail included an envelope that had money within it. I did not look inside. I continued to pull out the remainder of my mail. There were several large mailing envelopes used to hold important documents. My impression was that they held legal documents. As I was pulling out the mail, her son slipped and almost fell. That almost-accident caused her to say, "You know I helped a man collect money for an accident. Guess how much?" She was referencing his settlement. I replied, "A mil?" She smiled and said, "$1.5! And he didn't even get hurt!" I said, "I need a lawyer like you. Say, how do you do on harassment suits...ones that cause a person to lose a job?" She looked at me strangely. I said, "Well, I guess that sounds strange since I have given you no details." She laughed and asked if I could email her the details.

She went on to say, "My son and I like to do witchcraft over it." I thought she was joking by making a dark reference to a harmless line of work. But the more I have thought about it, I am no longer sure that I understood the context correctly. In response to her joke, I said, "I might. I don't like mixing business and personal together though." The lady pleaded with me to do it though. She seemed driven to help me (or hurt, depending on which way you view it).

We walked away from the mailroom toward the elevators. On the way I bumped into a girl carrying a purse. When we collided, I actually ran into her purse strap, rather than her body. My hand glanced off of her purse which caused her to turn around and make sure I had not taken anything. I laughed and held up my hands, apologizing. Everyone around – including the girl I ran into – laughed about it. Right as we approached the elevators, a photographer wanted to take all of our photos. He took individual photos that he showed me as

The Written (cont'd)

he took them. The lady and her daughter also took one together.

When he showed me the pictures, I realized the "boy" child that was with the lady was actually her daughter with long hair. I do not know if I just could not recognize her gender because of her youth, but she was clearly a girl in the photograph. As I looked at her, she had long brown hair draped over the right side of her face. The left side of her face had her hair pulled back behind her ear. Above her left brow, there was a symbol – a mark. It was blurry, but it was either the five-dots mark or a square. In reflection, I think it was likely a square, but it was blurry. It was only about the size of a quarter. On her right temple, there appeared to be a mark hidden beneath her hair. As I stared at the symbol, I realized I could be staring at the mark of the beast (upon the forehead). Perhaps it could be a different mark of God upon the forehead, but it was not the same mark given to me, so I have more questions than answers. If it is a square, I definitely feel that would be the mark of the beast since it is the opposite of what was marked upon my hand. If it is the five dots pattern, it leaves ambiguity since mine was coupled with a circle beneath the five dots (representing the whole).

November 8, 2014

This morning's experience is extremely tough to describe. It is as if I have reached another "level" in my experiences in the heavens. Recently, there seemed to be an emphasis on the abstract – lines and spheres, doors and hallways. This time, I found myself walking down a hallway that separated two worlds. I could not understand if they were entirely different worlds with separate people living separate lives, or if the worlds were different timelines of the world that I have come to know.

I stood in the hallway before two angels. They kept asking me if I wanted to enter. I was clearly standing between two points of entry and exit. Perhaps it was the entrance to the heavens. Most of the time, my ascent is such a blur that I can only realize I have left my body and am suddenly in the heavens trying to gather my bearings. Maybe my spiritual strength is opening up understanding what I have only known as blurs. Regardless, I stood there unable to fully comprehend what I was seeing.

As the angels continued to ask me if I wanted to enter, all I could do was walk around the room to try to gather understanding of the setting. It was as if I was dropped in a completely different interpretation of the way I have come to understand archetypal concepts. But, somehow, this was even more primal and archetypal.

I looked around and could see everything was constructed by lines. There were no walls. The lines were just markers and guideposts for my understanding. I ended up losing harmony before I was able to explore beyond the doors. But, I also recognized before my ascent and descent that there were three separate white flashes of light within my brain. That is the only

The Written (cont'd)

way I can describe it. I was in a dark room and no lights were flashing. But once my eyes closed and I began to meditate, light burst from within, filling my periphery of darkness in the whitest of light. This is not the first time this has happened. In fact, it happens quite frequently. But, I just realized I rarely write about it – so I thought I would include it here.

November 10, 2014

Yet again, I found myself in an abstract scenario in the heavens. I was speaking with an angel who I knew as "Tom." If I had to guess, I would think this was likely biblical "Thomas," but I hesitate to tie the two together without the angel answering that question. To date, it seems that I have met many of the angels and characters mentioned throughout various religious texts. I do not know any "Toms" on Earth, nor do I know of any other characters that would have a spiritual significance greater than Thomas, so I have to think that there is a strong possibility that Tom is Thomas. But, again, I want to clarify that I am merely guessing at a possibility in order to help define who I am writing about rather than just an abstract angel.

Regardless, Tom was my guide for the evening. This setting involved boats again – another common theme in recent weeks. All of the boats were represented by spheres, but they were all guided by poles. Tom was holding one pole. The boat he was discussing with me was spherical. He explained to me

Glory

that it was the best vehicle because it moved in the motion of the spheres. He then went on to explain that its motion was guided by the magnetic poles within the sphere. The reference to magnetism was the first time that any spiritual guidance involved that much specificity in the science behind the motion of the spheres. I was extremely impressed with the boat and how well it sailed.

After I was shown the spherical boat, I was taken by two other guides down a highway. We appeared to be walking south. Along our left (the east), was a beautiful ocean. There were beaches and rolling sand hills that separated our highway from the beach. The angels seemed extremely frustrated over a particular "major construction project" that was taking place along the beach. I kept asking questions about the project, but I never seemed to be given any answers that made enough sense for me to be satisfied.

Eventually we came to a point where the project had leveled a hill that separated the highway from the beach. Where the hill had been leveled I could see an artificial beach with sunbathers on it. I wanted to look more at it so I could better understand the angels' frustrations. I could sense the energy had changed in that particular location from the rest of the beach. After I looked at the leveled hill, I began to lose harmony and returned to my body.

After returning to my body I could not help but try to understand the metaphorical meaning. At the time my soul was in the heavens I tried very hard to understand the meaning, but it was lost in the magnificence of the moment. Upon returning, my best understanding was that the ocean and the highway representing the spirit and the heavens and that the beauty was slowly being overtaken. My best understanding in the immediate moments returning from the heavens was that the motif was another foreshadowing to the beginning of the end of times. I cannot be sure whether it was an indication of heaven versus hell, or rather that the most spiritual places on Earth – those places such as I am located in Fort Lauderdale – are on the verge of being destroyed, or altered enough to prevent clear angelic communication. Either way, the angels were unhappy at which I could not help but take notice.

November 11, 2014

Last night's experience was extremely muddy in clarity. At best, I can only remember a few images. One of those images was of smoke coming from the engine of a vehicle. I understood it to mean that my "vehicle" was overheating – meaning that my body was not regulating its body temperature really well for the journey to the heavens. The other imagery only pertained loosely to a lesson of some sort.

November 12, 2014

My travels to the heavens this morning began with me arriving in an abstract location before two angels. These would be the two angels that would guide me through the experience.

Glory

I should note that it has become increasingly common – if not the standard – for me to have a male and female angel guide me lately. And though they usually stay in the background, periodically they come to the forefront when their attention is required.

So as the experience began, I was led to a dimly lighted building that seemed to house a restaurant. The colors were mostly blues and grays. It seemed to be raining outside. The inside walls were made of a wooden or vertically-riveted metallic texture. I walked down a long hallway. Before I reached the end of the corridor, a large room opened up to my right. This room seemed to be the dining area of the restaurant and also had a large, dark wooden bar. I continued walking forward to the end of the hallway.

In the back, there was an elder angel sitting on a bench that was built into the wall as it came to an end. It was simple, with no ornate details. More or less, it was just a plank attached to the wall. The end of the hall was more like a cubby area. After the large opening on my right, this was maybe a 5 x 5 space where the hallway found its end. The angel saw me and immediately stood up. She told me that I could sit where she was sitting. I noticed rain was leaking through the roof and falling through in a steady stream in front of the bench. It was as if the bench was behind a waterfall, but not hidden from view.

As I sat down, I took notice of the angel's appearance. She was clearly elder, with long gray hair flowing in whimsical curls midway down her torso. Her face was aged with wrin-

The Written (cont'd)

kles. This may be the first female angel I have seen that was physically worn-down. She began to speak with me about her daughter. The elder and I seemed to know each other and were quite comfortable in conversation. She seemed to think that her daughter and I were a literal match made in heaven (pardon the pun). She never said it directly, but that was the impression I picked up in the conversation.

I asked her how "Zoey" liked Nashville. In earthly form, I had just returned from Nashville back to Fort Lauderdale. I had wondered how the angels felt about the location previously, so my soul's curiosity took charge. The elder angel laughed and told me how much she hated it. At that moment Zoey walked in. She looked so beautiful. She had long straight brown hair that reached her waist. Her skin was milky white. Her lips were a soft-red, small in definition. Her face was narrow, and all of her facial features were small. She had two strands of her hair pulled back around her crown to create a 1960s-inspired hairstyle. There were perhaps gold flowers in her hair as well – or it could have been a crown. Actually, now that I write this, I realize that she must have been wearing a crown that was subtle but enough for me to take notice.

She wore a long sheer robe that formed around her perfect body. She also wore a scarf around her neck. She seemed very "fashionable." I recognized in that moment that her appearance in the restaurant would be akin to a famous celebrity making a public appearance. At that moment I also recognized that every action I took, every word that I spoke, must be done with a delicacy so as not to be mistaken for a starstruck fan (again, no pun intended). In the conversation with her mother, I felt my infatuation with her daughter, but kept it playfully hidden... at least so I thought. Regardless, I was not sure if I had ever spoken personally with Zoey. This was most definitely the first time I had been shared the name Zoey, but I have seen a brunette angel before that was of similar majestic beauty – hence my pause at saying this was our first encounter. Perhaps she is the same angel as the bride I have seen.

As she approached, I knew others in the room would very quickly take notice of her in the room. Without missing a beat, I looked up at her as she approached and said, "We were just talking about you." Even though I felt her "greatness" and majesty (as could every one else in the room), I continued on, unfazed by her status. She sat down and felt comfortable having dinner with me. We spoke for a while without me ever seeming to make any social faux-pas that would have demonstrated a lack of maturity or respect on my part. This experience eventually faded as my body began to overheat. There was so much Love, greatness, and majestic beauty in the moment that it was very much a sensory-overload. How I managed to maintain composure must be a testament to my spiritual strengthening over the years.

The following day, I researched the origin of the name Zoey. I came to learn that "Zoe" which is pronounced "Zoey" is a Greek word that appears in the New Testament numerous times. The word "zoe" means "life" – but as in spiritual life, the life after our earthly bodies has passed. With further research, I began to wonder if I saw a personification of an

The Written (cont'd)

archetypal concept. Had an elder angel introduced me to my spiritual soulmate, Zoe, in my travels to the heavens? As in, had she introduced me to "spiritual life" after earthly life has ended? It was enough to boggle my mind for hours afterwards.

In my research, I also learned that it was thought that the name Zoe was the Greek interpretation of the original Eve. That too would make sense in the context of the original woman representing eternal life through the mating with Adam. All of these thoughts rattled my brain a bit because, to this point, I had believed that the angels I have met in the heavens are actual beings, not necessarily archetypes. So, during prayer, I asked God for clarity on my two recent encounters with Tom and Zoey – and with help in understanding who they were.

After prayer, I decided that I would also speak to Zoey aloud and at least explain that I felt terrible for not knowing if her name was truly Zoey, Eve, or possibly Anael (who is the brunette angel I have met before), or perhaps even something else entirely. Ultimately, I felt guilty for not knowing who she was, but wanted to humbly accept responsibility for my lack of understanding. After all, she knows my soul better than I do and hiding anything would just be childish. She and I had such a deep attachment I thought it was best to put all of the cards on the table.

Times before I have spoken directly to the angels aloud and have received responses, but it is a rare action I have ever taken. My conversation is mostly just between myself and God. But, I figured that it was worth a shot to express myself, regardless of the outcome. But, in the most humbling of responses possible, my Father spoke to me directly and shared with me that it was indeed Tom (spelled TM, which is Tav-Mem, which in turn means "the divinity of the water") and Eve that I had encountered in heaven.

Later that morning, I returned to the heavens. I found myself walking through another dimly lighted area. This time I was in the woods. A group of kids approached me and attempted to ambush me. They were younger and seemed to think they were clever in how they were going to attack me. As they tried to attack, I responded with a slew of amazing acrobatic stunts that caused them to stop in their tracks. The childish nature of their actions hit them instantly. They all stopped and stared in a sense of awe of my actions and shame in their own actions. We talked about their efforts in cleaning up the path in the woods. That seemed to be a job they were tasked with and had done a great job so far – they were just full of childish mischief. As we talked, they seemed uplifted. Eventually, we parted ways.

November 13, 2014

This morning I had one of the most surreal experiences I have ever had in my travels to the heavens. If it helps, I would say that some locations in the heavens are more divine, and others are meant as places to learn and grow. If our present existence of Earth is akin to a channel on a radio dial or a tele-

The Written (cont'd)

vision station, the heavens could best be seen as changing the station of the soul's perception of the world around it.

This morning's experience began with a near-identical setting as my apartment. I first thought I had awakened, but spiritually I knew that I was in spiritual form. I walked around my apartment fascinated by all of the tactile sensations. Everything was identical to earthly senses. The setting was almost perfectly recreated. As I walked around, I touched the floor, walls, and anything I could touch so my mind could attempt to justify that I was in a physical form and not in spiritual form.

I eventually noticed a few differences in my apartment which caused me to have a sense of relief from finding confusion in spiritual and physical forms. In particular, one piece of furniture was missing. At that point I shouted out, "I know that I am in spiritual form, and this is one of the best ones yet!" I eventually walked over to a chair to gain my composure since I began to lose the clarity in the moment. I sensed an angel was near. I asked, "Help me see what I need to see."

The setting changed to me standing outside of a club. There was a male and female angel in front of me. They kept talking to me as if I was a "driver" for them. I felt tipsy so I said I was not driving. They seemed unfazed by my response and asked me to find the car we arrived in, which I did. When I returned to them, I talked about the white walls surrounding the area. As I had searched for the car, I ran across an arbitrary ending to the setting I found myself in – hence the white walls I was discussing. They laughed and said they were glad I found those. We all got in the car and headed back to my place.

The male angel was convinced I had lost something that he needed. I kept telling him that he had it. When we got back, he sat down in a chair next to my bed. He kept looking for whatever it was he was on a quest to find. I lay on the bed underneath a sheet half folded to my waist. I placed a pillow over my face since I did not want them to see me having sexual thoughts. It was an absurd action and I had no idea where the thoughts were coming from, but at the moment, it made sense.

As I noticed how turned on I was under the sheet, the woman walked over to me, having also noticed. It was the brunette angel – possibly Eve. She said, "While he is doing that, I want to spend time with you." I sat up on the edge of the bed, having removed the pillow from my face. After saying those words, our eyes made contact. With one swift move, she put either arm underneath my arms and rolled me on top of her as she jumped up onto the bed. I rubbed my hands down her back. Her flesh was so real. Her hips and thighs were cool to the touch. It was what I can only describe as the perfect sensation of skin-on-skin touch where perfect body temperatures collide.

I searched for the wings on her back with my hand, but just found the places they would go. Sometimes the angels' wings are hidden from sight, but in this moment I felt the locations of the wings on her back. Her flesh was cool to my flesh. She was wearing something that covered her breasts, but it

The Written (cont'd)

was just for the front. Her back was exposed with her garment having no strap. I noticed her legs were wrapped around me. I playfully said that I could handle making out for a bit while he waited. As I said that my left hand caused me to notice how she was not wearing any clothes except for the small coverlet on her breasts. I kept my clothes on though. We began to make out passionately. As sensations increased, I eventually lost harmony.

November 14, 2014

This morning, I was sitting with a group of other heavenly beings on the beach. We sat beneath a palm tree. We were all wearing white and listening to our teacher. He was also wearing white and standing beside the tree. Overall, there were maybe twelve of us. I did not count the others, but that is the number I "knew" as the count of the group. I fully believe the man who was speaking was Jesus. I have encountered him many times in the heavens, and though this time it was less personal, I could still tell it was he.

As he spoke, he said something along the lines of "finding Israel." One of the men in our group seemed to only know the term "Israel," but not the meaning. Jesus looked over to me to answer. I chimed in quickly and excitedly. I explained that "finding Israel" was no different than concepts in Buddhism, Taoism, Confucianism, etc. I explained that "Israel" was not about what one religion deemed as "the way" for the truth could not be molded to a specific religion.

Several people in the group became uncomfortable with my words. I could sense that bringing into question religion was unsettling to those who were entrenched in the mindset of a specific religion. But as I spoke, my energy increased and angels gathered around me to cheer me on. The angels were smiling and said, "He gets it. He understands." I went on to explain how each religion took an inherent truth and shaped it by its own parameters. Jesus looked on, excited in my answer. He looked at the group and said, "Exactly. He knows."

Everything else following became hazy at best when attempting to bring the experience back to Earth. The only other thing I can recall with clarity is that I was given a sandwich. As I took a bite of the sandwich, I pulled it back to look at it. The sandwich had unleavened bread as the top and bottom, with several pieces of food between the slices of bread. One of the items appeared to be a slab of meat about an inch thick. It was sitting on top of another substance like an egg and possibly lettuce. I immediately decided to stop eating it because I thought I was eating pork. However, an angel walked over to me and told me that the meat was not pork and that it was completely okay for me to eat. I continued eating and savoring the sandwich. It was very good.

The Written (cont'd)

November 15, 2014

Though I have no understanding of the context, the meaning, or implication, I was shared the words "Milner Tyson fifteen ten." I thought that the numbers at the end were represented as 15-10, but because they were illustrated to me in concept rather than anything written, I am just notating it as I was shared.

After I returned and wrote down those words, I returned to the heavens. This time I arrived at another restaurant. There was a brunette girl that seemed excited that I was there while they were opened. But, as the restaurant closed, she seemed angry and bitter about something internally. I continued to want to know about a door that she seemed to be standing guard over. It continued to frustrate her, but I could not understand how she could be happy to see me yet frustrated at my question. She said she did not want to tell me about the door. I could sense it led to a demonic place that she wanted to keep hidden from me. And while it was apparent she liked me, she was extremely sensitive to that topic.

Throughout my travels, I spent a lot of time with this brunette girl. We were happy. When I tried to write lengthy notes of the experience, I did so in the "in between location" that periodically tricks me into thinking I have arrived back on Earth and am actually taking notes. However, upon fully awakening, I realized I had not taken any notes on Earth, but rather that was part of the in-between experience.

Glory

November 17, 2014

The last two days have been full of muddy memories of my travels. Yesterday seemed to hold only scant recollections of imagery of life tasks. This morning, my travels were again immense, yet the only thing I can clearly recall is being in a room where an electrician was wiring the ceiling. Above me, was an exposed grid. The electrician was on a ladder. He was pulling cables through and connecting the ends of the cables to different nodes on the grid. There were two colors of cables: red and white. The ends of each cable consisted of a bulbous connector unlike anything I have ever seen on Earth. The cables could also connect to each other at the top. So, perhaps the bulbous connector was at a T-angle with the cable.

I watched as the electrician connected a red cable and then a white cable to a node. The white cable was plugged directly into the red connector. I was asked to help out. I climbed up a ladder and plugged a few of the cables in. As I began helping out, an elder angel walked into the room through a doorway on my right. He looked up at me and said, "I didn't know you knew how to do that." I responded in a way that reminded me of all of the times I had recently had to respond in a similar fashion. I said, "Engineering. Yes. I do that too. Like I said when we first met, if I told you everything about me from the beginning, it would seem too unbelievable to be true. But it is, so I just do not say much about my past."

The Written (cont'd)

The angel responded, "Interesting. So you've done electrical work before?" I said, "Actually, engineering would be a better way of putting it. Electrical was a part of it. But again, engineering is just another piece of my past. There are many others." With that I lost harmony and returned from the heavens. Even as brief of an experience as that was to notate, the whole experience was much larger and grander. I just was unable to bring the details back with me. The experience the day prior was similar in that I had to answer questions in the same way about my past being too unbelievable to share with the person in the beginning. However, I have no context to place any of that conversation within my journals.

November 18, 2014

This morning's travels lacked tactile sensation, but were still a visual spectacle. It began with me standing inside a house that I thought was dirty. In looking around the house I did not see any dirt or filth, but that was my impression. I really did not want to be inside the house. I was accompanied by a few other souls. They seemed to be representative of my spiritual family – the type of experience which always leaves me a little confused. The house was made of wood and was ornamented with handmade wooden furniture. It seemed a lot like a house from the late 1800s or 1900s in both size and decor.

As we stood around the room, a voice broke through the silence. "You are crowning." I was not sure who it was directed to, but in front of me was a woman waddling around. My first understanding was that she was pregnant and that the baby was crowning, even while she was standing up. She eventually walked into a room full of shadows. I noticed there were gray bodies lying around the sides of the room. I could not tell if they were unawakened souls or rather dead bodies. She picked up one and was dragging it around with her. She seemed kind of crazy. When she found a cleared out spot in the room, she straddled the man and began having sex with him. He remained lifeless and dead. I suppose it is worth noting that all of the gray men were completely naked.

After she finished having sex, she tossed the dead man aside onto the stack of other bodies. As this happened, she turned around to face us and held a newborn baby, placenta intact. It was quite a disturbing scene. Though I struggled to retain a lot of clarity throughout the remainder of the experience, I remember walking through the house and slipping on something blue on the ground. I could not decipher what it was, but it caused me to nearly fall. I understood that I was in the role of a teacher in the house, but I never felt I was playing that role very well. It seemed more like I was experiencing and observing more than teaching. Eventually we sat down to dinner, which was either in celebration or preparation for a race – though I could not explain anything more in detail.

The scene changed, and I eventually found myself on the beach with a group of others. I watched upon the water where a group of people swam. As I looked on, I was instructed to watch two strange objects as they came across the water.

The Written (cont'd)

Though they moved across the water like boats, they were shaped much differently. Each of the objects was identical to the other. They appeared to be large platforms, perhaps twice as long as they were wide. The platforms appeared to be made of darkened wood. In the center of the platform was something that appeared to be the top of an outboard boat motor – black in color. It seemed to rotate seamlessly to change directions of the platform. My impression was that these robots were police of some sort. Eventually, they returned from the direction they arrived (my left).

In traditional cardinality, I would say they returned to the west. Typically the directions in these experiences are meant to be understood in relative cardinality to my initial alignment, so it makes sense to think that "robots" arrived and returned to the west. After the robots left, the group I was with left the beach to go get food. We went to a place that resembled a food court at a mall. We walked around in the inside of the food court surveying the choices. The structure was made of white marble or alabaster tile. The ceiling was open with glass panels and the blue sky appeared overhead. Inside, there was a lot of greenery ornamenting the walkways.

I finally found the restaurant I was looking for. It was Mexican. For some reason I thought I had eaten at this place many times before. It seemed to be my favorite. I ate so much during our dinner. I continued to go back for seconds and thirds, etc. When our dinner was complete, we walked to a dimly lighted parking lot. It was pretty much empty except for a couple of cars. The group I was with said their goodbyes to me and one other. At this point I realized I was with a girl (whether she was a Love interest or an angel, or maybe both, I cannot be sure). She was extremely beautiful, and it felt like we were in the early days of a relationship together.

As we stood beside the car, the girl and I talked. I did not want to return to Earth. It was one of the only times I can distinctly remember not wanting to return to Earth. The longer we stood there together, the stronger my spirit began to feel. The amount of Love and strength in that moment was so much that I just could not bring myself to depart. I am sure now in retrospect that the vehicle represented my exit from the heavens to the Earth. The girl seemed to want me to stay as well. Overall, it felt – between the dinner and this moment – that my spiritual life force had been depleted and this was all in an effort to refill it.

In truth, between two glasses of wine I had the previous Wednesday and my spilling of seed, I can feel a weakened spirit within my body. I cannot be completely sure why this happens, but it is apparent that it happens. It is as if spilled seed not in the warmth and Love of another, lowers vitality in spirit. The same could be said for alcohol. Even though I have reduced myself only to wine on very rare and select occasions, the results seem to still swing my internal pendulum to grounding on the earthly side rather than the spiritual side.

Again, perhaps if the intention behind the intake was different, the impact would be different. For example, if it was in celebration or in the company of another, the intention would be different than if it has no joy, Love, and happiness surrounding it. This is just a theory, but if the soul is influenced by intention, then it stands to reason all activities, all intake, all expressions of emotion, are the result of intention. Anger from Love and trust being broken is different than anger from judgment. The latter is inexcusable. Only Love is the source of all truth.

November 19, 2014

My first experience in the heavens was long, but I never felt like I had a grounding between my mind and soul to adequately bring it back with me. I tried for the majority of the experience to bring rationale to the spiritual experience. And while that may be hard to understand, the concept is that while the soul and all of the heavenly experiences may appear similar to earthly experiences, they are constructed and deconstructed entirely differently than in the manner we construct and deconstruct earthly experiences in the mind. To bring back an experience means that not only does the spirit have to have strength and maturity in the heavens, but it must also understand how to bridge the two locales in construct and deconstruct. It is as if the mind serves as a subconscious translator between two entirely different experiences.

So with that said, I struggled to bridge the experience from the heavens to my earthly understanding – though the experiences were seen as identical. In the first experience I can only recall being in the same cabin as I was in during the previous morning's experience in the heavens, but this time it was different. This time happiness radiated throughout. Yesterday's experience did not seem to have the same feeling of happiness. But this one was bright, happy, full of yellows and joy. It was like an unending sunrise engulfed in Love. And though it was long in experience, that is all I can bring back.

After taking notes, I returned to the heavens. I found myself in a house that I thought was my Aunt Karen's house. I never saw her, nor did the house look anything like the house she owns. I rarely talk to her, so it was an odd parallel to draw even in heavenly terms unless it had something to do with our earthly family in spiritual form – as in another time/space understanding of life. My uncle Steve and cousin Rob were also there. I also sensed my deceased uncle Gary who has appeared in other heavenly experiences. In fact, he was one of the first guides that appeared to both Bryan and me – each time initially without a face. So, it is also possible that the house was a construct of something he wanted me to see. Regardless, I knew I was in the company of my earthly family in spiritual form. But this is where logic begins to become blurred with some really tough concepts.

As I was in the house, I felt I was looking through a store. I searched through a kiosk with a rack on top. The rack contained bags with marbles in them. I continued to hear a voice tell me that I must find a glass marble to serve as a replacement for (what I could only gather as) Bryan's missing testicle. I could not figure out why he was missing a testicle, nor did I ask. I just knew that I was tasked with finding a glass marble

The Written (cont'd)

that resembled a testicle. There was an emphasis on it needing to be glass. I found a bag with seven marbles in it. One additional marble was part of the bag, but was not one of the seven. The other seven were perfectly round. I rolled them around in my fingers trying to decide what an appropriate testicle size should be. I only knew what mine felt like, so that is all I had to go on. Ultimately I decided that round was not the answer. I decided that oval would be better.

The eighth marble fit this definition exactly. It seemed large, but I figured it was the best I was going to do. I walked downstairs and up to the register. My uncle was ready to check me out. When I set the bag of marbles on the counter, he told me I probably would want the bag of marbles "with a mat in it." I replied that this was the only bag I could find. He told me that I should go look a little longer – that there were better replacements upstairs. I returned up the staircase, but became lost at the size of the house.

I did not want to awaken Rob whose bedroom was attached to the other rooms I was having to visit. Each room was dark and empty, aside from a double bed. I could not help but think about how many beds were in this house. I realized my aunt had been planning for everyone to stay at her house. I liked the warmth that was felt in her actions. I suppose my actions woke Rob because he eventually came into the room and asked me if I needed help. I explained what I was looking for. He walked me around the rooms and through his room. Every room seemed interconnected. In his room, he flipped on numerous switches on the wall and along a shelf that produced small glows of light. We eventually reached the "store." I was pointed to a wall that had netted bags hanging along the wall.

I began to sift through the bags searching for glass marbles – ones with a variety of oblong shapes so that Bryan could determine what was best himself. After all, the marble was for his body and he would know what he needed better than I. One of the bags I found contained ornately carved shapes and figures. They seemed to be made of bone or something of similar consistency. I was pointed to a specific bag while I was searching. I thought it would contain the answers. When I pulled it off the shelf, it indeed had marbles in it, but it also contained two white phallic handles that seemed to be carved from bone/ivory as well.

My first reaction was that they were some type of sex toy, which made me curious as to why I had been pointed to this bag. As I studied the contents I realized the marbles inside were not glass, so this was not my answer. But, I was curious about the handles. There was also a lot of streaming material inside. I realized that the bone handles were either pompoms or some type of fetish whip. Either way, I was unsure of why I was even directed to it. I put it back on the shelf and continued searching. I sorted through one last bag that had marbles made of glass and a variety of other glass pieces. One piece was the letter W or M (depending on orientation). It seemed like the bag had too many weird shapes and not enough marbles, so I put it back on the shelf. I eventually ran out of bags and decided to return downstairs to buy the bag I originally found. As I returned downstairs I lost harmony.

The Written (cont'd)

On November 20th, I spoke with Bryan on the phone. Fearing the worst possible interpretation of the vision – that he may have testicular cancer – I began the conversation by prefacing my words with "how weird what I was going to share may seem." I asked him if he had a physical recently to which he said it had been over a year. I told him that he may want to go get checked out because my experience pertained to him having a problem with his right testicle. I began describing the bag of marbles and eventually Bryan stopped me. He then shared with me something I never knew: he had to have a testicle removed as a child due to a hernia.

He went on to say he learned it was his right testicle, but had only learned it was his right one in his most recent physical (since it hangs in the middle). I obviously never knew that, but then he shared something even more interesting with me. He said that Matt (our cousin) was also missing a testicle due to a complication at birth. Matt's father is Steve who is the person I saw in my experience at the register. When I took the bag to the register for him to check me out, he told me to go back and find the one "with a mat in the bag." Now I see that he was saying that Matt also needed a testicle.

In the end, I think the experience was something that would send a great big celestial sign to Bryan during our conversation to let him know these have all been for a reason and very real. It also helped me emphasize the importance of him listening to the words I am writing and peace in the directive I have received in giving him all of my writing.

Glory

November 20, 2014

Today's entry is going to seem broken, disparate, and without a core storyline. But this morning's experiences in the heavens are some of the most important that I have had – and most importantly the longest lasting and most numerous set of experiences I have had throughout the morning hours. The nineteen separate experiences I had occurred over the course of five hours. As best as I can explain, the experiences happened without gaps for the entire five hours. And though the experiences may not contain five hours worth of detail, there is only so much I could bring back to maintain my balance between earthly body and spirit. That is always the biggest challenge.

At certain points in the experiences, when I recognized an important detail that I wanted to bring back to Earth, I would return to my body to write about the experience before returning to the heavens... nearly instantly. Before I even found a meditative state, my soul was already beginning to leave my body. It was as if all it took was for my eyes to close in order for my soul to detach and return to the heavens.

It is also important to understand that during my prayers I asked God for an increase in clarity and quantity in my travels, so I could better understand all of the questions that have been building over the last week for me. I shared with Him how two angels had visited a friend of mine (Cheryl) and me earlier in the evening on Earth and had spoken to me in San-

The Written (cont'd)

skrit in the midst of the very conversation they were having with Cheryl.

It was the first time that I was with another person wherein what we perceived from one situation was distinctly different. Cheryl only heard a couple of sentences from the man who was speaking directly to her, yet he and his wife spoke to me in a foreign language twice, as well as to her. We were sitting next to each other and there was no reason either of us would have so distinctly different recounts of what we had witnessed unless there was a split in perception of the reality around us. I knew the two people that approached were angels when they initially walked up to us. Cheryl is fearful of accepting the potential that angels surround us. In fact, those two angels appeared right after I shared with her my first experience in seeing angels. So this moment would go down as the first time there was a distinctly different experience that I witnessed in the company of another.

With respect to this particular experience, my prayers this evening centered around the recognition of that moment as well as the desire to understand more than I have been bringing back with me. In essence, I asked to be ramped up in spiritual lessons. And though I have made similar prayers in the past, this was definitely the most extreme response I have received.

The first experience began with my periphery becoming filled with pink azaleas. The flowers were everywhere, like the lushest blanket of flowers possible. As I gazed upon the azaleas I heard a voice exclaim, "All of my [a word that I best under-

Glory

stood as family] thinks I'm an antediluvian Rothschild." Obviously everything about that sentence was without basis in my mind, so I immediately returned to write it down. I do not know who spoke it, but the voice was male and sounded in what I could only describe as deeply masculine, bold, and breathy. The word antediluvian is one I had never written or spoken until now, but it means "pre-Biblical flood." The Rothschilds are a family that have long been thought to be part of a secret society that covertly controls the world. So putting those two concepts in a sentence as a descriptor for anyone, much less whomever I was unable to see, was compelling enough for me to take note.

When I returned to the heavens I found myself in a void. This time I was without vision, but I was able to hear. I suppose I was still finding harmony at that exact moment to allow my senses to settle in. In the distance I heard another voice. This one said, "Is it possible that one button will decide what you do?" I had no context to the question, nor an image to draw any better understanding. So with that I returned to take note of the question and explore the meaning later.

I once again returned to the heavens. This time I was greeted in a beautiful land. The grass was an inexplicable green. The sky was a perfect blue. I looked down to see I was standing on a path. Before me was an angel wearing white. His wings were not visible (as is usually the case). He was leaning against an alabaster wall. At the top of the wall was an incomprehensible wall of spheres. It was most certainly part of the equidistant bouquet, but blended seamlessly into the ala-

The Written (cont'd)

baster wall behind him. The angel was slender with a milky complexion. His facial features were very small but well defined. Though he was not muscular, his features defined his masculinity. His eyes were a steel gray. His hair was just beyond shoulder length and was a white-steel gray. He looked at me and said, "Water for you?" I just stared. His questions fell somewhere between rhetorical and caregiver.

I looked around and soaked in the world, but every time I turned my face ahead he was standing there asking me to take some water. I understood that water would help balance my soul and body in the heavens. I never said no, and I believe that he eventually gave me water, but not through traditional methods. The only way I can describe this is that by me not saying no, somehow my soul was replenished through the idea of water. I recognized the importance of this moment and returned to my body. Though the travels to arrive in front of this angel took a lengthy amount of time and the scenery was enough to cause me to explore every facet for minutes on end, the only aspect that I could bring back in full story-form was the angel standing before me asking me to have some water.

When I returned once again to the heavens, I was standing with the brunette angel. I could not be sure if it was Zoey because I was unable to get a good look at her face. All I knew was that she was wearing white and had long, straight brown hair. When she is with me it always seems like a special moment – a moment that seems like others would become jealous of or try to latch onto if they were to take notice of her. I

Glory

wanted to make sure that we diverted any attention away from us.

We seemed to be in a setting similar to a stadium. There were long wrapping walkways that led up several stories. They were made of concrete. The rest of the structure was made of steel painted in a high gloss black. There was an elevator that ran vertically down the center of the large walkways. The angel and I were standing at the top most level of the building. I walked with her to the elevator. I shouted out something into the reaches of the stadium to distract the others. We seemed to be hunted, but more out of fascination or fame than for game or lessons.

Truthfully, it was the angel I was with that was the cause for commotion. I was excited that she wanted to share her time with me but others seemed to just want to be in her presence. As we walked to the elevator, the doors opened. We stepped in, but someone was quickly on their way up the winding walkway. I suppose it should be noted the walkway ascended in a counterclockwise direction. When I noticed that we would be caught before the elevator doors had time to shut, I grabbed the hand of the brunette angel, and we darted out of the elevator and down a darkened hallway leading to double doors.

As we reached the double doors, the woman chasing us came into view. I tried to step in front of the brunette angel and shield her from the person chasing after us, but it was too late. The angel had already been spotted by two separate girls. There was not much else I could do to prevent them from

The Written (cont'd)

catching us. They were approaching from either direction. As the first one caught up with us I said, "Why does she have to spoil it for all of the others?" For some reason I sensed that this woman was friends with the angel – not close friends, but rather ran in a similar social circle (if there could be such a comparison made to the angels in the heavens). The two girls catching up to us caused the scenario to end, and I returned to my body to take notes and return.

At this point, I had noticed how vivid and numerous the experiences were becoming. I sensed that I was being helped by the angels for an evening of many experiences and lessons. I closed my eyes and immediately returned. I stood in the void and took notice of what first appeared to be spirals beginning to fill my periphery from the east. As I studied the spirals, I realized it would be better described as a waving blanket of translucent spheres interlocking from radius to radius.

These spheres were all smaller, maybe the size of a golf ball relatively speaking to a human. The spheres were all waving in the wind like a blanket which caused their intersecting arcs to appear as spirals. And, in understanding the equidistant bouquet, this makes sense because the direction of travel through the equidistant bouquet is in a spiral akin to that made in demonstration of fluid dynamics – a three-dimensional Fibonacci sequence. As I stared at the spheres beginning to fill the right half of my periphery, the left side remained in blackness.

I must have tried to ask a question about the next place I was going to visit because a voice spoke to me in a way that

Glory

would be a response to that type of question. The male voice said, "They need you as a general in the war first." My mind raced with possibilities. This was not a game or a lesson – not this time. This was an order, a call to action, and an answer to part of my prayer earlier in the evening where I asked to help better understand my role during these times. I looked around and wanted to ask for clarity, but whether I decided or I was forced to return to my body to take notes, that is what ended up transpiring. I was beginning to think at this point that any control to and from the heavens was not being governed by my intentions in these travels, but rather only as the angels seemed fit. I had a sense that there was a lot to understand over the course of the evening and this was the time I would be inundated with the most information I have ever been shared.

I took notes of the spirals and the words spoken to me and immediately returned to the heavens. This time I was leading an army of spiritual soldiers. I headed east with the small group of soldiers behind me. I had something in my hand like a staff, or perhaps a sword. I held it up with my right hand in a way that a commander would do leading his army into war and shouted out in a commanding, victorious voice, "We are the Bayersayach!!!" As I shouted this out I immediately realized I had no idea what the word meant though my soul knew so boldly how to exclaim it in strength. It seemed like a proper name, and if I had my best guess at what I felt the word meant in that moment, I would best define it as "God's Army."

The Written (cont'd)

As we marched onward I repeated the word over and over unraveling how the word was formed from the Hebrew letters, "Beyt, Resh, Shin, Hey, Kaph." My mind was actively attempting to understand the archetypal meaning even though I already understood it to mean "God's Army." In Hebrew, the letters would string together to mean "the house or embodiment of hope radiating through the revelation of the anointed." Whether or not this is a Hebrew word known in modern times, I am not sure. But, this was a word I was shared that held significance in the moment.

I have never sought to understand Hebrew from a modern interpretation – only in archetypal form. I initially wondered if Aleph would be included between Hey and Kaph in the spelling, but eventually decided that it would likely not be included (even as a silent character). I think that having five letters would hold a much greater symbolic meaning in reference to the five pillars, the five books of the Torah, etc. when used as the formation of a word meaning "God's army." So henceforward, I will refer to God's Army as the word that the angels shared with me: "Bayersayach" (phonetically).

When I returned to the heavens I appeared in the courtyard of the location I had been previously where the angel asked me if I would like some water. The courtyard was beautiful – alabaster white walkways and retainer walls. Palm trees were placed throughout. The sky was a beautiful blue. The courtyard was extremely large. I was tasked with assembling an army. My angelic guides told me that I would need to assemble them "five to ten times." I understood it to mean to

Glory

walk to five different locations in the courtyard and assemble the army, but that I would have to return a second time to each location to collect any remaining souls.

I walked toward one large white wall. The men and women could be seen over the top. As I walked to the wall with the same army I had when I shouted, "bayersayach," trailing behind me, I saw the soldiers above the wall raise their hands in victory, in God's name. They began to jump over the wall and form behind me. I headed toward the second wall but with everything happening so vividly, I wanted to make sure I was able to write down everything I was witnessing. The angels continued to reiterate that I would have to assemble the army "five to ten times" even as we headed toward the second wall. I returned to my body to take notes from the experience.

When I returned I was placed back into a scenario I was in earlier in the evening. It took me returning to be able to recall the events that preceded it, but I will start by describing the loose details from the first experience. There were so many moments that I tried to find the line between balancing the experiences and returning. But, apparently I missed this part upon initially returning to take notes. I now recall it occurring when I met the angel offering me water. That particular experience was quite long, but it was very broken – as if the angel offering me water continued to interrupt the other storylines involving me taking place in the heavens.

During that experience I was greeted by the same angel that I saw earlier in the month. I originally described her as reminding me of Taylor Swift. Mostly, the comparison can be

The Written (cont'd)

drawn due to her height, facial features, the color of her hair, and the naturally curly/bouncy/springy appearance of her hair. She is beautiful though distinctly not Taylor Swift. Even in the experiences I do not recognize her or mistake her for whom I am comparing her. Rather, it is just a way for me to try to reference the angels.

I met her in something that would resemble a large, hitchable camper that was parked behind a house in a subtle neighborhood. At the time it was attached to the vehicle that took it there. It was as if when she visits this particular area she brings her own chamber with her. We spoke inside of her mobile chamber, but I cannot recall it in much intricacy. The inside of her chamber was ornate. There were two other angels with me, or perhaps protecting her, or perhaps both. I have recently noticed that I have a certain admiration and reverence for some of these angels I am speaking with. In the beginning, I had no fear and approached them as I would anyone else. But now, even though the conversation is held in the same manner, inside I feel differently. I suppose that is because I recognize their spiritual significance more and more each day. And, the warmth of their Love is so overpowering it is almost impossible to put into words.

So though that is all I can recall from the earlier experience, and our subsequent parting of ways, on this particular journey to the heavens I was able to recall these details of the previous encounter. But, for the present experience, I found myself standing in an empty parking lot with two angels. We were about to walk down the street of a neighborhood to meet other angels. It seemed that it was supposed to be a discreet location – one that others would not notice the royalty within.

As we walked down the street, I took notice of the neighborhood. The houses were small, one story buildings. Each of them sat off of the street and were surrounded by tall trees that resembled southern pines. As we walked past one particular house on my right, I recognized it as the place I had walked with the angels in my earlier experience where I met the angel in her mobile chambers. As we passed the house, I peered backward over my shoulder to see if her chamber was still behind the house. I had a longing, a sense of hope, to see her again. I took notice that the vehicle that guided her chambers was no longer parked within view from the street. My heart sank. But, just as quickly as it began to sink, I noticed that her chambers were still parked behind the house, cleverly tucked out of view.

When the angels noticed me looking for her chambers they smiled at each other. They knew I was enamored with her. We continued walking to the end of the street where we reached the house belonging to the friends of the angel. We did not go inside, but rather walked through the gate of a privacy fence to the right of the house. I walked along a pathway that curved to the left. The backyard was extremely well manicured with numerous trees (like large oaks). Tucked to the left was a small pool. In the pool was an angel that I have seen since the beginning of my experiences in the heavens. She is a blonde angel that I have said reminds me of a girl I once knew

The Written (cont'd)

named Nicole. I have never gotten her name, so I am not sure what to call her.

I walked up to her and gave her a greeting-kiss on her right cheek. She returned the greeting and told me she was glad to see me. I looked to see that there were other angels in the backyard. It seemed this was a secret meeting location for many of the angels that had been part of my spiritual journey so far. I wondered if they were all family or maybe even of similar rank and role. A child ran up to me and asked to see pictures of my nights because he had heard a little bit about me and wanted to know more. It was clear he was not privy to my background (nor did I understand what my background exactly was) but that he had overheard the elder angels speaking about me and wanted to learn more. I obliged by showing him pictures.

The curly haired angel I had seen earlier in the experiences appeared in the backyard. My heart fluttered for a myriad of reasons due to the presence of the angels around me, but she caused my heart to flutter just a little more acutely for some reason. She came over to me and said, "Hey!" in greeting. We all sat down as the sun began to set and share stories. A small dog ran over to me and jumped up in my lap. It was wearing a puppy-shirt. It jumped out of my hands and fell awkwardly onto the ground. The female angel to my left laughed. I explained that the dog's name was Alex. I said it was named after Bryan, who was named after his father, and his father's father before him.

Glory

The child who wanted to see pictures of me asked questions about how old my granddad was in a picture I was holding. The picture was black and white. He was facing left and wearing a sports coat and fedora in the picture. I said, "Just before I came down yesterday...so around nine-thirty." The child was mesmerized at the photo. He also seemed mesmerized that a photo existed of someone so recently from a different time/space. I even became more fascinated in the details of the picture since I had not really thought of it being out-of-place in the location I was in at that time. I decided to return to my body to recount this part of the experience.

After I finished taking notes, I was immediately able to return to the same place in the heavens I had been before. My soul was understanding the dynamics of traveling to specific locations a little better each time I journeyed back. Time had passed from when I had left. To me, it was only minutes on Earth as I jotted down my notes. In the heavens, it appeared to have been hours. When I returned, there was an angel sitting on the back porch of the house. I did not have to ask any questions, for it seemed like she was waiting for me to return to answer questions I had not yet asked.

The angel said, "She quit using the term 'mentor' in regard to you." The angel was talking in reference to the curly haired angel. My eyes perked up. I understood in this dialogue I was learning that the curly haired angel had been a mentor to me, but now saw me as having moved beyond that point in our spiritual companionship. It gave me hope that she saw me as more than needing help – that perhaps she saw me in the

The Written (cont'd)

way I admired her or, at the very least, stronger in a spiritual sense.

The angel that was speaking to me went on to say, "She disappeared at half of the strength that she appeared. She arrived twice as strong as how she left." Throughout my travels back and forth in the heavens, I was grasping for a higher understanding of the spheres in the equidistant bouquet. The spheres doubled in size and subdivided into smaller spheres during my travels. This was the math behind understanding how to move from location to location. It was also the principle behind energies and understanding our arrivals and departures. So, part of the dialogue from the angel was also to re-emphasize to me the importance of understanding the law of doubling/halving in this experience. I felt a peace that the angel had waited for my return so that she could grant me answers to some of the questions I did not even know I had at that point. We chatted for a little longer and I returned back to my body to journal.

Again, a quick trip back to the heavens resulted in my strengthened understanding of the motion and the movement of the experience itself. I was by no means becoming an expert, but I was much further along than I was before the evening of travels began. When I arrived back at the house, I decided it was important to start understanding the names of the angels I was speaking with. When I arrived at the house again, I walked to the front door. I was greeted by another angel. This angel shared with me that the house belonged to an Elder Angel named "Charles." That name seemed so familiar,

Glory

but I could not place it. I decided to return to write about the experience.

I returned to the heavens once again. This time I found myself standing in the void with the blanket of equidistant spheres beginning to fill the right side of my periphery. Before me stood an elder angel. I am not sure it was Enoch, but that was my initial impression. I only had a brief look at him though, which is the reason for my pause. As I stood before him, I felt anxious to travel back to the heavens. He did not seem to be moving quickly enough for me, so in my haste I realized I could use the equidistant bouquet to travel. I leapt into the blanket and began to understand how to follow the spheres for navigation. As I did so, the voice of the angel bellowed out, "You do not need to joke around with it. It is to be used for serious purposes." I felt I was getting scolded, but at the same time I knew that I was learning how to use it, so I did not understand why I was being scolded.

As those thoughts were filling my mind, the voice boomed out again, "You are learning serious things." As the angel spoke, I understood the latter to be more of a nod of approval than of a scolding. In earthly terms it would be more akin to a parent warning a child that seems to understand how to ride a bicycle, "Be careful, but you are doing well. Keep it up!" With the angel's words still resonating in my head, I decided to return again to make sure I recounted the experience with as many details as possible.

I returned to the heavens. This time, I was standing before an elder angel on a beach. The ocean was behind us. The

The Written (cont'd)

angel was instructing me on "how to make a sphere around myself." I watched as this elder angel that appeared to be Enoch (gray hair, white robe) knelt down and began moving his hand in a circle just above the surface of the ground. As he did so, the sand began to turn white, and the consistency changed to something that appeared to be a paste. As the angel moved his hand he said, "This is one of two kinds of spheres that you can create. This is the kind that others can see on Earth."

As I watched him continue to make the same circular motion I asked, "Counterclockwise?" but quickly corrected myself as I watched his left hand move in a clockwise motion. "Clockwise." I said. He nodded back. It was hard to understand the directions because I was acutely aware we were always in a constant state of spin. Whether the world was spinning around us, or we were spinning within it, I was not sure. But, it seemed like it was some combination of the two. The angel's hands lighted up in the glow from his palm. The whiteness of the sphere became a great white light.

He asked me to step closer. When I did, the light of the sphere surrounded me. About halfway up my body, it appeared I was standing in a bowl of white light. Above the edge of the bowl's rim, the white fell flush across my body forming a bond with the sphere from below. The top half was as if I was in a spandex bath of white light. The bottom half held the bulbous shape of a bowl, but it was firmly rooted within the ground. I understood how I can learn to draw light energy from the Earth to root my body within its strength. The angel did not show me how to make the other sphere. He walked away, pleased that I had understood all that he shown me. I have to believe he showed me this to learn how to make this same type of concept manifest on Earth, but I do not know how much of it (if any) will be perceivable. The angel was specific to say that "this is the one that others can see on Earth" – implying that it is able to be seen with the eyes. Whether that results in the same phenomena I witnessed or some other form to others, I cannot be sure. But, the implication is that I was shown something important that can be used on Earth due to the strength of my spirit.

After he walked away, another angel walked over to me. He was excited to share with me that he had been working on a device for my daughter based upon my traveling abilities. He explained that the device would give her "the gift of travels" like me, but that her ability would be even stronger than mine since these light workers were able to build this device off of my abilities. I understood it to mean that they have a genetic understanding of my spiritual body and could use that to help my daughter travel back and forth with even greater clarity and ease than I am able to do. It seemed that they work to assist us from their plane as much as we strive to find them from our plane. The device he showed me looked similar to a backpack made of aluminum pistons, pipes and lights.

I returned to my body, took notes, and returned to the heavens. This time I was in a more abstract form. I was spinning counter clockwise. It was a slow spin that felt nice – like floating along in the current of a river. I looked below me and

The Written (cont'd)

saw two sets of white cans. They appeared to be circles, but the spin gave them depth. As I spun around the two cans (side by side), they turned into a grid of four (two by two). I was with another soul at this same time. This person was either a teacher listening to me explain, or a student who understood part of the equidistant bouquet already.

I began to wonder if my time on Earth was drawing to a close. While I was spinning I was instructed to make sure I gave Bryan everything I had written before I took my trip to Nashville. I was not sure why he needed it. I debated if it was because he needed to catch up on all of these experiences as he can fit them into his schedule, or whether it was because my time here was nearly complete.

As I asked God whether my days were drawing to a close, light filled my periphery and I fell back into my body. My phone was vibrating under the pillow next to me. There was a LinkedIn notification on the screen. It said, "Parkinson's D. has invited you to connect." My mind raced at the thought that maybe I was about to be diagnosed with Parkinson's. But the more I meditated about it, the more I understood that I was potentially being led to solve the Parkinson's problem. Later in the morning I looked up information on Parkinson's and realized that the tremors all occur in the range of 4 hertz to 7 hertz. Immediately I understood how to cause the effects of Parkinson's to be suppressed if not cured completely.

I returned back to the heavens and arrived back in the void. I looked to my right and saw the equidistant bouquet blanket rolling in the wind (or in the flow of the aether). As I

Glory

stared at it, I saw a white spherical wall form along the right side of my periphery. It was a solid wall, but created by white spheres. The top layer of spheres was translucent. There were two angels with me. I shouted over to them jokingly about how I was seeing the same wall I saw in my other experiences. They were amused. I lost harmony and returned to my body.

I once again arrived in the heavens. This time, I was with (what appeared to be) a family I met here in Fort Lauderdale. In fact, I met the two parents first who really wanted me to meet their daughter when she arrived a few weeks following their departure. As it turned out, the days of meeting their daughter were the best few days I have had in Fort Lauderdale, though I never pursued her in any dating sense. It was purely just getting to know her as a person. But that can be expounded upon at a later point. She has a beautiful soul.

In this experience, we were all having dinner at a restaurant I had never been to. We were eating in the upstairs dining area. The inside had white linens on wooden chairs and tables. The carpet seemed to be a rich green. During the dinner, her dad shouted out "T'allez-vous modi" (or something that sounded similar). Technically, T'allez vous is not a word in French, so maybe it was just allez-vous. Either way, when he said the phrase, I was curious about the word modi (which I had never heard, and actually I am not sure if I even spelled correctly).

We all had a great dinner and great laughs. We drove back to the condo where we all live. On our way back, someone forgot an item, and we had to return to the restaurant to

The Written (cont'd)

retrieve it. On our second attempt home, Joe (the father) was searching for something in his pocket. He could not find whatever it was and feared he had left it back at the restaurant. So, we returned to the restaurant a second time to retrieve it.

On the second trip, I understood us to be traveling to Pompano. We were ascending a tall hill when Joe realized he had lost whatever the item was. He shouted out that same French phrase again, "T'allez-vous modi!" I asked if the word I did not understand (modi) meant "quickly." Joe seemed intrigued I would have figured that out. I explained he had used the word twice and that the context seemed to fit for the definition of "quickly." In French, the word for quickly is "vite," so I knew it was a strange thing for me to rationalize, but nonetheless, that is how the conversation transpired (right or wrong).

When we returned to the restaurant, we decided to walk back. As we walked past the restaurant, Joanna (their daughter) waved up at someone in the upstairs of the restaurant. She was being playful and fun. We were all still in a good mood. When we made it back to the condo, there were two moving trucks parked out front. One truck was smaller with a lot of color on the outside. The other truck was a large white unmarked semi. The conversation I was having with Joanna turned into her moving into the condo. I playfully asked if she had a lot of stuff. She avoided the question, which was enough for me to think she must.

As we reached the trucks, the rear trailer doors to the large white truck swung open and two angels jumped out.

Glory

They were wearing white robes. The truck was packed full of items. At the edge closest to us, there was a short, wide wireframe shelf packed with items. They were neatly stored and evenly distributed. When Joanna saw the two angels and that particular shelf she became excited. She exclaimed, "They are SO my movers!" I could not tell if she liked the way everything was packed, or if she was indeed surprised in recognition of her stuff being moved in to the condo.

She jumped into the back of the truck, tossed the shelf onto the ground in front of me, and began to run upstairs in excitement. Until this point I did not know we were that far along in a relationship (in the heavens), so it seemed like a surprise, but one that I was eager to welcome. It was almost as if the universe was saying to each of us, "You two should be together," in an archetypal story-form, more than anything else. Perhaps that was the whole point. It is also important to note that Joanna looks strikingly similar to the brunette angel with straight brown hair I keep seeing – but not the angel named Zoey.

I returned to my body, then back to the heavens. This time I was standing in front of a Christmas tree. It was clear that I was experiencing a moment from someone's past rather than the present. I found the last remaining copy of a homemade Christmas movie on a flash drive for a set of parents. They were extremely excited and surprised I was able to produce the video for them. Their "recovery guy" had not been able to help them find their old videos which caused them to think all hope was lost.

The Written (cont'd)

The video was grainy. I watched it play. It was a video of Christmas morning with a mid-twenties year old girl with curly brown hair. My mind flashed to the times I had spent with her and how she and I had some type of relationship during the same timeframe the video had been shot. I recalled us being intimate just after that particular video was shot and us joking that it would be funny if our intimate moments were caught on camera. But they were not. In earthly terms, I have no idea who the girl in the video is. It does not seem like anyone from my immediate past, yet it seemed so familiar...

I wrote down notes and returned again to the heavens. This time I was standing with the same girl from the video. We were in front of a beautiful suburban home. The yard was lush green and well manicured. The house was a mixture of brick and white wood. It was the perfect suburban home. The girl grabbed the For Sale sign out of the yard in an action that meant we had either just purchased the home, or she did not want anyone else to have the home but us. She was excited, looked at me and said, "Three Peterson Whitesview Circle." She had the biggest smile on her face. I assume that it was an address, but I am not sure from what period or where. I also was unsure if "Three Peterson" could possibly have represented me, her, and a child and our name was perhaps Peterson. All of this was racing through my mind. I decided to return back to my body to write it all down before returning again.

Once again I returned. I had become extremely lucid with all of the experiences and decided I should be more productive in the remaining travels. I prayed that I may have some clarity with names again. I spoke to the angels, to the void, and to God about my desire to identify to whom I was speaking. I also pleaded for forgiveness that I may have been shared their names before, but was unable to correctly identify them. This process seemed to go on for a while. Scenes changed. I moved from the equidistant bouquet blanket to an area of white light.

Eventually an Elder angel appeared. He was the elder black man wearing a white toga that I see on occasion. He had short white hair. When he appeared, I thought "Uriel" but was not shared a name. I lost harmony and returned again to my body. It became clear that it was becoming more difficult for me to maintain my balance with so much earthly intention to understand. It almost has to be surrender and acceptance of what is learned rather than desire to ask something specifically in order to maintain the best harmony.

The final experience of the evening involved my ex-wife, Stacey. She and I were in a house. I was unfamiliar with where we were, though. It seemed like Georgia had already gone to bed and that it was just her and me left to catch up with each other. Stacey jumped into my arms, straddling me. She tried to make out with me. She had a long tongue and was being really extreme in her actions. Honestly, it was very sexy and a little bit fetish driven in the manner she was attempting to lick my face and use her tongue on my body.

I never kissed back. I tried to pull away from her the whole time. Somehow she had managed to restrain my arms with her legs as she used her hands to try to pull my face into hers. I fought the internal urges. I could remember the good

The Written (cont'd)

times when we were intimate together. Never had she tried to take control as she was in this moment. I could sense that our intimacy could be perfect if this was not just a one-time attempt to win me over and then have her return to being bitter and disinterested in me.

  She somehow forced me to carry her back to the bedroom. She was wearing really short jean shorts that reminded me of the summer we were first together. Those were the times she wanted to dress the most revealing. Over the years she began dressing more tomboy-like which was not quite the same for me – mostly because I thought it was unflattering to her beautiful body. While she is more beautiful today than she was when we met, I thought she chose to wear the strange clothing as a subconscious way of projecting her unhappiness onto us. I never said anything about it, and this may be the first time I have ever voiced those words, but her clothes mirrored her unhappiness the worse it became.

  This time was different though. This time, it was reminiscent of when she was happiest and we were young and in Love. Only this time, it felt like there was a much more mature intimacy. I fought the desire because I have never quit loving her. I never will. True Love transcends time and space. It does not mean it has to be, but rather that it never will be undone. In this moment, though, I knew that us having any intimacy would only end in more anger and frustration on her part.

  She looked at me and said, "You know that time when you were a freak once…" Her voice trailed off. She was not talking about me. She was raising a question to me from her perspective about herself (though I have to say it did not hold any actual earthly references). Obviously, my thoughts whirled around my head at breakneck speeds. I wondered if she was basically telling me she was now an untamed carnal pleasure in bed. Of course it turned me on even more. That was her plan.

I replied, "Oh, you mean you are going to get freaky with me?" She gave me a dirty smile as if I had no idea what I was about to experience. Fortunately I held strong. I never kissed her, never willfully held her, and before we made it to the bedroom, I jettisoned my soul back to my body so there would not have to be any decision made. I would rather not experience it at all than be faced with a dilemma of whether I would have her back with all of the hurt I had experienced in my past or break her heart telling her no. Just to clarify my thoughts in writing: I would not have her back, even in a spiritual form, where she would likely never know that moment occurred.

In reality, I believe that she likely experienced that moment with me in a shared consciousness. We have never talked about it before, but I know that she has "very real dreams." However, to say they are anything else makes her clam up and not talk. My perception recently has been that she never quit loving me and is possibly angry at herself for the decisions she made. In this experience, she thought she could win me over with intimacy – and that would definitely have strengthened our marriage since it was absent from an early point. But, I would never truly know if it was all a show, and therefore it was not something I was willing to explore with my heart.

The Written (cont'd)

November 21, 2014
Afternoon

During afternoon meditation, I was intent on returning to the heavens in the same manner I learned to travel during the early morning hours. As I found myself in a great vibratory state, I heard a voice speak to me. "You were extracted. You were working for Lion forty-five D." That seemed to be in response to a question on whether I was allowed to willfully travel to the heavens or whether I was taken there. As it turned out, it seemed as if I was taken there from Earth. The second part of the sentence does not make a tremendous amount of sense on the surface level though.

Upon looking up the number 45 (which sums to 9...the whole) in biblical context, I learned it was mentioned only three times. One of those times is in the book of Daniel, where he mentions that those who make it 45 days through the Lord's trials is a part of Jesus's returning. If one were to assume that October 3rd (the start of Yom Kippur) of this year were to be the specific date Daniel references, 45 days following would bring us to November 17th. If the letter D represents four as well, this would put us on November 21, 2014...tomorrow. Also, Lion 45 D directly references Daniel and the den of lions, the mysterious number 45 in the bible in correlation to Revelation, as well as the D for Daniel. So, essentially, this specific day and time somehow manages to tie exactly – all without me having any underlying information about any of those numbers.

I jotted down the notes and returned to the heavens once again during meditation. I prayed for help understanding the names of the angels again. I opened a door to an "information" building. I observed a long line wrapping through a maze or railing. At the end of the line was a woman. I began asking her if she knew anything about the angels I was describing. As we talked, the door slammed behind me. I was committed to going through the line at this point. The woman seemed to want to distance herself from me as I described the angels. She made her way through the line as swiftly as she could so as to keep her distance from me. I told her not to be afraid, that I was just seeking names. As she seemed to let her guard down, I found myself speaking in a strange language.

I heard myself ask if she knew Kal-ev. My own reaction to the recognition of speaking a name caused me to become disoriented. Hearing a foreign language come out of my mouth was enough to make me lose harmony. It took a lot of work to maintain balance. I realized I was being tested on my spiritual strength. I continued through the line.

As I neared the dark windows where the line met its destination, I emerged from a crossbeam overhead. The room was all white and fairly well lighted. When I emerged, I saw that there were three angels standing in white, all watching me, smiling. They were happy in my actions. As we made eye contact, they bathed the room in blue light. It was enough to cause me to have to work harder to maintain harmony. I felt a

The Written (cont'd)

peace in the angels' actions for me. The blue light was in recognition of my strength.

I told the lady in front of me not to be scared of the angels, for they were happy in my efforts. I then spoke directly to the three angels. I said, "I'm just hoping to bring back the white into blue." The words flew off my tongue with ease. I assumed I must have meant "bring back the divine information to Earth." The angels seemed approving of my statement. I eventually lost harmony, just shy of making it to the information window...but only for a moment. I regained my strength, but found myself outside again.

I walked to another building. It was white on the outside and had a couple of steps leading up to a set of double doors. As I gazed upon the doors, two angels opened the doors revealing a bar table. A very large elder black angel was sitting at the table. He seemed to be pushing the two angels' patience as if he was not supposed to be there. However, since he was already there, I also acknowledged it was an opportunity for me to walk in. The two angels that held open the doors were female. The one on my left had short auburn hair. Each angel had a milky complexion and delicate features. I sensed their unrest with the man but chose to nod and continue walking on. The two angels nodded back at me, and I returned to my body.

Glory

November 21, 2014
Late Afternoon

The experiences from this afternoon were shortened as I have been traveling much of the day. My meditations have been aboard aircrafts. While most of the experiences lacked complete clarity, they all seemed to involve the same theme. The first several travels involved me helping others find Love. There were maybe three or four separate experiences where this was the case. In each one, the angels around me watched as I helped a man and a woman find happiness together.

One experience set itself apart from the rest. Perhaps it was from the clarity, or perhaps it was meant for me to understand it contained a special message from the heavens to my soul. In this final experience of the day, I was able to see myself as an older man. I had lived a good life. I cared for my daughter who was the center of the experience. I Loved her so much in it, and I wanted to protect her from a broken heart. I also spoke with Stacey and shared with her how much I Loved her, though we never appeared to have gotten back together. I spoke to her about finding her inner peace. The conversation with Stacey did not hold any romantic interest. Rather, it was focused on helping her grow. The experience weighed on my soul more than others because it felt as if I was meant to understand the experience as closure. Maybe the closure was so I could have confirmation that my divorce was as it was supposed to be, as well as it is to remain in the future. But, it also

The Written (cont'd)

felt like the closure I felt was earthly – as if (again) my time here may be reaching the end of its journey.

November 21, 2014
Evening

After having a very good meeting with a client in Nashville, I again felt the weight of the decision on next steps with a contract with this company. The opportunity was no doubt divinely introduced into my life, much as it was this past February (when I had three jobs presented to me simultaneously). Again, it was one of three. But, just in the same way that I felt when Wilson extended his opportunity to me, I feel very strongly that God could be telling me to let go of earthly contracts. But, on the flip side, I also think that the contracts could be purposed into my life since I think I still need to feel stability financially. I have been completely conflicted on what I should do, and I continue to pray for guidance.

After the meeting I felt led to watch a movie. I went to Opry Mills to catch whatever movie was about to start when I arrived. There were a couple movies I had not seen yet, so I was okay with whichever movie I saw. It happened to be that the latest Hunger Games was playing on the biggest screen just a couple of minutes from when I arrived. I went ahead and chose to watch that movie.

As the movie began, I heard God tell me to pay attention. I knew that this movie would contain something special for me to understand at this particular juncture in my life. As the movie began, the spiritual story was very apparent. I was able to immediately see His story being shared with me through the movie everyone else was watching. Perhaps someone else would also see a story specific to his life. Truthfully, that did not matter. The only thing that mattered was what was being spoken to me.

There came a time in the movie when the government broadcast a video to the rebels that said, "Take the contract. If you don't, there will be seven times the amount of destruction, etc." Immediately I knew that this specific part of the movie was tailored exactly to my situation. On one side, the evil entity was telling me to "take the contract." The numbers of seven were clearly scripted for me to understand the message to me. After the movie ended I was left with the question. Was God telling me to "take the contract" or was He telling me to pay attention that the evil side was telling me to "take the contract." Again, it seemed to give me a double meaning. But most importantly, whatever decision I truly believe God is sharing with me will be the correct one... at least until I am redirected or receive confirmation in my understanding of the decision.

November 22, 2014

This morning's experiences were again numerous, but I was extremely tired when I lay down to rest so it was hard for

The Written (cont'd)

me to awaken my earthly body in order to take notes from each experience. Each time I would return to my body I could not awaken it. I only found an in-between state that left me feeling a little helpless in a spiritual sense. I continued returning to the heavens since that doorway had been opened to me, but I was unable to write much about the experiences except for the last one. The only takeaway I had at all from the earlier visions comes from the last one.

In this experience, I was visited by the four archangels. All four were large and adorned in white robes. Their faces were so bright that I had to look away. I could see that their hair was variant in color, each one containing curls, but that is all I could initially discern. The angels were there in response to my prayer earlier in the evening. When they arrived, I was initially wearing red boxer briefs and a t-shirt. It was as if they visited me on Earth to take me to the heavens. When we arrived in the heavens, I spoke to all four archangels for a while. Snow fell around us. The setting seemed surreal.

The way I initially journaled the setting was that we were standing in "a very ornate snow background." We talked about life on Earth, my travels back and forth, my stress in determining whether to accept the next financial contracts. Part of the conversation led to me showing the angels photos where I helped make people happy. The conversation seemed to be intended to help me understand my purpose. When we talked about finances, I told them that I was not concerned about it, just that I like to understand my plan in how to handle any financial decisions. I acknowledged that I had been blessed

Glory

beyond any expectation, but it was hard to understand when I would no longer need to rely on money and instead, purely follow the spirit.

As we talked about this, three of the angels walked into an adjoining room and began to chat among themselves. The fourth stayed behind with me. We sat down at a table next to the doorway. Though I could not look at the angel's face due to its brightness, I could see the angel's hand resting upon the table. Our conversation was fluid, and I spoke to them as if we were old friends or acquaintances. There was not any awkwardness or missteps in the conversation. As the conversation turned to small talk, I complimented the angel's nails in being made of gold. I could not discern whether the nails were materially made of gold or whether it was a form of nail polish, but the best way I could describe them was similar to a glitter paint. Light reflected off of the nails causing them to shimmer in their golden glow.

The angel joked with me about my observation of its nails. It said, "Oh, you can see that? I'm glad you like it." The angel seemed amused and entertained at my playfulness in the conversation. At that point the angel joined the other three angels as they were returning through the doorway. They chatted among themselves, conferring about the conversation that just took place. When they stood before me, or I before them, one of the angels spoke about my observation of the gold nails. It was a much more masculine voice. He seemed jolly and amused as well. One of the other angels extended its hand to show me that its nails were made of a golden-purple.

The Written (cont'd)

Again, the best way I could describe it would be similar to a purple-glitter paint, but I could tell the nails were materially made of this inexplicable substance.

There was small talk made about the purple and then the angels spoke to me. One of their voices said, "We will return to you again." With that, they turned and vanished into the distance. I knew in that moment that the subject matter of their conversation had caused them to go back and discuss next steps for me. Perhaps it was my willingness not to be bound by money. Perhaps it was my stress about having a plan for the future. Perhaps it was because I was not fully in harmony with the moment. In truth, it could have been stronger so I could understand more and return with greater details of our talks, though it was a very overpowering experience nonetheless. Maybe it was all of the above. I cannot be sure. All I know is that I was visited by the four archangels. My future was at least part of the subject of their conversation. And, finally, I know they will return to share with me next steps.

After the angels left, I was able to awaken my earthly body so I could write down the experience. At that time, I also recalled there was another experience earlier in the night where both my cousin Bryan and his deceased father, Gary, were present – however, I cannot recall any details. Finally, I was able to recall there were numerous experiences similar to those I had on my flight to Nashville the day prior. These experiences from the day prior were all about helping others fall in Love, and there was a continuation of that theme when the experiences first began for me this morning. In all of these par-

Glory

ticular experiences (including the prior day's experiences on the plane), the details were unclear. Only the feeling of helping others fall in Love remained after they ended.

November 26, 2014

This morning's experiences were extremely numerous, though the details were lacking and each experience was very short. The first experience began with me in a darkened room. Looking around, I noticed that the room had many twin beds surrounding the walls and a couple of larger beds in the center of the room. It felt like I was a child and this was a place for all of the children to sleep. I heard my name called and turned around to see my cousin Bryan.

He was very excited to see me and extremely excited to share with me something he had just experienced. I heard him say, "And Lucifer made a noise like this." Bryan let out a quiet, but eerie shrieking sound. He was quiet enough to make sure he did not wake any of the others in the room. I repeated, "Lucifer?" I was surprised at why he would be excited at this particular experience. As my question rolled off of my lips, the door to the room opened and two young girls came in. I recognized them to be my sister (not my earthly sister) and her friend... perhaps a cousin. Bryan made a gesture at me to be quiet, as if he did not want the girls to hear his story for fear they would be scared. He said, "Shhh." The two girls looked

The Written (cont'd)

startled but crawled in the big bed in the center of the room. I lost harmony.

I returned to the heavens and found myself in the same room. I was in the middle of a conversation with Bryan. I said, "I used to follow Aileen's (or maybe Alene's) breath when she fell asleep by putting my arm around her." My mind filled with a vision of me wrapping my right arm around this girl. My best understanding of the context of the conversation was to tell Bryan how to best find a meditative state before falling asleep – especially in the company of another in his bed. On Earth, I know Bryan has been frustrated at his lack of travels to the heavens and seems to think that it is due to being newly married and having to determine a way to find a meditative state in the company of his wife's sleeping habits.

As I thought about the image of this girl under my arm I felt a twinge in my right arm. I looked to see that I was lying on top of a black wolf that was trying to bite me in order to get me to rise up off of it. I immediately sat up and turned to look at the wolf. I sensed the black wolf carried an evil within it. It looked at me angrily, but hurt. I could see I had dislocated the wolf's jaw by lying on top of it. In fact, the bottom jaw was jutting out to the side at a 90° angle. The wolf was in obvious pain. And though I knew the wolf was there to attack me, I tried to help it. I grabbed the top and bottom jaw in either hand and tried to pull them back together. That hurt me inside as much as it physically was hurting the wolf. The wolf winced. I winced internally at its pain and let go. The wolf whined and ran off into the distance.

Glory

When I arrived back in the heavens, I was intent to understand why I would be in a room like that, aware that I was dreaming while my body was on Earth in a deep meditative or sleep state. I repeated the question into the void. "Why would I be dreaming in a room like that?" I saw a hand enter into my periphery. It was glowing with a white light. It was a right hand pointing to my left. A voice said, "Aileen knew…" I said, "Why would Aileen know?" I lost harmony and returned to my body.

Almost immediately, I returned back to the heavens. A robotic voice that sounded like it was in a can said, "Another's thoughts were inside of you." My vision was filled with an image of a great tree with a golden sky behind it. I was walking with an angel to the tree. I had not quite found my harmony and the sight of the sky and tree caused me to return to my body.

I took notes as quickly as I could and returned. I found myself again in the void. I asked, "Why is it so difficult for me to see vividly right now?" I kept repeating the question hoping to receive a response. I began to think that if I saw any more vividly I would lose the trip altogether. My thoughts rationalized I was walking a fine line in a suboptimal travel state. As those thoughts filled my head, a female voice spoke from the void, "Would you like it better if your son was a/the surgeon? That may make it easier." It seemed like a nonsensical thing to have been said at that moment and it caused me to lose harmony. But now that I am writing about this voice in my notes, there are numerous possibilities as to why those words may

The Written (cont'd)

have been spoken. Unexpected? Yes. But nonsensical? Not necessarily.

I returned to the heavens and found myself in the bedroom with all of the beds for the children. I overheard a female voice say to me "Daddy says…" The rest of her words trailed off as I realized that my sister was speaking to me. This time it was not a thought of "my sister in heaven." It was an actual moment where family ties were involved in the conversation. This thought jolted me inside and caused me to lose harmony. I took notes and returned to the heavens.

I found myself back in the gorgeous setting of the great tree and orange sky, standing with my angelic teacher. We began to climb the tree. The angel said to me, "We are only given three rocks." It was implied that I was not to lose the rocks, or drop the rocks, though I was unsure what the context of the rocks was. When we reached one of the branches of the tree, we sat on it and stared at the fiery sky. To my right the sky burst into a yellowish-orange fireball. This fireball grabbed all of my attention. I wanted to see the fireball with clarity. I wondered if it was like the fireballs written about in the Bible where angels descend from the heavens. As I focused on the burst of yellow and orange, I was transported to a room filled with carvings all over the walls. The walls seemed to be made of emerald, and the carvings appeared to be God's records written in Sanskrit upon the walls. Everywhere I looked, words filled the walls. As I focused on the walls – in particular, a beam of stone overhead with words – I over focused and was

Glory

returned to the branch. The experience caused me to lose harmony and return to Earth.

When I returned, I was standing before a giant female gatekeeper. She was without form, speaking to an older, funny, creole man. He was black skinned and jolly in nature. They laughed and she let him by. Suddenly, I saw the creole man as a sphere floating down a calm river to the east.

When I returned to the heavens, I found myself standing before an elder angel with a gray beard in a room of white. The angel seemed to be Enoch, though he did not identify himself. He was standing in a white robe. He said, "Jonathan, I'd like to remind you where you will be returning from and what you will be doing." As he said these words, I watched as two white cylinders rotated on top of each other. The tubes were about four feet wide and a foot tall. They were horizontal to the floor and attached to a machine that swung them over and above the other much like the way a chamber in a revolver spins the shells around. However, there were only two of these white cylinders in the machine. The angel stood on the far side from me. The chambers obstructed our line of sight. The lighting in the room was a soft cyan. When the cylinders had rotated, he opened a hatch on it. The hatch was essentially half of the cylinder that was spring loaded to open 90°. He motioned for me to get into the capsule. At this point I lost harmony and returned to my body.

Again, returning to the heavens, I found myself standing in a doorway similar to the hatch to board a plane. An angel in all white walked by. He said, "Are you sure you don't have

The Written (cont'd)

anything to ask me? You can ask me anything…" For some reason I was nervous that I would ask something unimportant. So, instead, I just replied, "Nope. I'm all good." If I had nearly the control of the words that come out of my mouth in the heavens as I would like, I would most certainly have attempted to ask other questions. But, instead, it was as if I was on autopilot. I held onto the top of the doorway, enjoying the moment. The angel shrugged, smiled, and walked on.

I returned again to the heavens, this time in a void. I twisted through something that I understood to be a black hole. Somehow the motion of the black hole turned everything purple. A voice spoke from the void. "Why did you go through there?" I really did not have an answer. I replied, "I don't know what I am doing. It just seemed like the right thing to do." At that point I was taken to a room where I was handed a white pot. The pot contained a beautiful plant – one unlike anything I have ever seen on Earth. The plant was budding. I wanted to take it back to Earth with me and give it to my sister (I am unsure why I would give it to my sister. I rarely talk to her.) However, I was told that I could not take it back with me, which saddened me. This was the first time I had ever attempted to take something physically from the heavens with me to Earth. My curiosity had been increasing as to what could travel between the heavens with me.

On my return trip, I was standing in a room. A beautiful red-headed angel walked by with two children trailing behind her. I could not tell if they were patients, students, or maybe even her own children. I suppose it does not matter. They were angels of young age. The angel that led me to the room called out to the red-headed angel, "Hey Darcy!" I wondered if maybe I did not hear it correctly. But, regardless, my thoughts were cut short when the angel turned to me and said, "You should be together." It was enough to cause me to lose harmony and return to Earth.

Upon returning, I saw myself standing between two spheres. On the right, I saw the most beautiful garden. It was lush with the greenest of grass, trees, and plants. The sky was ignited in a bright yellow. The world I could see to my right was as real as it could be, but I was left standing on the outside staring in. To my left, there was an artist who was reproducing everything that I could see on my right, upon a canvas with some type of bring-to-life paint. I could not look upon the artist, for he was too bright to see with my eyes. I was left having to gaze upon the scene to my right. I could, however, see as he brought to life portions of the painting on the left.

I asked the angel that I was standing with about the colors and why I could not see everything on my left. I was told that the man allowing me to watch had six canvases that made up everything I was witnessing and that he chose who would receive them. I heard a voice say, "I want to be king." The voice caused me to lose harmony and return to Earth. I also want to note that the "artist" was extremely large. His hand and paintbrush dwarfed my body in size. In one of the previous times where God revealed himself to me, I was barely the size of his big toe as I stood next to his foot. This was a similar feel-

The Written (cont'd)

ing at that moment – especially in that I could not look upon that sphere, nor could I see anything beyond His great hand.

Once again, I found harmony in the heavens. This experience was shorter. I was standing in a chamber and overheard conversations of others around me. They were all discussing how they wanted to become king. As I tried to make sense of the voices in the void, an angel spoke to me directly. The male voice said, "She can't be. She is not trained like you." I knew in that moment the angel was giving me peace that I was excelling in my journey, faster than the others that were desiring to become king. I lost my bearings and returned to Earth.

Of the last three experiences of the morning, I found myself in a strange suit inside of a metal ship. A female angel seemed to be walking toward me. I was not sure if she was actually walking to me or just in my direction, so I jumped upward to the ceiling defying any gravity that may have existed. When she was close, I jumped back down to catch her attention.

I startled her, but then she looked at me with that deep angelic gaze that halts everything in its tracks. I heard a voice speak to me. "Who is she?" I must have been being tested, but as usual, I fell short on name associations. I just stared at the angel. She was wearing a strange suit too, but her face was very distinguishable. As I stared, I heard violins begin to play and then an orchestra begin to break out in song. It was a sweet song…like one that would be played at a wedding, or a song that could be waltzed to in the passion of the moment. The song was so strong in my spiritual ears that I became lost in its wonder. I returned from the heavens and journaled the experience, never answering the angel's question.

I returned to a group of soldiers standing before an angel. We were being sent out into the void. I was confident I would return, though the angel that was sending this legion into the void did not have as much confidence that I would return. I became aware I was speaking fluently in a language to my angelic guide that I was unfamiliar with. He seemed to understand me. Spiritually, I seemed to understand as well. The angel told me I was given a "ruby-shahbi." The spelling may be off, but I repeated the word several times so that I could bring it back with me. This "ruby-shahbi" seemed like something that served as a form of recognition. With the word repeating in my mind, I returned to Earth to write it down.

In the final experience of the night, I found myself playing guitar to a song I had never heard. It had a beautiful melody and there was another angel singing. At the end of the song, I turned and looked at the angel. She said, "I want them to hear me sing. I'm gong to bring them over here so they can hear." With that, the angel walked over to another group of angels in the room. The room we were in formed a perfect square. It is one of the only times I have been able to see the entire perimeter of the space I was in.

As the angel walked away, I lost harmony and returned to my body and journaled this last experience. These seventeen experiences in the early hours of the morning took place only in the time frame of a little over an hour. This was the highest frequency of travels I have experienced to date. A few days

The Written (cont'd)

ago in the morning when I had the twenty-plus experiences, those took place over the course of three or four hours. So, this time was much more frequent, yet I did not seem to have as detailed of experiences as several days prior.

November 27, 2014

The experiences this morning were difficult to bring back. And, while I know I had several experiences, there are only two that I was able to bring back with me. The first experience took me to a soccer field where I played in a soccer match with other angels. I suppose much like we use sports and physical activity to help keep our body in shape, it makes sense that our souls have to remain conditioned and receive strength through coordination exercises.

At first I was unsure why I continued to find myself on football fields, hockey rinks, and soccer fields. But, the more I travel back and forth, the more I realize that my mind-body-soul alignment is strengthened through these activities. This time was no different than the other experiences. I was on a soccer field and realized I was becoming much better at it than I had been in previous experiences. We were playing on teams of three. It seemed we were only playing on half of a field. My team scored easily. I scored one goal when the ball was passed to me.

The second experience took me to a more divine location in the heavens. The setting seemed familiar from my heavenly travels. I was in a room with two female angels and one male angel. At the time, I thought one of the female angels was named "Shamain" (which sounded like Shannon with an M instead of an N). However, I found out later that particular name was not of the angel, but of the location.

As we stood in the room getting ready for church, I spoke to the female angel twice. I was also meeting a male angel named Paul. We left the room we were in and entered into the church. The walls were a light beige color. The sanctuary contained pews that formed a slight arc around the pulpit. There were four seating sections with walkways between. As the double-doors opened up to the sanctuary I inadvertently called the brunette angel that was with us "Shamain" when I went to tell her that I would see her after the service.

But, just as the incorrect name rolled off of my lips, I quickly corrected myself with what sounded like "E" before quieting myself so as not to bring attention to my correction. I was sure she knew I called her by the wrong name, but I tried to cover it up. I walked down the aisle and decided I would return back up the aisle to the angels I arrived with. A beautiful ash-blonde female angel was in the doorway. She was extremely familiar, and I am always mesmerized by her beauty. Her hair had so much body and reached down below her waist.

As I reached her I said, "I almost called the other angel by the wrong name. But I think I corrected it in time." The ash-blonde angel smiled as if she wanted me to feel comfort, though still knowing that I had goofed up the angel's name.

The Written (cont'd)

She said, "I know. I heard." As she finished her sentence I said, "Your hair has gotten so long!" At that moment, it seemed her hair was much longer than the last time I had seen her.

She smiled again, this time flattered by my words. She said, "I know! It reminds me who I am." She turned and walked down the hallway mid-sentence as if to allow me to see the beauty of her hair as she walked away. She continued speaking as I gazed at her. Without missing a beat from her last sentence, she said, "I am Schyphaen." I immediately was overcome with a tremendous amount of excitement which caused me to lose harmony and return from the heavens to Earth.

The loss of harmony was completely okay with me though because I was returning with another name of an angel. Though the name was tough to understand in spelling, the first syllable sounded sort of like "Scah." The second half of the name had two syllables but her voice faded out as she walked away and I lost harmony. It sounded sort of like "peter" but without the T and the ending possibly being an N instead of an R. And while I had never heard this name before, I researched every angelic name that I could possibly find on the internet. It turns out this name is only mentioned once and is found in a Latin text called Liber Juratus (The Sworn Book of Honorius). Not much is noted except it is an angel of the Descending Node.

This particular resource had pulled together many names not found in any other text. On this same site, I was able to find the proper spelling of Shamain and came to learn that it was the name of First Heaven. Of course I read up on the subject of First Heaven as much as I could find. As it turned out, not much is known about it, save for a short note about some of the names of the two hundred angels that purportedly dwell there. I immediately knew that this particular location that I travel back and forth from (which is just one of many locales I journey to and from) must indeed be First Heaven.

One of the short notes about First Heaven that I could find mentioned that Adam and Eve are reported to have lived in First Heaven. This particular note was located in the Testament of Solomon. This excited me so much because I recognized this particular locale as the same plane where I first met Zoe (Eve). As I reflected on the events, I realized that the angel that I inadvertently called "Shamain" and corrected myself to "E" was one and the same as Zoe, but it was the first time I had called her by her real name, Eve.

All of a sudden, the setting and the understanding of the angels began to fall into view. Though there is nothing else that is publicly available that could help me decipher my experiences, I can safely say that this particular setting is First Heaven. And while it may take some time for me to decipher these locales spiritually, it is important to note that every experience is much like understanding actions through a set of third-party eyes that have no control over the actions. Once full harmony occurs, the senses become one and the same as the senses on Earth and there is a limited amount of control that can be invoked. But this ability comes through the

The Written (cont'd)

strengthening of the spirit that has been occurring over the years of my travels. I wish I could get there faster, but I am doing all I can do. When that harmony is found, it generally overwhelms my strength and eventually causes me to return. But, these are also the most memorable moments – the ones where I ask questions, receive answers, or learn names. Now I know when I return that I can ask about the heavens – First Heaven, and which heaven my travels have taken me to…at least that is my intention so I can bring clarity in my writing of these experiences.

November 28, 2014

While some of my experiences this morning were clear, the first several were very hazy. In the beginning, the best I could explain was that I was in the heavens with my family. I thought my "family" was my spiritual family though, and not my earthly family. That is really all I could take away.

The second experience took me to a city location in the heavens. The building I found myself in was surrounded by a walkway in the shape of an H. I was in a restaurant with a female angel. The restaurant joined another restaurant on its backside. But, to reach the restaurant, you would have to walk out, down, and around to the other side of the H walkway.

For some reason, I felt it was important to excuse myself from the dinner I was having with the angel to go to the restroom. When I walked toward the bathroom, I decided to go

Glory

ahead and walk around the restaurant to the adjoining restaurant to say hey to my "friends." These friends were angels as well. They were happy to see me when I arrived. They knew I was having an important dinner and showed me how to return through the inside connecting doorway. They were amused I chose to say hello to them.

As I walked back to the restaurant I was originally dining in, an elder female angel approached me and asked me why I was in the back part of the restaurant. It was apparently off limits to patrons. I explained my situation and that I was told to return this way to get back and have dinner at the adjoining restaurant. The angel began by explaining that I should not be back there. An elder male angel took notice of our conversation and came over to understand the situation. He felt sorry for me due to my innocence and told the other angel to allow me to pass. He then helped me find a glass and filled it with wine so I would have a good story as to why it took me a few minutes to return to my dinner partner angel. I could say that I wanted to grab a drink for her while I was up. It made me smile that I had angels looking after me. I returned to my body to take notes of the experience.

When I returned to the heavens, I found myself in another group of angels in the same building as I was in before. We were sitting around a table having a good conversation. In the midst of the conversation, one of the angels brought up the subject of astral projection (by those specific words). When he said those words, it caused all of the other angels to pause and show him their undivided attention. Some seemed curious.

The Written (cont'd)

Others seemed like it was a subject they were fascinated with. He went on to say that "this area has a large group of people doing it." The others that were listening to him seemed somewhat confused by his words.

I took the opportunity to chime in and explain many of the benefits. My words managed to grab everyone's attention. Every person seemed eager to know more. We spoke for a while over dinner. I shared with the group how one man had a piece of property that he devoted as a memorial to astral projection. After dinner we traveled to the property for everyone to see. At the entrance of the property, there were angels standing guard over the entrance. They allowed me to enter with the group behind me. There was a long, twisting road that lead to the manor. It was twilight when we arrived. The property had a lot of trees, but certain areas had been cleared out for gardens, etc. I shared with everyone how the man had built the estate and left it in a trust for others to see upon his passing.

One of the larger attractions to the property was a garden with large, megalithic stone structures on it. It was surrounded by a black, iron fence. And though it may sound absurd, the garden was called something that sounded like "boob stone garden." I assumed this was because of two large stone spheres that were in the middle of the garden. We walked through the "boob stone garden" and looked at the large stone structures. I noticed there were others visiting the garden as well.

We eventually wandered over to a "pool" with an impossible shape. If one can imagine a deep swimming pool that

Glory

contained no water, but elevated a hundred feet in the air in an almost inverted fashion, that is the best way I can describe the shape. We climbed into the pool. I watched as some slid down the pool and made gravity defying leaps onto the ground. Everyone landed safe-and-sound. However, I was nervous about the leap, so I backtracked and climbed down the ladder that we first used to ascend. I am never fearful of anything in the heavens, so I was even curious at my own fear of getting hurt. I suppose this unrest caused me to lose harmony, since I found myself returning to my body. I took notes and returned once more.

This time, I again found myself with a group of angels. It may have been the same group as before, but it was hard for me to know for sure. I did take notice that the brunette angel was "out of town." I think the brunette angel must again be Zoe. This seems to be a recurring theme as of late. I knew I had a longing to see her, but her presence was absent in the moment. The group I was with jumped in a car (for lack of a better word) and asked me to follow them to a house outside of town.

When we arrived, we all celebrated the company of each other with a wonderful dinner. Most people over indulged in food and drinks. Time flew by as we were there. We were all involved in the best conversations and camaraderie. As some of the angels began to leave, I looked at my watch and realized it was 7:00 a.m. As it turned out, whether it was 7:00 a.m. in the heavens was irrelevant because I came to learn that it was actually around 7:00 a.m. back on Earth.

The Written (cont'd)

I knew I needed to head back "home," but I needed to drop my vehicle off on the way. I guess my vehicle must have been a rental, or possibly stored in another location away from my home. I did not really have any rationale for why it had to be dropped off. I just knew that the vehicle would only get me part of the way back to my "home." Some of the angels must have sensed my confusion as to what I should do because as I headed to the door, a brunette angel offered to follow me and take me the remainder of the way home (once I dropped off my vehicle).

While we were standing at the front door of the house, a male angel walked up and spoke with her. I could tell she was enamored with him. Whatever he said caused her to decide to stay with him. I thought it was romantically driven, but I was not upset at it. It seemed like her invitation to take me home caused that particular angel to decide to make his move. It was apparent they had a history together. As I watched that situation play out, another angel offered to follow me and take me home. On the journey back I lost harmony, returned to my body, took notes, and returned once again.

I did not miss much from my brief detour back to Earth. When I returned home, I was greeted by a group of female angels. The sun was now coming up in the heavens. It was a bright morning. The skies were orange. The female angels seemed excited to see me. One of the angels in the group was the red-headed angel that I have seen a lot recently. She always seems distant to me, but judging by her friends' interactions with me, it is easy to see that the red-headed girl likes me and is just unsure how to show it. Her friends continue to serve as matchmakers. Though I have never crossed any line with her that would indicate my interest, her friends all seem to want us to be together.

Time transitioned to some point in the future. The setting remained unchanged, though. This time the red-headed angel was returning home from something akin to college. There was a celebration for her at her house. When I arrived, I sat down next to her. I was on her left side, she on my right. We were sitting on backless barstools at a table in her family's kitchen. The table top was made of a light gray marble. As we sat there I could sense that she was nervous, but hiding it well. I noticed on her left hand – slightly offset to the left near the top of the hand and the bottom of the wrist – there was a circular marking. And while her skin was a milky complexion, the marking was lighter than her skin, though nearly indistinguishable in contrast. It looked like a seal of some sort with an intricate Celtic knot or floral pattern inside the rim of the circle. There were other markings inside of the insignia as well, but I could not make out any more detail.

I pointed to the marking with my right hand and began to ask her about it. When I touched her wrist with my index finger she did not shy away. I took her left hand in mine and asked her what the marking was. She said, "Oh? You can see it? I have others as well." She raised the sleeve of her white gown that was covering her arms and the rest of her hand. There were two other discernible markings. There was a mark that looked like a triangle on the right side of her left hand lo-

The Written (cont'd)

cated just above her thumb. The third marking was in the shape of a square and was on the top of her left hand in the very center. The triangle and square markings were much more intricate than just the shapes themselves, but the shape is all I could see with clarity. I suppose being able to see markings on the hands and foreheads come from an increase in spiritual strength. I can only guess this because the responses of some of the details I have been observing recently have generally been responses of pleasant surprise like, "Oh? You can see this?" She seemed proud of the markings but I did not understand what they all meant.

Up until this point in my travels I was unsure if she really liked me or whether it was just her friends playing matchmaker. But, in this moment, she seemed to enjoy having her hand in mine. I took the opportunity to interlock my hand in hers. She did not let go. It seemed that she wanted to hold hands. We placed our hands on the table for others to subtly see without drawing attention to it. Her hand in mine was so soft, so real. This was one of those moments that my senses in the heavens were flooded with sensations indiscernible from earthly sensations. It was the kind of moment you feel the reality of the spiritual world as it compares to Earth's. The sensation overloaded my mind and I lost harmony and returned to my body.

I journaled the experience and, again, returned to the heavens. When I returned, I found myself in the same setting as before. Some time had passed from when I had lost harmony. We finished our meal and she became upset about something. After trying to understand why she would be upset, I realized that she was upset that I might perhaps like the brunette angel. I did not know how to handle the situation since I had not made any forward action with either angel until we held hands. In retrospect, there was a time the brunette angel kissed me, but understanding the spiritual world in storyline context is incredibly difficult. I am as monogamous of a person as definitively possible, but experiences in the heavens have so little context that I am just now beginning to understand there is a consistent storyline taking place with my travels – not just abstract lessons and instructions.

The heaven I have been visiting most recently seems to be as tangible of a place as here on Earth, with storylines and order to everything that is taking place. And while I assured the angel that my actions were just with her, I now have to sort through the possibility that I have to experience the heavens as I would on Earth. This is different than experiencing Earth as if it is Heaven. This is taking that concept and flipping it upside down. But I suppose before I could experience Heaven as it is on Earth, I would first have to experience Earth as it is in Heaven before I could truly understand the former. Everyday is a lesson. Everyday is another chapter in my travels.

November 29, 2014

The experiences this morning were difficult for me to retain harmony. Prior to going to sleep, I had a coffee drink with

The Written (cont'd)

several shots of espresso in it, so I have to believe the excessive amount of caffeine did not help my circumstances. My first experience seemed to be a continuation from previous experiences. I shared stories with the angels where I talked about traveling to and returning from the heavens. The angels sent me somewhere I am unsure how to describe. When I returned, I was shown the "Seal of the Owl." As I was shown the seal, my right hand became very itchy on Earth. It was the same hand that was being "shown action" in the heavens, so I think my mind must have struggled with understanding the dichotomy of my soul and my body at that moment. Either that, or the angels affected the right hand of my spirit in a way that my body recognized the change on Earth. Either way, it caused me to return to my body. I recognized that the interaction in the heavens directly affected the sensation I was having on Earth.

When I returned, a man I did not know walked up to me. I thought of him as "the mystery man" as he spoke to me. He wanted to find God. At first I was unsure how I could help him, but then I thought about the motion that Enoch had showed me a few days earlier. I began to make the motion and have the mystery man step into the "first sphere." But as I made the motion, it became clear I was not quite strong enough to form the sphere and retain harmony. I lost my bearings as it felt like my soul twisted and inverted itself upside down, causing me to spin out of control. An angel stepped into view and said to the man, "Tell your wife we will be visiting you soon." With that, I returned to my body.

Glory

I returned once more to the void. While trying to figure out how to travel to my next destination, I was shared the angel names that sounded like "Jahiel" and "Uriah." I was not given any context – only the names. I immediately returned and wrote the names down. These are two names I have not heard before in my travels to the heavens. I also have no idea of their context, so I plan to research their origin as well.

When I had some time to research, I searched out the names I was given. The only place that I could find information on anything similar to either of the two names was in one of the Books of Solomon called Ars Paulina, which is part three of Lemegeton. I have no idea what the book is, but it is interesting that on the 28th day of the month of November for those with the sign of Taurus, "Javael" is the angel that governs the plane. My experience began in the late hours of the 28th and continued into the early morning hours of the 29th.

November 30, 2014
Early Morning

My mind races at the possibilities of the message communicated to me this morning. Prior to finding sleep, I prayed that God would help me understand how to find clarity in my travels. Whether that meant increasing my eidetic memory, or somehow understanding a way to bring back messages from the Divine in a better form, it really did not matter. My prayer focused around understanding the details that I struggle to

The Written (cont'd)

bring back with me. I also spoke to Gabriel. I apologized for my naiveté in understanding who she was as the brunette angel. In my journaling, there has been a distinct difference between Zoe/Eve and the more elder brunette angel that appears regularly to me. Up until tonight, Gabriel had been the archangel that I have felt I had never met because I had always thought of this angel as male. However, after doing some reading earlier in the evening and researching ancient artist depictions of the Archangel Gabriel, I now know – without a doubt – that the brunette angel I have seen for the last several years is indeed Gabriel. So, this evening I spoke to Gabriel, asking for her forgiveness in my naiveté. I also asked that when I see her again, if she would give me some sort of confirmation that she heard this message. After my prayer, I fell into a meditative state.

While it took me awhile to find my way to the heavens, when I arrived I was overcome with the raw energy in the moment. I was standing in something that resembled a parking deck. There was an angel approaching me from the distance. The angel wore a white robe and its wings were visible. The angel was so luminous (like how the moon glows) that it appeared a spotlight was on her. As she approached, I thought it may be Gabriel, but was unable to look upon her face to know for sure. I could sense her intelligence and wisdom radiating through the light.

The angel wanted to ask me questions about how I had arrived in this particular location. For some reason, the questions seemed like I was being baited into a trap of some sort. I had never felt that way in a spiritual conversation before, so it was a strange feeling that overcame me. It was the first time I felt uneasy in how I replied to the angel's questions. I took notice that the angel desired to show affection with me. She approached me and we kissed passionately for just a brief moment. But nearly as suddenly as my soul was ignited from her kiss, we got back to business.

The angel had the austere demeanor of a lawyer. She wanted me to do something for her, which again, I felt uneasy about. It seemed her request (which was without words or definition) would mean I would be sinning, so I refused. I turned and walked down the parking deck structure to the levels below. The angel continued pursuing me. It seemed like her desire for me was to have sex with her. She did not deliver her request for me in words, but rather in intention. Up unto this point, sex in the heavens has almost always been a bait-and-switch tactic to test my spiritual strength. It was a tactic used by Lucifer's forces in disguise. But this time was different because I was being asked for consent. I took notice of the difference, but again, without words in the request, it was hard to understand.

The angel followed in the distance and eventually approached me again. As she began speaking with me once again, a male angel approached from my right. I assume it must have been Michael, since the direction of their approach is important in understanding their identities. I was unable to look upon him either. He listened to her questions for me and

The Written (cont'd)

decided that we should "help" her find resolve in her questions.

When we reached the bottom of the structure, the female angel wanted to spend time with me alone. She pulled me aside into a room where it was just her and me. She kissed me again, and I returned the kiss. There was so much electricity in her kiss. I could tell she was trying to warm me up to her desires. As we stepped back out of the room, the male angel took her arms and held them behind her back in a way to demonstrate strength and submission. She did not resist. She allowed him to walk her over to a white wall and push her body up against it. She seemed to enjoy the role-play that was going on. It never seemed like she was struggling, or he was controlling her. It was more of a demonstration of voluntary submission. She communicated to me that she wanted to submit to having sex with me. She pulled her robe up half way over her buttocks. She straightened her legs to make her figure more provocative for me. I walked over closer to her.

It was perhaps the most conflicted I have ever felt in the heavens. On one hand, I knew I was in the presence of Divine angels – angels I thought to be the great Archangels Gabriel and Michael (though again I will emphasize I could not look upon their faces due to the light). There was nothing being forced upon me, but there was this conflicting emphasis placed on sex in this moment. The male angel called me over and told me that I should have sex with her. I said that I thought it was wrong, that I was being tested or that she was not really willing. He told me to reach between her legs so that I could check myself.

There was a large part of me that believed the archangels did not have the anatomy to even have sex. I reached my right hand between her legs. She repositioned her legs around my hand to help draw me close. I could feel a loose cloth over her parts (like an undergarment), and as I pressed my hand to her body, I felt the wetness of her desire for me. I pulled my hand away and decided that maybe there was a reason for all of this. I began to slide my pants down, but then my mind filled with all of the conflicting thoughts. This caused me to return back to my body.

When I returned, my heart was beating wildly and my earthly body was as turned on as it could possibly be. I have held true to my abstinence and have fought off bodily urges at every opportunity. This time would be no different. But, in having to fight off the urges, I was unable to find a meditative state again for the rest of the night. When I eventually did find harmony again, it was only for the briefest moments.

I found myself standing before a taxi driver and his yellow car. He opened the door and said, "I quit." I looked at his door and there was a list of how he received payment for his fares. There was a cost-per-mile line, and others that one would expect. But one line in the middle caught my attention. It had a circle with a dot in the middle and next to it "-100." I recognized the circle and dot as one of the symbols from the Testament of Solomon, but I was unsure what it meant in the context.

The Written (cont'd)

After returning to my body and praying this morning about the experience and confusion in the moment, I realized there were some important takeaways. First, I had prayed for help in understanding how to have better clarity in the heavens. I suppose there is a distinct possibility that my celibacy and removal of any sexual pleasure in my life could have a negative impact on the vitality of my endocrine system (the system that balances hormones). I am not saying that having sex on Earth would help, but rather that the act of sexual stimulation – in the right circumstance, with a person of like intentions – could bring forth an energy that could help balance my soul in the heavens. I took the time to research and read about the history of ritualistic sex, since that is a known concept within the occult.

I had always thought it must just be some form of earthly desire interfering with the spiritual journey. But now I have to be at least open to the possibility that there is an underlying truth, regardless of how diluted the actions surrounding that truth may have become over the ages (and with improper influence). Let me be clear: I am not approving of ritualistic sex or saying I would break my vow of celibacy. Rather, I am just saying that the concept of finding a balance of sexual energy with the rest of the body may help in the clarity of the experiences in the heavens.

The other reason I have to be open to the possibility is that I was not "tricked" in my situation. In fact, dismissing the possibility that I was talking with archangels, any negative spirit that has attempted to have sex with me has never once asked

Glory

for my consent. This experience was distinctly different. And when I did not give my consent, there was an effort to help me understand that my consent was because the female desired to be submissive to me in that circumstance. If one is to believe that the two angels – of which I could not look upon their faces (again, another situation that only happens with the holiest of angels) – were teaching me something new, I would at least have to ask, "What am I being taught?" It breaks the mind because it crosses into the most delicate territory of all. And regardless of how the question is answered and how hard it is for a person to grasp the scenario as a "lesson," in everything else I have written and experienced, it has all been transparent and true. This time would be no different. So it stands to reason that there is something to be explored in the scenario. And honestly, it could just as easily have been a test of the strength of my vow to God. If it was not a test, the only possible thing I could have been shown in that moment was something pertaining to sex as a method in how to use it in the way it is intended – not in the way of the ego.

And for the final takeaway, if I am to understand that what I was shown is an answer to my prayer (which almost certainly every experience in the heavens is fueled by my preceding prayers), then it only makes sense that however abstract it may have seemed, the experience was meant for me as an answer to my prayer…regardless of my preconceived personal bias in the answer given. So that is how I have to view it. Obviously, more prayer and seeking of wisdom is critical. But, at least this is a starting place.

The Written (cont'd)

November 30, 2014
Afternoon

This afternoon I tried a myriad of experimental things to help me find clarity in my travels to the heavens. I won't write them all down in this entry, for the experiments are unimportant – only the results should be written. There were no chemicals or anything of the like used. This all pertained to inspired ideas on how to find spiritual alignment. Until today, I have mostly just dealt with meditative tactics. With this particular day committed to trying to improve my clarity in my travels, I eventually found a meditative state and subsequently traveled to the heavens.

The first image I saw was a male angel standing in a kitchen that looked similar to mine. He had a black eye and wanted me to see it. This was the first time I have ever seen an angel not in perfect health, so I think it must have been a symbolic message to me. The angel did not belabor the subject of the bruise on his eye. Instead he just smiled and said, "Hi," to me. As I studied the angel's face, I began to lose harmony. In the moments when my vision began to leave, a female angel walked over to me. I could not really see her since I was losing harmony, but I sensed her presence. She said, "Hi, Jonathan. I just wanted to say hi before you leave." And with that, I returned to my body.

Fifth Revelation

There is a moment that stands out above all others, a moment of spiritual truth and recognition. That moment is best understood as when God unveils a grand revelation. His words are strong and powerful. His delivery is surgically precise. But the weight of understanding His words can take hours, days, and weeks, if not longer to reveal His intended meaning.

This Fifth Revelation was a moment of such delayed revelation. In the moment it was presented, I understood the highlights of His story, but I did not understand the intimacy and gravity of His intentions until much later along the journey. It took right at two months of slowly digesting His message to fully come to grips with all that He had revealed. For the hardest concept that I have ever wrestled with is the embodiment of ego versus acceptance of servitude to divine duty. It is a place where most falter, and few seek to carefully listen. It is a place where Satan can slip in and attempt to wreck His grand intention. This Fifth Revelation is symbolic of the fifth pillar. It is the construct of the Pilgrimage to Mecca. For within this revelation, He answered my longest standing question.

Glory

"Who am I?" is how the question began. In the beginning I sought the answers through the angels and the Lord, as each circumstance allowed. It was along the journey that I learned I was a "what" and not a "who." For this vessel is only an embodiment of a doorway that opens to His Divine Spirit. It took years of learning just what that meant to understand the divide of body and spirit. And just as long as it took for that concept to sink in, it took another period of time to understand the role the vessel plays for the embodied spirit.

The role I am to play was revealed in the Fifth Revelation. While the journal entry is unchanged as it was written when it was revealed, this introduction is written after hindsight allowed the meaning to fall into view. For this was the day of His confirmation, that I am truly One of Two. And while it took some time for it to sink in and accept (mostly accept), in retrospect it could not have been clearer.

This revelation is the embodiment of all that was revealed in Revelation 11:4, over two thousand years before. However, in the words written at the time of the experience, I was still cautious to even bring up the idea that "one of two" was a possibility and that Revelation 11:3-4 could even possibly apply, though Bryan and I have discussed this possibility for nearly the duration of the three years. Call it being cautious, or extremely guarded to prevent misunderstanding. Either way, God eventually revealed the meaning with clarity, though the following journal entry still leaves room for His eventual revelation.

...

Fifth Revelation

December 1, 2014

This morning's adventures in the heavens were again numerous and rich with meaning. In the beginning, the first few experiences were shorter and lacked clarity. But, as the experiences continued, I was granted more strength in vision so that I could bring back better details of the experiences. I suppose if one is to view stamina and strength versus endurance, there must be a balance. The heightened number of experiences and the messages I am able to return to Earth with must be more important to the angels than fewer experiences of greater clarity at this particular point in time. That is how I have to view it at least. Perhaps I have only so much capacity to travel, and in so, the angels must decide whether to stretch it out for more numerous messages that can be researched for deeper meaning, or for fewer, more direct messages that may have a greater "wow factor" but may not hold as much vital information. Why tell a story over fourteen days when fourteen days can be condensed into a night?

It is important to note that I spent the previous day seeking God's guidance in trying to understand better ways for me to increase my vision in the heavens. And while I again will not talk about all of the methods and tactics I tried (for they are unimportant), I spent an entire day in search of how to improve my potential in the heavens through earthly practices. And though no method involved anything external, I was unsure how some of my experiments would be viewed in God's

Glory

eyes. Maybe He was able to get a good chuckle out of me that day. After all, I was only seeking reason from the messages the angels have been delivering to me. Nothing was out of bounds. This was purely me saying, "Father, I do not know what I am doing, so I am going to use today as if I was a child in a sandbox learning how to build a sandcastle. I hope that anything I do today will only be viewed as a day of schooling."

I am sure, to the reader, this leaves a lot to the imagination. But, the methods are unimportant until I understand what – or even if anything – can help strengthen the spiritual mind for a heightened level of communication. Regardless, I hope that my actions at least demonstrate to my Father that I long to do more for Him, and through that action, hopefully receive His grace. So as the experiences began, I had one underlying question: Did the actions I took earlier in the day affect (for better or worse) the experiences I would have throughout the morning hours?

My first experience began with me standing in the aisle of a plane. A great angel in a white robe was standing about thirty feet away from me toward the nose of the plane. He did not speak. Rather, he seemed to give a nod of approval and acceptance of my arrival. Obviously, the plane was archetypal as a vessel for me to be taken to the heavens by my angelic guide. Maybe the angel was just nodding at me as if to say, "Hello." Regardless, the nod was subtle but most certainly there. For my first experience, it seemed as if some of my efforts earlier were viewed at least favorable in intention.

Fifth Revelation

The second experience was, again, brief. Upon the plane's arrival at our destination, the angel took me to a large building that resembled a hotel. I wandered through the lobby and through each of the conference rooms before losing harmony. The building was ornate, classy, and grand in presentation. The ceilings were extremely large and there were white ionic columns throughout the building.

Upon returning to the heavens, I tried to consciously ask where certain angels were that I have seen in previous experiences. I wanted to make sure Gabriel forgave me for not recognizing her greatness in previous experiences. I also wanted to strengthen my "relationships" with those that I continue to see so that I may have a better sense in understanding the angels that I do not know quite as well.

I am sure I sounded like a broken record with my question in this particular travel. The only way I knew how to consciously ask the question was to repeat it ad nauseam so I would not forget my intentions in asking the question. I am sure there are better ways, but for me, this is how I have to ask for now. It must be how a child must feel when he begins learning how to ask questions. Children repeat questions over and over because that is the only way they know how to resolve all of the questions in their minds. The sheer amount of information coming into the minds of children is enormous, and they have just reached the potential to begin filtering it in understanding. This is how my travels should be seen.

As grandiose as some of the travels may have seemed, they have been nothing more than the way a parent would care for a child they Love. Each time the parent shows the child attention, the child is overcome with such a feeling of warmth and Love that it becomes a feeling they long to have all of the time. Other family, friends, and acquaintances will appear in the child's life – each one demonstrating his own unique ability to Love the child. Like the child, this could be seen as how the angels appear to me in the heavens. They continue to care for me and nurture me. And even though I can rationalize that I am an adult in earthly terms, I am still a child on the spiritual plane. So as I continued to ask the question – repeatedly – of where Gabriel was, or where some of the other angels were, I heard the voice of the Spirit speak from the silence. The words spoken were directed to me to answer my question. I heard, "Don't follow after one angel, for there are seventy watching over you." The gravity of that moment was so strong that I immediately returned to my body to write down the words verbatim.

When I returned to the heavens, I was greeted by an angel that took me to a place that felt so familiar. It was as if I had been there many times before, but had been unable to bring back the experiences with me to Earth. Perhaps other parts of the experiences returned with me prior. Perhaps I was not allowed to share what I saw because I was still gaining my vision. But this place was familiar, sacred, and special. I was taken into a garden. There was a waterfall pouring down in front of large, moss covered rocks. Everything was greener than the greens on Earth. I was wearing a blue suit with a white shirt. My belt was brown as were my shoes. I was fasci-

Fifth Revelation

nated by my belt and shoes mostly because I never wear brown on Earth. The only color dress shoes I own are black (with black belts to match).

I took notice there were angels all around me. They were wearing white gowns, glowing softly like that of the moon. The location contained a circular pool of water to my right. It was elevated. If I walked down a short but steep decline and immediately back up to the other side, there was an altar made of rocks. It too seemed to be filled with water. The water poured out of the altar and into the pool of water to my right. I jumped over the crevice and climbed the rocks of the altar to see. I almost slipped on the rocks because they were covered in moss and damp from the water in the air.

I returned from the altar, still fascinated with my brown belt and brown shoes. As I gazed around and back upon my clothing, the voice of God cut through the sounds of nature and water. He said, "These are the best days of your life." I was taken aback, soaking in His words. The angels around me were giggling. They seemed to find my reaction to my shoes and belt humorous. My attention was on this tiny detail while I was surrounded by something so Divine and so great...I suppose I would have laughed at myself as well. As I heard the laughter, the words of God bellowed within my soul. I lost harmony and returned to Earth to journal the experience.

When I returned, I was standing in the void. To my right was something that looked like the blanket of spheres that I saw days prior in my travels. But this time was different. This time there was a face created from the spheres. However, just

Glory

by me changing perspective slightly, I could see the dimensions of the spheres that comprised the face. The spheres had an indigo hue. But most importantly, it was critical for me to see that, what appeared as an object was in fact, comprised of the spheres from the Equidistant Bouquet. In that moment, I could see how a hologram worked, yet understood form and factor of how the Equidistant Bouquet was the foundation of all that is seen, and the way motion is perceived.

I returned to the heavens. I arrived back at the altar and pool of water where I was taken before. The angel that was with me dipped her hand into the water from the altar and asked me to feel inside. I reached into the water and felt two bulbous rocks that were almost touching each other. She said, "Did you see anything else?" I said, "The large rocks. These were the two I touched in the water." I made a motion toward the bulbous rocks in the water below. The angel pressed onward. "Anything else unusual?" she asked. I said, "Tomato juice. Yes, tomato juice flowed from the rock." The angel gave me a strange look as if I just replied with the most unexpected answer possible. I knew not why I said, "Tomato juice." However, I felt very confident in my answer.

While the angel was searching for a way to reply to me, I looked back to see how I arrived at that particular answer. I could not see anything that even resembled tomato juice in the water, yet I still remained confident. Without missing a beat I said, "Have you not witnessed strange things with me so far?" The angel gave me a look of acknowledgement, yet still seemed without a way to properly reply to my tomato juice

Fifth Revelation

answer. In that moment, I felt like I was someone showing the angel something she had never seen, yet I knew she was explaining to me things that I had never seen. It was a strange moment where I felt confident in an answer and had to assure my teacher that I was correct. The confusion in the moment caused me to lose harmony and return to my body. As I journaled the experience I wondered if I had witnessed blood flowing from the rock and not "tomato juice." Either way, I wanted to make sure I wrote it down as it happened rather than upon reflection of the moment. For, if others are to understand the way God communicates with them, it is important to understand how I learned to understand God's communication to me.

When I returned, I found myself in the void. Light began to fill my periphery from my left. I heard the voice of a male angel. He said, "I'm here to help you. The other angels had to leave for a few years." He unrolled a blank scroll before me. I could not see anything written upon the scroll. I was unsure if I was to write something, if the intention was symbolic that I was supposed to be writing everything upon a scroll to share it with others, or if there was something upon the scroll that my eyes could not yet perceive. I arrived at the fact that I was supposed to write. I asked the angel to reveal his name to me. Though he would not step into view, he shared with me images of my sister here on Earth and said, "Michael." His name reverberated through my body. I immediately returned to Earth so I could write down all that he had shared.

Glory

It is curious to me that Michael revealed my earthly sister to me upon the blank scroll. In symbolism, I could see that I may be supposed to share my writing (or upcoming writing) with my sister. Her husband leads a church, and she is an ordained minister. I have wrestled with whether to tell her anything about my experiences thus far since I knew she would likely dismiss anything I would have to say. But perhaps I am supposed to write my story and share it with her so that she may do with it as God wills.

As soon as I returned again, I recognized I was still in the presence of Michael. Though I was in the void and still unable to see clearly, I knew it was a good opportunity to speak with Michael. I asked him, "How can I see better?" With that question, Michael took me back to the altar and circular pool of water. I saw myself kneeling down in the direction of my feet. He said, "Take the brass vessel and place it to your temple to grant sight."

I looked upon my form (from first and third person points of view). I was wearing a white robe. My hair was brown and shoulder length, flowing around my head with body. In my hands I held a brass Aladdin's lamp. It was small – maybe seven inches in length. As I kneeled down, I lifted the brass lamp from the area of my feet and placed it against the center of my forehead. I immediately recognized the conflict of the imagery I was seeing with the words Michael shared, for the lamp was placed upon my forehead and not my temple. Michael stood in a white robe beside me, to my left. As the imagery soaked

Fifth Revelation

in, I was returned to my body to make sure I was able to write everything that I had seen in detail.

The imagery was extremely vivid. This was one of the most detailed moments I have ever experienced. However, in response to my initial question, the answer left me with more questions than resolve. Was "my temple" referring to the temple on my head, the body as a temple, a physical temple to worship and praise, or maybe even all of the above? What was the brass vessel, and why did it look like an Aladdin's lamp? And, why was brass emphasized?

After all of the experiences were over in the early morning hours, I sought Bryan to help me understand the message being shared. On the surface, I first thought that I was searching for a way to spiritually see better in the heavens. If there was an earthly action that could help strengthen my spiritual eyes, I was open to learning. As I waited for Bryan to free up from his daily routines, I researched brass as it is used in the Bible. In almost all circumstances, brass seems to be a reference to an impure metal – such as a metal representing earthly man, where as gold represents purity in spirit. There is mention of God appearing with feet of brass, again representative of the earthly vessel. But when Bryan and I found time to speak, he pointed me to both Exodus and Revelation.

The first book of Revelation is where John of Patmos is shown a vision of the Son of God, with hair white as wool and feet of fiery brass, kneeling down before a pool of water. The similarities were striking! The depiction John gave was nearly identical to the image I saw. However, John also described seven lamps upon seven lamp stands – of which I only saw the one I was holding. He also described the Son of God as having a gold sash, though we were both wearing white linen robes. Even as I write this, it raises so many questions. Is it possible that I was shown the same imagery as John? If so, why the variances? Is it possible that I saw a different perspective of the image, such as the seven lamps written about would be held by seven churches on Earth. This could easily have been a directive to me. But the more humbling question that has to be asked…is it possible that if I truly saw myself in the same position that John saw "someone like a Son of Man," wearing the same clothes (albeit without the gold sash that would mean receiving God's anointing), holding one of the seven lamps, being asked to place the brass vessel to "my" temple – could that mean that my body may serve as the vessel for Christ?

This seems sacrilegious at first blush. But, if one is to understand as Jesus was the embodiment of Christ, and that Christ is within each of us, then it stands to reason that since Christ is flowing through me presently as I become nearer to my Father, then the Son of Man could be the brass vessel through which Christ returns. And, though I would not say I am Christ, I would say that I have given my body and soul to Christ, so that Christ may live through me for others to see. Could it be that the Son of Man is to return through the devout? Maybe there are seven anointed that may carry this potential upon this Earth. Perhaps all that is needed is that One may understand the calling. Most certainly this is just a starting point to understanding a truly amazing message from

Fifth Revelation

God. If, for no other reason, to know that I have been shared a similar vision to that of John's in Revelation is grand enough for me to forever humbly pray thanks. But as it turned out, the conversation with Bryan continued to reveal more information.

As I researched the verses more thoroughly, I was led to a theologian who mentioned that the angel in Revelation that says "Babylon has fallen" is none other than an angel named Uriah. Now, while the theologian also offered the possibility that Uriah was a concept for a light of destruction (such as that of a nuclear bomb), I had never heard of the name Uriah mentioned in the Bible at all. In fact, just a few days prior I was shared the names Jahiel [or Javael] and Uriah as angels of importance. They were not revealed to me in form, but rather in name. I searched for references to Uriah (assuming it may be an alternate interpretation of Uriel), but found no context of the name. It was only upon happening over this particular theologian's work that I found reference to Uriah (or Urias).

As it turned out through more research, the Septuagint translation of the Hebrew biblical text into Greek is the only place this name is revealed. The name Uriah is written about in Isaiah 21 where Isaiah is shown a vision of an angel in the watchtower exclaiming "Babylon has fallen." This is the same reference given in John's Revelation in Chapter 18. Aleph-Vav-Resh-Yod-Hey is the Hebrew word used in Isaiah to describe the angel in the watchtower. Later, Masoretic translations used the Hebrew word Aleph-Resh-Yod-Hey (without the Vav) and translated it as Lion. In meaning, both

Glory

words mean "Light of Yaw" or, rather, "Light of God." If one is to take the Septuagint translation (the oldest known translation, and therefore likely the most accurate translation between Hebrew and Greek at that time), then it is easy to see that the vision of Isaiah and John's Revelation were based on the same angel. So, the angel that instructed me to take the brass vessel to my temple – without directly saying – passed on two messages to me: the first being all that I discussed about the correlation to John's vision (and the variances within); the second being a reference to Uriah exclaiming "Babylon has fallen."

In the context of everything, this most certainly is God saying to me, "This is the end. It has been seen from the watchtower. Babylon has fallen." In the words of John's Revelation, "And he cried mightily with a strong voice, saying, Babylon the great is fallen, is fallen, and is become the habitation of devils, and the hold of every foul spirit, and a cage of every unclean and hateful bird." This most certainly is a hearkening to the end of times. Where my body falls in context to the brass vessel and the lamp, will be revealed to me in God's time. But, in the immediate moment, I understand His message that "Babylon has fallen." And while I have deviated from my usual method of journaling about my experiences in the heavens and then placing any additional analysis at the end, it is important to place this analysis here, for the next visions I had continues to pertain to the same symbolism (though I would not understand them in full until after Bryan and I would talk much later in the day).

Fifth Revelation

When I returned to the heavens I saw two angels walking toward me with a great light behind them. The surroundings were not immediately clear. As I faced the angels, I took notice that the angel on my right side was wearing a black robe and had reddish-purple hair pulled back in a bun and was wearing black sunglasses with broad straight edges. Her hair was not purple per se, but rather had a mauve tint to it – like a mix of dark chocolate, strawberry, and a hint of mauve. The angel on my left (to her right), was wearing all white and had long, blonde, flowing hair. The image shook me, and I returned to my body to journal the experience. This was the first time I have seen an angel in black. As I understood it, this was a divine angel and a dark angel walking to me.

As I worked on finding my harmony on Earth, I repositioned my male parts. This would typically not have been worthy of even my own attention except for no sooner had I readjusted myself to be comfortable in my meditative state that I heard a voice exclaim, "We [or He, hard to understand] won't be coming back here again. At least not Beelzebub." I was immediately thrown for a loop. I have known Lucifer by name and many appearances in my travels. This was the first time I heard the name Beelzebub. My impression was that he was distinctly different in form and spiritual entity than Lucifer, but I did not have time to ask the voice. I was jarred enough to lose harmony. I had not even fully finished readjusting myself, which is what caused me to take notice. So, right or wrong, relevant or not, I was at least touching my body (non sexually) but in a place that the devil knowingly works as I heard those words. Perhaps the voice was telling me that I have personally overcome Satan's ability to tempt me through fleshly desires and that now, my body has been purposed to be used divinely in all aspects. Or, it could be that the message was a continuation of God's words to me pertaining to Isaiah and Revelation. Maybe it was both, or even some other context I am unsure of as of yet. Either way, I journaled the experience and once again returned to the heavens.

This time, I was standing before "the judgment of council." There was a list of demonic names that were recited by one of the members of the council. The room was filled with negative forces that seemed to be under some form of judgment by the spiritual elders. As the names were listed, I tried to recite and remember them, but they came at such a fast rate that I was unable to recall any. After the evil names were recited, the conversation by the Judgment of Council (which seems like it should have been called the Council of Judgment, and maybe it was…twisting of words and phrases does happen to me from time to time in translation) turned to the angel whose name began with "Scott" or "Schah." I immediately recognized the name as the angel who told me its name in the church a few days earlier. The name was something like "Schyphaeon." But even this time, the second half of the name failed my ears. In trying to remember all of the names, I lost harmony and returned once again to Earth. I wrote down as much as possible and prepared to travel back once again.

Just for humor's sake, the first words I wrote down after I returned from the heavens this last time were, "Gah. Names

Fifth Revelation

are so hard to come by." Again, this was a time I would be riddled by the recurrences of angels I have seen before, angels I had not yet seen, with no names or recognition of familiar names to help me be able to write about the experience with any more clarity. Now that I think about it though, I suppose it makes sense that God would only allow for some of the angels' name to be written about.

This next experience began in a bedroom. The walls of the room were white, and there was a bed with white sheets, pulled tight around the body of the mattress. The bed was larger than a King bed...either that or I was smaller than an adult body upon the bed. The posts were squared off – modern looking – and were stained in deep brown. The wood grain bled through the stain. I was lying on the bed next to a beautiful brunette angel. I could tell she really liked me, but we were not doing anything more than talking and staring above. She would roll over on her side and face me from time to time, gazing at me. We were both clothed and neither of us were making passes at the other, just enjoying the moments.

While we were talking, a male angel walked in. He lay down on my other side. He seemed to be motivated by the girl's curiosity in me. I could tell that either he liked her, or had a previous relationship with her, which is why he wanted to make his presence known. She must have sensed my questions because she immediately began telling me how she met him over a massage. Confusingly to me, as she was reminiscing over these great memories between her and the other guy, she drew her body closer into me to cuddle. I began answering questions she had about me. I never once felt threatened that the other male angel was in the room, or even on the bed with us. It was almost as if she wanted me to know how great her attraction was to him, so I could understand that it paled in comparison to her attraction to me.

At one point the male angel placed his hand upon my back shoulder blade. It was not sexual or anything similar. If I had to guess specifically the intention of his actions, I think he was trying to sense if I had wings, or gauge the size of my wings or even if they were beginning to grow. Whatever the case was, it was a little awkward, but not annoyingly so. I joked with the girl about how her questions would be easier to answer if he did not have his hand on my back the whole time. I eventually decided to stand up and remove myself from the situation. Maybe he was making it awkward for me intentionally so he could spend time with her. I was not quite sure.

When I stood up and turned to face the bed, he tried to get closer to her, but she did not want anything to do with it. This was the first time I was able to see his face – and one of the few angelic faces I have seen. He had sharp features and looked to be in his mid twenties by earthly standards. His hair was brown and was messy-spiked up top. His hairline was lower down his forehead than mine and he had strong brow and jaw lines. Given that I have very little points of comparison on a heavenly level, this angel could easily serve as a model on Earth.

She motioned for me to get back on the bed. The angel rolled away to make room for me and decided to get up and

Fifth Revelation

leave. Honestly, it was a little bit of a relief, though romantic emotions are a lot different in the heavens. We snuggled up to each other face-to-face and continued talking.

I began to hear a noise from the back corner of the room, and then I noticed a smaller twin-sized bed was tucked away in the corner. The person in the bed reminded me of my friend Jason on Earth, but I do not think it was him. The girl asked me about my hair and continued to compliment me on its length. The male angel that I thought had wandered off was still somewhere near because he also chimed in with words of admiration for my hair. They kept saying, "It really is so cool."

Now, on Earth I cannot say I am very excited about my hair, but I have been trying to let it grow out. There are days I like it and days that I do not. Overall, it is just my hair, so I do not really think much of it. But, it was nice to hear compliments. As they continued to sing praises, I said, "I've had it for twenty-two years." In earthly terms, I have only been growing my hair out for almost three years. I am not sure why I said "twenty-two years" but it is possible that it relates to the twenty-two steps in the Hebrew alphabet and progression of a soul. This would be the first time I heard those numbers in context to my age, though.

The angel that reminded me of Jason sat up and repeated my answer. The girl and I laughed at how he sounded. We were not making fun of him, but rather enjoying the moment. I recognized that his speech was slurred and sounded strange because he was still learning how to communicate in the heav-

Glory

ens. It made me think about what I must have sounded like earlier in my spiritual growth. The girl and I laughed about those thoughts as well.

A fourth angel walked into the room at this time. He was a male angel with short brown hair and a beard. He was a little on the beefier side of things, but not fat. The angel that reminded me of Jason became excited in his recognition of this fourth angel. He instantly wanted to blurt out every secret that he knew. He began by explaining that a man named Van was in the mob and then proceeded to reveal someone else's secret identity. I could not make out the second person's name or occupation because his words became heavily slurred again in his excitement. He then wanted to tell me about how someone he knew had to repaint their car so they would not be caught after an accident that could have revealed their identity. He pulled out a picture of the rear end of an old Mercedes. It was olive green and had a European plate on the rear. The picture he showed me revealed a scratched and bent up rear end – as if someone had hit the car from behind. The scrapes and scratches were white. He then pulled out a picture of the car after its touch up job on the rear end. The rear of the car looked immaculate, but made to resemble something used, not something recently fixed up and repainted. The car tag had an image on it that resembled something like "the rat pack" or maybe "Lucy and Desi Arnez." None of it made any sense in the immediate moment, but it triggered the memory of another moment in the heavens which I had been unable to recall and journal about until now.

Fifth Revelation

Based on that recollection, I apparently had dinner with the brunette angel and her mother recently. While we were at a restaurant in that experience, her mother told me about some theory she had over a mystery. She had said, "Arnoldo [or maybe Ernesto] was a suspect, but [she thought] Desi was the real suspect." The memory was interesting, but I still did not understand how it all intertwined.

Back to the current experience… the angel and I decided we would get up and go have dinner. On our way to the restaurant, a child walked by. I am not sure why the child caught my attention, but it did cause me to take notice. It was a younger girl maybe around the age of seven wearing an olive colored shirt. The brunette angel and I continued to talk about the mystery that was alluded to by the pictures of the car while we were in the bedroom. The angel remembered that her mother had mentioned the same story to her growing up – and had included one other person as a suspect – but she could not recall the name.

We reached the restaurant. It was made of white alabaster. It looked like a one story structure from Greece – simple on the outside, but beautiful in its simplicity. When we walked in, there was a bench with two ladies sitting on it. They were sitting directly in front of a hostess table. The angel on my right reminded me of someone familiar, but I could not place her. As I tried to place her, she began waving at me. Then, the angel on her right (my left) began waving at me as well. It took me a second to recognize them and realize they were actually waving at me and not to someone near me. The two angels

Glory

thought it was cute that I forgot who they were again because they knew my travels to the heavens caused me to be forgetful. I suddenly recognized them as two of the angels that take me from place to place in the heavens. I began to lose harmony and returned to my body.

Once again I returned to the heavens. Once again I found myself in a familiar setting I could not quite identify clearly. It was definitely familiar from my travels to the heavens and not on Earth. I found myself sitting with an angel at a table. Another person entered into the room and walked up to another table asking for directions. There was an angel that pointed over to another building. I could see it was the church that I had visited before.

A different angel walked in asking for a password. The angel was given a sheet of paper that contained a word above and a word of gibberish below it. The gibberish was supposedly the password they were looking for. Not much longer passed before the angel I arrived with and I walked over to the church to attend the service. The service consisted mostly of praise songs. The songs were beautiful. There were clear, multi-part harmonies with parts written for soprano, alto, baritone, and bass. My angelic guide stood by my right. Most of the angels in the church were elders. They were all extremely large compared to me. I was handed flash cards for the pronunciation of the words as we sang along.

The main song I remember was a praise song that focused on the word "Uriah." I was handed three cards. The first said "U -" pronounced "YOU." The second card was "- RI -" and

Fifth Revelation

pronounced "RYE." I did not read the final card – even though it was handed to me – because I recognized the word. At first I began to sing "EL" for the archangel Uriel, but I realized that it was more of an open "AH" sound as we sung. I looked around the crowded sanctuary as everyone dwarfed me. Everyone was wearing white robes. I came up to their waists. As everyone sang the word **URIAH**, the melody repeated and eventually I heard the whole chorus of song break out with an orchestra supporting the melody. It was one of the most overwhelming songs I have heard in the heavens. It was so beautiful and moving. Words cannot explain. The power of it caused me to lose harmony and I returned once again to my body on Earth.

The final experience in the heavens was the lengthiest and most vivid of all of the experiences I had this morning. It was the fourteenth experience. It began with me in an older house. The inside was washed in green lighting. The green was flattering though. It was more akin to the way modern movies have a green tint sometimes rather than washed in an emerald color. Whether days passed or I just kept repeating specific actions in the beginning, I am not sure. I continually found myself wandering through the house and into the kitchen. I would make a bowl of cereal (which I almost never eat on Earth) and sit at something equivalent to a kitchen island. The seats were taller than the proportions for a table I am used to on Earth. They would have been more akin to barstool height.

Every time I ate breakfast, I noticed water dripping from a leaky pipe above. The rafters were not exposed. There was only this one spot that was removed in the ceiling to expose the bottom end of a cylindrical pipe. At first, the leak did not seem to be relevant. But, with each passing meal, the drips became more frequent and invasive. I decided I would eventually see if I could resolve the problem myself rather than tell anyone else about it. It seemed like telling someone would only prove my dependency on others and cause them to carry the burden of something else going wrong in the house.

I walked up a great staircase to the third floor. I knew it was the third floor, though it was the floor immediately above the floor I was on. I am not sure if the kitchen just had overly tall ceilings or if there was a floor below it. Regardless, I was now on the third floor. I searched all over – in the bedrooms and the bathroom. I could not find the origination of the leak, or a place to access that part of the ceiling from above. I eventually realized it must be coming from a room that was closed off to me. This room was the "rental apartment" that was always inaccessible to me and the others in the house.

I walked back down the large stairwell. I noticed the thick mahogany railing on either side and the carpet that covered the majority of the hardwood staircase. As I walked down the stairs, water began pouring out of the ceiling above. It was pouring out onto the staircase and the hallway. When I had walked upstairs, I noticed three exposed valves in the ceiling. The valve on the left had been replaced and looked newer than the rest. However, it now appeared that same valve was spilling forth the water from above. I walked to a female Elder standing in a room in the front of the house and told her about

Fifth Revelation

the leak. She became visibly upset since she had just replaced that valve. I told her I thought it was somehow connected to the apartment above. We both walked back to the leak.

I found a towel and began trying to mop up the water, but it was an effort in futility. Eventually, the Elder needed to call someone for help. We walked into a bedroom. I jumped up onto a large bed. This bed was, again, larger than any King bed by earthly standards. There were dark mahogany posts on each of the corners of the bed. Each of the posts was very ornate. The comforter on the bed contained a very intricate pattern adorned in dark greens, browns, and golds. The elder sat across from me on the bed. I sat near the head among the pillows. The Elder picked up a phone to call someone for help.

As soon as she picked up the phone, a beautiful girl about my age walked in. She looked part Asian, but did not have the more identifiable traits an Asian typically has. She lay down next to me on the bed and told me I should come out to wherever she worked on Monday. And while she said Monday, my mind interpreted it as Wednesday. She seemed to work at some sort of restaurant and had many beautiful friends. I, of course, asked her why she wanted me to come out. She replied that she had several friends that liked me and that we would have a fun time together. Then she said, "Or worst case, it won't be any fun but you will get laid." I laughed and she laughed.

While the conversation was entertaining, it went against any moral principles I have. But, I chose to just laugh it off with her. I told her that if I come out, she will have to reintroduce me to her friends because I can never remember names. I told her I would play it off well – to just say something like "_____, you remember Jonathan right?" She laughed and liked the plan. She knew I struggled with names and did not mind helping me. It was like I had a spiritual wing-woman to help me look like I was not missing a bead on my interactions. I did not sense any attraction to her, nor did I feel she had any toward me. It seemed we were just really good friends.

My legs were extended in front of me, almost reaching the Elder who was still on the phone. The brunette climbed on top of my legs and reclined on the elder. I am not even sure how to explain our orientation, but it seemed like my legs created some sort of support for her, like a chair. She extended her legs and feet out and placed them on my body. She played with her feet by moving them over my body. It was not intended as sexual or flirty…it was more like a comfort we had in another, and she was just biding time while we sat there together. The elder eventually stood up and walked a few steps away from us since the girl was lying upon her while she was on the phone. I paid careful attention to the elder's reactions to whatever was transpiring on the bed with the brunette and me.

The elder seemed unfazed and was not in any way disapproving of whatever was going on. I wondered if this was some form of "acting out," but it seemed acceptable. On Earth, it would not be acceptable social behavior in the company of others. But, again, this did not seem sexual in context. It just seemed like two friends sitting together and talking. I tried to

Fifth Revelation

better understand the context of the moment, but my senses started to fail, and I began to lose harmony. I returned from the heavens to write about this experience, though I still do not have any understanding of the interaction that transpired with the brunette.

In symbolic terms, I believe that one of the three valves breaking and spilling water was metaphorical to my life. Perhaps it was implying that one third of my mind-body-soul needs to be further refined, nurtured, and fixed. Or, perhaps it means that one of the three pillars of my mind-body-soul is overflowing in abundance, but the other two need further nurturing. Either way, it left me with an understanding that I need to further nurture my spirit, my mind, and my soul on Earth and in the heavens.

The Written (cont'd)

December 2, 2014

It has rained all morning. I have never wondered if rain has an effect on my travels, but I have to think that it is a distinct possibility. There is a scene in the movie, Adjustment Bureau, where the angels tell the main character that water prevents the angels from hearing his thoughts. Later on, rain plays a role in helping the main character hide his thoughts from the angels. I have not really paid much attention to the idea that rain may block my travels until today because (a) I have not been traveling consistently enough to think that something naturally occurring (like rain) may prevent my travels, and (b) I have not experienced a full morning of rain when I feel as if my body is in a heightened state for travel.

So, as it would be, this morning I tried to travel numerous times. Just prior to the rain arriving, I was allowed to walk around the heavens, but there was no angel present to answer my questions. I feel like I spent the entire time I was in the heavens just regurgitating all of the questions I have for God pertaining to the role of Uriah and whether my vision from the previous day that involved raising the brass lamp to my temple

Glory

was indeed the same as John saw on the Isle of Patmos, or if it was altered enough for me to understand my role. I discussed these questions in depth in the previous entry, so I will not rehash them. But, I did want to make note in this entry that I sought clarity from God.

December 4, 2014

This morning I felt my soul travel to the heavens, but I was unable to return with any words to write.

December 5, 2014

I stood before the feet of Jesus Christ. He was clothed in linen and wore a gold sash around his neck. He appeared with dark brown hair, shoulder length. I fell to my knees before him. I struggled to hang on to harmony in that moment. The images became blurry, but refocused. Jesus was attempting to give me guidance to my earlier prayer concerning all of the writing I have been tasked with completing and also the proper time to share with others all that he has shared with me. And while he did not tell me a specific date, he gave me peace that I was doing all I was supposed to be doing for him and that he would let me know when the time was right. I was to have faith in his timing.

The Written (cont'd)

December 6, 2014

This morning was filled with numerous travels to the heavens again – fourteen to be exact. I have felt "off" over the last several days where my experiences have been extremely muddy or non-existent. But this time I was granted sight again to see everything with clarity. The experiences began just a few minutes shy of 2:00 a.m. (generally the time everything starts to come into focus the most clearly). I became aware that my soul was alone in my apartment. I felt a terrible presence permeating the air. I walked through the house checking behind all of the doors. There is a set of double-mirrored doors in the entrance of my bedroom. These doors go to a closet that I use mostly for storage. The evil presence felt strongest to me in this particular area. I was not sure if it was hiding in the mirror, or behind the mirrored doors.

I called my mother, and she told me she thought that the presence was hiding in a painting I had been given by an artist named Paul. I assured her the demon was not hiding in that particular painting. In earthly terms, Paul painted a picture of my daughter and me where I was represented as a white tiger holding my daughter (a baby tiger) in my paws. It is the lone painting in my bedroom, and he created the painting without me asking him to do so. It was purely how he perceived me symbolically.

My mother and I discussed where the demon could be hiding, and even if the demon was just a figment of my mind.

Glory

We both concluded that the demon was hiding in the double mirrors. As the awareness of the presence overcame my soul, I knew this was going to be a situation similar to when I was confronted by Abbadon. In fact, the demon could be Abbadon in hiding. I knew I had to return to my body first to pray.

I prayed to my Father for help in ridding the presence from my home. I spoke out in the air to the demon and warned it I would invoke the hand of God and extinguish it if it did not return from where it came. I closed my eyes. Light filled my periphery, but then the light became extinguished by the beast. It became clear that it was not just a demon, but the Beast. Its voice sounded like a doubling of the same voice passed through a series of audio filters that made it sound deep and brooding. The voice was choppy, as if it was unable to find full focus in its communication. I watched as the Beast slithered from the abyss to come kill me. I returned to my body.

This time I walked around my apartment physically on Earth. I spoke directly into the double mirror and warned the beast one more time to leave. I then returned to my bed and spoke aloud. "Beast, be gone from my presence. Father, I ask that you have no mercy. I have warned the Beast and it remains. I ask that You take Your forces and cast out the Beast with all of your might so that it may never return. Father, if the beast is a lost one trying to communicate with me, my heart breaks for it. I have warned it as both the beast and as a potential soul trying to reach out to me. I have asked it to leave for it is hindering communion with you. So with a heavy heart,

The Written (cont'd)

I ask that you cast it out. Cast it into the depths of the Abyss." I closed my eyes.

My soul was taken to the heavens and I saw a great light descend from the east. The light was brighter than the sun. It enveloped my soul and became an armor of light. I walked northwest, casting out all of the demons overcoming the Earth. The buildings on my left were single story buildings painted in cerulean. The windows were akin to how an old elementary school would have been designed. The light felt like the sun, and I embraced the fire. It was a conflicting feeling because the source of fire is generally seen as evil while water is used as a symbol for redemption. But this was a fiery light that seemed to expand and withdraw with the pulsing of my breath. As I walked by the building I heard the beast writhe in pain. It was ridded from the shops that I walked by. The destruction brought upon the Earth was unclear, but the destruction brought upon the beast was what I was to understand in that moment. In fiery light, I returned to my body.

As I closed my eyes after journaling, I heard a voice in the void. The voice said, "The enemy of our society is society itself where the beast is found." The voice arrived quickly after I closed my eyes. I immediately journaled the words.

I once again returned to the heavens. Inexplicable shapes filled my vision. The shapes came from the west and moved across my field of vision to the east. They were not clouds as we know on Earth today. The clouds were almost like geometric nonsense bathed in a misty white with a touch of gray. I watched as one part expanded horizontally before me, stretching out in the shape of a distorted H. A soft orange bead of light moved underneath the shape as it stretched. I asked myself if these were "clouds" since that is what the Spirit was imparting to me in that moment. The word "cloud" conflicted with physical clouds I knew on Earth. As I watched the shapes and wondered of its significance, I even debated with myself if these shapes were even worth returning to my body to describe, or whether I should continue to observe. A voice told me "it was" and returned me to my body.

When I returned to the heavens I saw a group of four women. Each one was beautiful, but scantily clad in lingerie. They represented the flesh of a prostitute. I was tasked by an angel to divide a twenty dollar bill into four stacks of five and take it over to them. We were standing in a glass building. I could see behind the women and slightly to my left the green foliage outside. It was lush and very healthy. Slightly to the right of the women, but in my field of view, was a hallway. The floor was made of Spanish-inspired tile. I walked over to the women and placed the stack of bills between them on the floor.

At this point they were all sitting and facing one another. I sat down in the very center of the women and explained to them my intention of Hope in the gesture. They immediately stood up and turned their backs to me. The money was not for anything sexual, though that could be the perception since they were scantily clad. The money was without strings, without reason. It represented Hope, which they did not want to receive. It was important for me to see that the backside of the

The Written (cont'd)

one girl most prominently in my view was pushed toward my face as she stood up, revealing her satin black underwear. The sides of the panties were tied together by a crisscrossed webbing of a black string on either side. The black symbolized their lack of light and her backside being pushed in my direction symbolized their intentional denial of Hope that God willed to share with them. I understood this as I have written as it was all occurring in the heavens. I returned to my body.

I arrived back in the heavens. I was standing in a garage structure. I noticed that periodically something would whiz by me in a blur of vapor. When the next movement caught my attention, I stopped it to ask it a question. The shape revealed itself in the form of a middle-aged person, though it represented a business. It identified itself as an "escort business." This particular question and response seemed familiar from recent experiences. It was a portion of the experiences I could not bring back.

I said, "Escort service? You can go on." I thought to myself, "Why do I keep running into escort services?" As the thought filled my mind, a mousy female voice asked, "Are you in jail?" I replied back immediately, "Of course not." Then, I started to think about the question and my answer. I wondered if I was being punished by God for something I had done. I returned to my body. As I wrote down the experience, I realized that my dismissal of the "escort service" was due to me thinking it was a sexually oriented business. But as I write these words, I realize that the escort service could just as easily have represented an angelic guide that helps souls see in the

Glory

heavens. Either way, it did not resolve the answer to the question about jail.

I returned to the heavens and found myself in a similar setting. I was asked by an angel to deliver a "cord" to an angel with the initials J.C. Though I use the word "cord," the word given to me was an archetype that I understood. It did not have sounds or letters that I understood. The angel wanted me to find "a cord with power" (again an archetypal concept rather than a word). I understood the cord was supposed to have form and not be weak and flimsy like in earthly definition.

I looked down and saw I was holding two cords in my hand. One was longer than the other. I was not sure which one J.C. would want, so I decided to take him two and let him decide. I found a white porcelain cylinder and began screwing it over the top of each of the cords. I said, "I know this isn't what is being asked for, but I know it will work." I immediately flashed to a vision from the day prior where I was tasked with the same challenge. The shock of the flashback caused me to lose harmony with the moment. The flashback was the moment that preceded me standing before Jesus in my hazy experience yesterday.

I returned once again to the heavens. I saw a beautiful brunette angel on the ground before two male angels. Her legs were wrapped to one side of her on the ground, revealing their beauty. The angels were clothed in white. The female angel's robe appeared to be sheerer than others. Her hair was black or extremely dark brown. It was pulled back tightly into a ponytail. One of the male angels reached down and took her left

The Written (cont'd)

foot in his hand. Her skin was an olive complexion, like someone of Greek decent. The angel's hand was large and thick, larger in mass than her foot. I was enamored by the beauty of her foot. It was small, but appeared long. It was thin and delicate, but held strength. It was of perfect proportion to any other foot I had ever seen. I could tell that she was annoyed at the other two angels, but maintained her composure. It appeared that she was secretly desiring the moment they would walk away and leave her and her feet alone.

Though I do not know for sure, it appeared as if this was a common interaction for her that became tiresome in repetition. I walked over to the group and placed a mason jar full of strawberry jam at her feet. My action was enough to cause the male angels to lose interest and walk away. She looked at me as though thoroughly entertained. I told her, "I did not put the jam by your feet." It was nonsense, and I had no rationale why I took those actions or said those words. She was definitely pleased that the others had left her alone and maybe it was the absurdity that caused it to happen. She laughed and thought it was a game. I asked her if she had ever tried putting the jam on her feet.

My mind saw an image of her foot with strawberry jam on the soles only. Though I did not recognize it then, in hindsight the image reminded me of the vision Noah experienced looking down at his feet as it was portrayed in the movie "Noah" that came out this past year. I explained to her, "I know it may seem odd, but it goes well with beautiful feet." She laughed and asked what I liked about her feet. I said, "They are small and fragile, delicate but not breakable." She placed one foot in my hand for me to admire briefly and then pulled it back down. She asked me more about the jam, intrigued at it. Something I said caused her to say, "So you've ridden my bone?" She batted her eyes playfully as she asked that question. In context, I realized I must have said something about a bone that she decided to turn into witty wordplay. I just cannot tell you what I had said. I am sure I must have looked puzzled because I had no idea what she asking me since I could not recall what I had said that led her to that play on words. I took it at surface value and assumed she was twisting it into fun innuendo. I replied back, "Oh, I believe I would remember if I had ridden your bone." She laughed because even my reply was senseless. She stood up and we walked away together talking about the heavens. She seemed thoroughly entertained by my presence.

 I returned once again to the heavens. I was standing upon red brick cobblestone. This was a walkway leading away from a mall and to a road ahead. An angel behind me was about to ask me if I knew where I was going, but I wanted to figure it out before he asked. I looked around. I had no idea where I was, how I arrived, or anything at all aside from what I could see. I realized I needed help from the angels to help guide me, though I wanted to figure it out without responding to his impending question for help. I reached the end of the walkway and observed a large circular entrance to the mall. The entrance was at the top of a slightly inclined hill to my right. Cars, taxis, and black limousines continued pulling up, drop-

The Written (cont'd)

ping off their passengers, and picking up others. I was enamored by the scene, but still knew I was going to need help understanding everything I was witnessing. I lost harmony and returned to my body.

When I arrived back in the heavens, I was sitting at a table in a room with a great angel before me. He was standing across the table from me. I have been in a similar room before. Each time before I had been shown a book, scroll, or parchment. This time was no different. The angel placed a large book on the table before me. It had a reddish-brownish-gold cover. There were four words that looked to be written in something similar (but different to Hebrew) stamped in gold foil on the cover. One of the words had a circle with a dot in the center. I thought I saw that same symbol twice, but I did not have enough time to see anything else. The angel said something to me that I did not hear clearly and pulled the book away so I could not see the words. It was as if he wanted me to see it, but not read it.

I said, "Jonathan's Book" in reference to trying to say the words that were on the cover. The angel looked impressed and though I asked, he would not place the cover before me again. Each of the words was comprised of only three or four characters. The first word may have had five. I understood the words to read from right to left, top to bottom. There were two words on top and two words below. The final letter of the fourth word was the circle with the dot in the middle. I returned to my body.

Glory

Once again I returned to the heavens. This time I found myself among others at a funeral. A female was saddened and supposed to speak to everyone. It seemed like my funeral. She was off to the side and speaking to me while crying. There was a wall to my right side that was straight, but had two slight angles in it. Light poured horizontally across the wall in geometric rays. The light came from behind her and poured past us. The streams of light were her words. They were brown with glimmers of cerulean pouring out along a taupe wall. I asked her that when she found strength to speak those words, to speak them "the other way" indicating that the light should flow in the opposite direction. I lost harmony and returned to my body.

I returned again and found myself standing before a male person who seemed distraught. I told him that "all he needed was in these words." The person was resistant to my words. I saw a book placed upon a table with writing scrawled all over it in random directions. I recognized the opened book as containing my words, but I have never written like that in any book before. My thoughts caused me to lose harmony and I returned to my body.

In my final experience, a woman stood before me. I sent her floating down a river telling her to relax, that she would be blessed, and that it would all come to her. All she had to do was float down the river without any stress or concern.

The Written (cont'd)

December 7, 2014

This morning I awoke to my air conditioning unit malfunctioning again. It seems like the times I struggle most with finding harmony with the heavens are the times when the air conditioner has stopped working. I know that it should not prevent a divine experience from occurring, but too much warmth pushes me out of balance. It is as if my body overheats much more quickly. This morning's experience even demonstrated that.

The portion that was clear was that in my travels, I arrived before an angel. I was sharing a house with another grumpy female elder. She was a stereotypical grandmother. The thermostat that controls the air conditioner was just inside the door to her bedroom. A few minutes prior, I had been told it was time for bed, so I turned down the thermostat to 72° (I generally turn it to 74° on Earth, but remember that messages are shared through all of the actions in the heavens). I walked over to my room but realized I forgot something on the floor of the older female's room. I returned to the hallway and stood before her door. I watched as she got out of bed and turned the thermostat back up to 78°. She went back to her bed unaware I watched her change the temperature.

My angelic guide continued to stand beside me. He explained (without words), that the rise in temperature in my apartment was not my fault and that there was another force at work intentionally trying to prevent me from traveling. The

Glory

grumpy woman knew I needed the air temperature to be lower, but she was determined to not let it be. At this point I returned to my body. I checked the thermostat when I awoke and sure enough, it was 78° inside – much too warm for me to find the most opportune balance when I am under the sheets and covers on my bed.

December 8, 2014
Early Morning

  This morning I witnessed a fight taking place in the water. The water was calm, like a pond or a lake. I watched as a girl saw the brawl and filled with fear. I walked over to the fight to see if everyone was okay. As I stood around the two children fighting, I noticed others had gathered near. A mother and a father began talking to one of the children telling him to go apologize to the other one. One child had lost a permanent tooth in the scuffle. And while I did not quite understand the significance, it was important to see that the child thought he lost his third tooth over from the middle, but it was actually his second tooth that was missing. I helped the child see which tooth he had lost before returning to my body.

  When I returned, I saw "the four coats." If I had to wager an initial guess, I would say that that the coats represented the four horsemen. One of the coats said, "He won't know what he lost without help." In the moment, I did not quite understand their message. I replied, "I don't wear stripes. I only ever

The Written (cont'd)

wear blue or gray suits with a white shirt. That is all. No stripes." The "four coats" wanted to make my suit with gold, but I feared it was too flashy to be worn as a humble witness.

I returned once again to the heavens and found myself in a hallway that followed a zigzag path. I followed the path to a grand room where a meeting was being held. When the meeting was called to order, I noticed my Aunt Karen and my sister were placed before a committee (being judged to enter the Kingdom, I assume). I was not privy to the words that were said. But I was allowed to witness the event. I returned to my body to write down all that I saw.

When I returned to the heavens, I stood with the four elder angels from earlier. We were in a church service. One of the angels seemed like a father figure to a girl that was in the service with us. This particular elder angel looked at me and motioned to a chair in the corner as he said, "There is one more seat over there." He wanted me to make a decision to go sit in it, or to remain with the girl in which case he would go sit down in the other chair. Either way, the elder appeared frustrated at a "fifth wheel" status in the conversation. Typically the analogy is phrased as being a "third wheel," but since there were four elder angels and me, it made sense to my soul that he indicated himself as a "fifth wheel."

After the service ended, he took me to a grocery store. He was insistent on buying "old meat" at a discount. Most of the service staff did not want to help him, but he eventually found the owner of the store and explained that he was going to cut the old meat out of the packaged meat. He pointed to a table

Glory

with old beef wrapped in saran wrap on Styrofoam trays. The meat was turning gray. The angel asked for something sharp so he could cut the old meat out of the package. I lost harmony and returned to my body.

During final return to the heavens this morning, I arrived at an outdoor location. I was talking with someone at a table, though I could not distinguish any features. As we spoke, another person walked up and killed a dragonfly that had landed on the table a short while earlier. It was an extremely large dragonfly – abnormally large. When the man smashed the dragonfly, I felt a sudden wave of sadness fill my body. Seeing this dragonfly killed was like the feeling of seeing a close family member pass away. The sadness overwhelmed me and I returned to my body.

December 8, 2014
Mid-morning

In my earthly life, as I walked to the coffee shop this morning to begin my writing, I saw the world through eyes I have never seen through before. The street was much busier than usual. I passed the landscapers for our building. I passed a couple walking together. We smiled at each other and said, "Hello," as we passed each other. I saw another lady walking by herself. I smiled as we approached and made sure to shine light upon her saddened heart. I could see hope. I saw in the distance a man that lives in my building. He is an odd fellow

The Written (cont'd)

by earthly standards. He is extremely smart and well educated, but he is ridiculed by other residents because he goes through the dumpsters that line the street each morning. I have seen him as he collects food and other items that he finds interest in. But his actions are viewed unfavorably by other residents because most of the residents have spent a lifetime building wealth. His actions contradict the minds of his neighbors. "Why would a man able to live in such a wonderful place resort to digging through dumpsters?" they frequently ask among themselves. Today, would be no different.

He was sorting through several dumpsters as I approached. In our conversations, I have come to learn that he does not like handshakes. He prefers a fist-bump to say, "Hello." He says it is more sanitary. So, in passing by him this morning, I made sure to say, "Hello," and give him a passing fist-bump; an acknowledgement that I placed no judgment upon his actions as well as to share Love and hope. He seemed ashamed that I saw him, but my actions brought a smile to his face as he seemed to understand everything I was saying in that one action. I continued onward... and this is the real reason for this entry.

As soon as I turned forward after passing Abe, I saw the head of my building's security department walking toward me. He is always friendly. And, while I describe everyone as mortal, I believe that each and every person in my life here is an angel purposed into my life to see me through all aspects of the journey. In all ways, I believe my Father's eyes are watching me through each of their eyes, and that they have been placed to test me and also to share messages. So today when I saw our head security guard walking from the distance I took note of how abnormal it was to see him away from our building.

As he approached he said, "Hey John! Have you seen the video of the dead shark that gave birth to three sharks on North Beach? Everyone is talking about it." There were no pleasantries exchanged. This was the conversation. How more direct could God's messenger be? I replied that I had not seen it yet, but I would be sure to watch it. He was glad. I could see that the message he was supposed to tell me was heard in the way he hoped. To some, they would have heard a passing comment about something interesting that happened and was now posted on YouTube. To me, I heard so much more. As he turned and walked away, I knew immediately that God was using the sharks to symbolize the "horns" spoken about in Revelation. One of the horns gave way to three. In the words of God's message, another sign of Revelation has been revealed to me. And though it may not seem as such in context of the conversation, in the context of the journey it was black and white.

December 9, 2014

The struggle to bring back information from the heavens seems to be getting harder and harder. But while it may be harder to put into words, the experiences are more lifelike than ever. This morning's experience was one that I can only

The Written (cont'd)

describe as possibly one of my last before our time on Earth is complete. As of a few days ago, I realized that from the date of the very first time God showed me visions to the very last day of my 33rd year here on Earth will be 1260 days. These are the number of days written about in Revelation and Daniel wherein both John and Daniel shared the amount of time God would have two people prophesy in the end of times.

Even as recently as a week prior, I felt like I was maybe just one of seven people representing the lampstands written about in 1st Revelation. But as I started calculating the number of days surrounding my upcoming birthday, I realized the 1260 number was more than a coincidence. It was one of the signs. Not only did the number align, but it should be seen as no coincidence that my spiritual journey began on my 30th birthday and has proceeded through my 33rd. So, if it could be seen that God has been revealing the picture to me with a little more clarity through each vision, this morning's visions only continue to reveal His message.

The experience began with two separate visions of the antichrist in one heavenly experience. The first way I was told cannot be put into words as it was more of a message instilled to me as I stood before My Father. After He delivered His message to me, I was instructed to visit my family over Christmas. While my soul was still in the heavens, my mind raced at rationalizing if God had really just revealed the imminent coming of the antichrist. I did not fully understand it at that moment, and expressing how it was shared with me through earthly words is impossible for me to do. But as God continues to deliver messages in pairs to me, He did so on this particular message as well. In the heavens I was shown a vision of myself sitting at a table for dinner with my family for Christmas, with gifts unopened. I knew I was there because I had been instructed to go see them. I revealed to my family that God had been speaking to me over the last three years. I went on to tell them that we were in an important time as written about in the Bible. In order to lead into the antichrist conversation, I posed a question to my mother. I asked her about her thoughts on the End of Days.

As she began to speak, my mind filled with God's voice continually reiterating to me "antichrist" and "thirty days." My mind raced at understanding. I could tell that my mother was wrapped up in a conversation with herself and that God used this moment to give me a confirmation in His first message. I repeated His words to myself over and over again. I then repeated His words from the first conversation. I saw the viewpoint of having the message delivered from My Father and my mother in the same experience in the heavens. This was one of the most powerful messages that God has shared with me. I returned to my body to write down the experience, but God took me back to the heavens to see more before I could write.

I journeyed to a department store. This was the second time I had been in the store. In bringing me back to the heavens, God placed me in this setting initially, but I could not recall all He showed me. Once again, through His grace, I was placed back in the store a second time (since I needed to re-

The Written (cont'd)

peat this particular course of His lessons). This time, I ran into the store wearing only a small piece of linen around my waist. It was barely big enough to cover me up. I knew when I ran in the store that people would view me unfavorably. But I was on a mission. I had to find something to wash my hands.

I looked around the store and realized I did not have enough time. I told one of the clerks that I was just looking for something to wash my hands before running back out. I was frantic the whole time. It was as if I was able to experience it in first person and third person simultaneously. When I ran out the door, I turned left and began running east down the road. I ran in soldier-like form. My arms moved almost robotically, thumbs pointed straight upwards. It seemed like I hoped running in that manner would distract others from thinking my clothing in the linen cloth was indecent. Everyone around me wore suits.

As I ran, it became more pressing to get to the destination more quickly to tell others. I crossed paths with different groups of people on the street. Most of the people were business men. As the last person came into view, he gave me an austere glare – like that of an angel. But this time was different. I had a bad feeling about this one. He was wearing a blue fedora pulled low on his brow. His gaze was one of strength, leadership, but also of judgment. I passed him and turned around, sensing something was wrong.

As soon as I turned, I saw him running at me with an umbrella raised over his head. He was going to swing at me and try to kill me with one swift blow. As inexplicable as this sounds, it was as if he had carried a dislike of me for quite some time – longer than my days on Earth could rationalize. I sensed jealousy because God had continued to grant me strength and show me favor – and perhaps I sensed I may have carried myself pompously in my youth. I thought about whether I had been arrogant in my spiritual past (a past that had not been lived on Earth). All I could justify was that I could understand how my faith in God's faith in me could rub someone the wrong way. All of these thoughts galloped through my mind as I saw him about to swing the umbrella. And, just as suddenly, one of God's great angels appeared and stepped between the man and me, protecting me from harm. The man froze in his tracks. I turned to continue running onward in an effort to try and wash my hands and share this message with others.

I returned to my body, journaled, and immediately returned to the heavens. This time I was walking by a clothing store in a mall. A female was decorating it in a way that would grab my attention. She noticed that I saw her decorating, but tried to slide away hoping that I really did not see her. I walked into the store and watched her backtrack through the crowd of people and eventually behind a register. Another couple saw me walking over and decided to help the lady avoid conversing with me. They tried to help her play it off.

The blonde female said, "Jean armor! (or perhaps a name – Gene Armour) Great to see you." They began talking at the counter so as to look too busy for me to approach. Undeterred, I pushed my way up to her through the line of people.

The Written (cont'd)

When I reached her I said, "Why do you keep setting things up to distract me?" She said, "My husband" as her eyes gazed above my head at someone behind me. In her voice I knew she was telling me that the angel she identified as her husband was calling the shots. I turned around to find myself staring at a great archangel, towering in size behind me. This was her "husband." The site of the great angel caused me to lose harmony and return to my body.

When I tried to return to the heavens, I asked My Father for help in understanding the thirty days he shared with me earlier. In truth, I asked if my time on Earth would end in thirty days, just begin in testimony, or if it was all just part of a Divine bulletin sent to those with eyes to see and ears to hear. In response to my question, I was taken back to the outside doors of the store I had just seen. I stood outside those doors asking the same questions in spirit as I was asking in body. In spirit, the question was phrased as, "Where can I find my answer?" I hoped for God to respond.

An angel appeared before me and told me "Messiah" and pointed East. I realized that the word "messiah" had been used several times throughout my travels this morning, but every time I heard the word, I spiritually interpreted it as "I am a ____" – which spiritually frustrated me for a while. This time, when the angel pointed east, I repeated the angel's phrasing of the answer over and over seeking clarity in the words. After the third repetition, I realized that I was interpreting the syllables of the word as a phrase. Then it all hit me with the weight of the world. The angels had been telling me

Glory

"Messiah." As the meaning of the word sank in, the context faded in clarity. But it was enough for me to return with this much.

I returned to journal the Messiah experience and one more experience that occurred just after the previous one. The second one contained even more clarity on the meaning of Messiah and how it applied to my spiritual walk on Earth. Careful to not place the word upon my shoulders or even just within my words to others without understanding the context, I sought additional help from the angels. And while the angels did offer the answers I sought, when I returned to write, I began writing about the first experience to make sure I did not miss any details. I thought the second experience was so fresh and important in understanding that I would be able to recall the details more readily than the first. Unfortunately I was wrong. I was unable to bring back any of the additional answers I sought.

When I returned, I heard two angels talking. One said, "Through and through" in reference to the last experience that I could not bring back in words. They witnessed my inability to write it down. I said to them, "I know it went through and through. Let's go again." But, I lost harmony before anything could happen.

I returned once again and heard the following words spoken by an angel, "The one of leadership takes office." This was in regard to my question about the Messiah and my upcoming role in the eyes of God. I returned quickly to write down the words delivered to me. I was not sure if the words were in ref-

The Written (cont'd)

erence to me taking all that God has shared with me and using it in the role he has planned for me here, or whether he was describing a physical establishment of where a Messiah would be found in the next thirty days. Perhaps both. Perhaps neither. When I returned to the heavens, I bore witness to a man who resembled the Son of Man once again in this series of experiences. I was twice told that I had to find him and that "the latter time was because he must be sought." I returned to my body to write down the words he shared.

As I journeyed back to the heavens, I wanted my Father to know I was willing to serve Him in any capacity that He desires of me. He knows I am unafraid to leave the Earth and join Him. The whole series of experiences this morning has been overwhelming, and I was left trying to better understand how my role fits in His plans (if at all). I said, "Father – if You need a vessel, use mine. I can watch on from above. If you need me to be a door, I can hold it wide open."

God took me to a building where I stood before a pillar that was holding up a piece of gray marble. The marble was in the shape of a square and was approximately two inches wide, by twelve inches tall, by twelve inches wide. Those dimensions formed the frame. The interior was inset, centered, and half the two inch thickness. Inside of the frame, a circle was carved out that was the size of the interior of the frame. When viewing the whole piece in its entirety, I saw that the piece of marble was divided along the center horizontal and center vertical axes, forming four corners. This was the message God showed to me in response to my question. As he shared it with me, an angel stood to my left, just out of sight.

I returned one final time to the heavens tonight. Again I prayed on my travels, seeking further guidance on what exactly occurs in thirty days. When I arrived in the heavens, I stood before a group of angels. They told me "canto thirty-three" referring to Dante's Purgatorio. With that, the angels morphed into great granite stones and formed a horizontal wall of seven blocks. The angel that told me "canto thirty-three" said, "that is all for tonight" as the angels formed a wall of stone before me.

When I returned to my body I tried to travel again, but it was clearly not going to happen. Perhaps God wanted me to research the words. If anything, I feel extremely pressed to write everything I can before the end of the thirty days. That is my only mission. All other earthly priorities shall be pushed aside.

The first thing I did in my research following the visions was to seek out what date thirty days from now falls upon, and what dates are 1260/1290/1335 days plus or minus from today as a point of origin. Nothing was readily apparent. Initially, I was disappointed because the 1260 days falls so perfectly in alignment with the duration of my thirty-third year on Earth. The symbolism is so rich, I hoped that God was placing more divine dates into my life to help others find truth in these words, and all of the other parts of God's words today.

As I dismissed my search on the dates, God spoke to me in the silence. He instructed me to look at the calendar accord-

The Written (cont'd)

ing to His words. If one is to take "a time, times, and a half time" in context, it is a Hebrew method of keeping time. A year was 360 days, which was represented by the word "time." In total, the number of days equals 1260. That specific number of days is mentioned in John's Revelation. However, in Daniel, 1290 and 1335 are mentioned in comparison to "time, times, and a half time."

This morning is December 9, 2014. If we are to view this point of time in reference to the Hebrew calendar, we would subtract forty-two months that contain thirty days. Relatively speaking, this would take us to June 9, 2014. If we are to view the number of days referenced in Daniel as corresponding to months, then the 1290 days represents one additional month. The 1335 days represents two additional months and a half of a month added to the original 42 months. So based on the Hebrew calendar, looking back 43 months (1290 days) from today returns us to May 9, 2011 – my 30th birthday and when my spiritual journey began. And 42 months forward from my day of birth, the date is November 9th – my sister's birthday. Immediately my mind began to spin. Everything about my life is suddenly proving to be a biological representation of everything that has been foretold. Initially, it was all overwhelming. I wondered at the possibility of what will happen in the next thirty days.

1320 was not a number that corresponded with any of the numbers discussed in Daniel or Revelation. Then I remembered, I was shared the knowledge of "antichrist" and "30 days" in the context of having dinner with my family over

Glory

Christmas. As it would turn out, a half month from now (15 days), takes us to Christmas Eve...the very day as a child I chose to be baptized and gave my life to Christ. It would also put the message delivered to me this morning from God right on track to correspond with Daniel's 1335 days, since thirty days after the dinner is the landmark the Lord gave me. And just as 1260 sequential days from the day the first vision occurred after that phone call to Bryan takes us through the very last day of my thirty-third year, the relative dates involved in understanding the next fifteen days takes us through my baptism in Christ, with the following 30 days as the day the antichrist arrives.

Daniel's dates are relative. Revelation's dates are absolute. But, the key to these numbers would not have been unveiled had Christ not delivered this message. It is also important to see that the conversation I held with my mother and father was over Christmas, where the gifts were unopened and dinner was late at night. On Christmas in our household, gifts are always opened first thing in the morning. Traditionally, Christmas Eve is when we have our Christmas dinner together. So, it would make sense that the Christmas dinner shown to me in the vision was the Eve of Christmas where gifts are still unopened. Thirty days from Christmas, is one of the dates foretold.

In Daniel 12:12, the angel says to Daniel, "Blessed is he who waits, and comes to the one thousand three hundred and thirty-five days." Most certainly 1335 relative days from the antichrist's arrival will also usher in the other half of the next

The Written (cont'd)

forty-four and one-half months. But the events did not stop here. I also looked up Canto 33 of Purgatorio. I recently read the entire Divine Comedy by Dante, but even so, I could not recall much of Purgatorio. Purgatorio was the most tedious reading of the three books. Instead of reaching for my printed copy, I did a quick search on the internet to see Canto 33. The first lines read:

"O God, the Heathen Come," alternating "Now three, now four, melodic psalmody, The weeping women now began to sing."

The very first line of Dante's inspired literary rendition of the apocalypse ushered in the arrival of the antichrist. I could not help but become even further convinced of God's message to me. It was not as if God just shared one seven and seven moment with me. They continued to come. For the reader of these words, one might ponder whether I subconsciously recalled that particular verse from the only time I read the book. And, that might actually have some merit in thought. However, later in the morning I spoke with Bryan on the phone. I shared with him all that had transpired with the visions. I then began supporting the numbers from Daniel and Revelation with the landmarks of my life. I continued on with the reference to Dante's Purgatorio.

Without the ability to recall those first three lines word for word, I reached for the book on my shelf. It was easier at that moment than going to grab my laptop to pull up the text online. As I read him the first three lines, I nearly had to do a

Glory

double take. The translation from my book differed from the rendition I found online. The printed copy of the book I read had the phrase "O God, the Heathen Come" entirely in Latin. Additionally, the remainder of the verse was translated differently. The only time my eyes had ever laid sight upon this Canto, I read the words in this written form:

"Deus, venerunt gentes" – the Holy Seven, in alternating chorus through their tears, first three, then four, raised a sweet chant to Heaven."

While the verse carried the same theme, the words were entirely different in translation. Both are an ode to the Deliverance of the Church. This particular canto's third line refers to weeping in the first translation. John Ciardi's translation (from the book I own) uses the word "tears" in place of "weeping." Regardless, this is a subtle callback to my vision from December 23rd of 2013 where I was told by The Lord's Angel that "I weep be" was "what I am."

If one is to take the first translation of Canto 33, it is again a reference to this first time I stood in the Kingdom of Heaven. Later in Canto 33, there is a call to action for Dante, and then a prophetic revealing of the number 515. With the number foretold to Dante from Beatrice, the truth was intended to be shrouded from understanding until the right time. Though I do not profess that the symbolism I am about to reveal is the meaning intended in Dante's thirty-third canto, it is extremely interesting to me that the month of May in the year of 2015 (5-

The Written (cont'd)

15) will be the end of my 33rd year on Earth and draw to a close the timeline of the 1260 days of prophecy. All that I have shared is enough to make even my strongest doubts of understanding the message from God vanish entirely – but this was still prime moments for His divine delivery of messages to me today.

In my conversation with Bryan, he shared with me how he had a vision this morning of an intruder in his house. In his vision, he chased after the sound in his house recognizing the filth of a demon. Bryan and I rarely talk about demons, and it had been days since we last spoke of anything happening in either of our experiences. In reality, I never truly believed in demons and only in the last month or two have I grown to realize that possession is real.

I think it was my childlike desire for goodness that led me to believe that demons were just souls searching for light. Bryan was unaware that I, too, had just chased a demon (Abbadon) from my apartment a few days prior. He was also unaware that I had cast out my first demon from a person on Earth (from a distance) by merely invoking the name of God. And while I will discuss that story in another portion of my writing, it is important to note that I became a believer of demonic possessions just a few days prior.

As Bryan shared with me the story, he also mentioned that he heard Marilyn Manson's song "The Last Day On Earth" playing in the background during the entire vision. Like unto how God shares messages with me through movies, Bryan is led through song. The lyrics that Bryan heard in con-

Glory

cert while he chased away the demon from his house are as follows:

Yesterday was a million years ago
In all my past lives I played an asshole
Now I found you, it's almost too late
And this Earth seems obliviating
We are trembling in our crutches
High and dead our skin is glass
I'm so empty here without you
I crack my Xerox hands

I know it's the last day on Earth
We'll be together while the planet dies
I know it's the last day on Earth
We'll never say goodbye

The dogs slaughter each other softly
Love burns it's casualties
We are damaged provider modules
Spill the seeds at our children's feet
I'm so empty here without you
I know they want me dead
I know it's the last day on Earth

The conversation between Bryan and me evolved into understanding the meaning of the words he heard. Bryan immediately found a more impactful meaning on the coattails of

The Written (cont'd)

the vision God shared with me. It was a Divine script, penned for Bryan and me to see from different viewpoints, but to discuss all that we saw through one set of eyes. Bryan went on to elaborate on the meaning of "dogs" in the song. Historically, the perversion of homosexuality was seen through the symbolism of "dogs." And without making this particular writing an argument of the spiritual rights or wrongs of homosexuality, the reference should be viewed as a landmark in humanity's time. This same landmark permeates numerous historical texts and fuels the repression of homosexuality within many churches. So, with that said, the symbolism of dogs gave rise to one more vision I experienced.

In writing down everything that has transpired today, I have not yet been able to mention that I took time to meditate after arriving at the divine numeric Revelation of my life. I prayed and asked God for further clarity. My King showed me three objects that were made of gold, circling around a central point. The visualization would be akin to drawings depicting the dreams of children floating over their heads while spinning in circles. The three objects were a dog, a snakeskin, and a cow. At the time of the vision, I understood the cow represented prosperity. The symbolism in the snake was pretty obvious as well, but Bryan continued to add value to the symbol by explaining that the snakeskin was symbolic of a seasonal change of the serpent – another way of foreshadowing the end. Finally, the symbolism of the dog came into view – but only now that the lyrics to the song had been disclosed through

Glory

Bryan's vision. All three objects were adorned in gold demonstrating the worship of idols.

And while I spent much more time discussing everything that God shared with Bryan, I made it clear that, above all, I wanted to ensure the words that God has shared with me are actually the words he intends me to share in order to help lead the Church home to Him. I have prayed many times – especially today – that I did not want the naiveté of my spiritual actions to be a downfall that played into the hands of the antichrist. And, for that matter, I wanted to take extra care and be a steward of His word in the most humble way possible. Lucifer's downfall was that he Loved God so much that he allowed his ego to become his identity. That is most certainly what I want to avoid in my efforts with God. I only want to please Him, and through Him, be all that He intends for me to be.

One more experience cemented Gods words for me – and it was important that I share this experience with Bryan as well. After writing much of these words, I returned to God in prayer this morning. This was the moment that he shared with me the vision of the three idols. But prior to the vision, I prayed aloud asking God for clarity on the dates and if I had interpreted them correctly. As I said the words, "So it seems that the 1335 days discussed in Daniel aligns with the coming of the thirty days after Christmas that you shared with me. And on that day, the antichrist would arrive." Immediately upon those words being uttered, my phone vibrated beneath my pillow. I smiled and knew that God was responding to my words. I told God that I had to respectfully check the message

The Written (cont'd)

to make sure He was communicating with me. I picked up my phone and noticed there were no new messages. I realized it must have been an email, so I clicked on my email icon. What happened next could not have been any more Divinely scripted. As I opened my emails, the iOS mail client read as follows:

All Inboxes	6
iCloud	
Gmail	
Outlook/Hotmail	6

Accounts	
iCloud	
Gmail	
Outlook/Hotmail	6

From top to bottom, my screen read 6-6-6. As I stared at my screen, my phone was simultaneously syncing with Gmail (it will not do this unless I open my email app, though Hotmail syncs through "pushes" hence the reason my phone notified me of the new emails). Instantly, after I read 6-6-6, my eyes welled up with tears in recognition of God's confirmation to the words in my prayer. I was correct in understanding the return of the Beast. Immediately in synchrony with my tears, my phone vibrated and refreshed the screen with updated emails. It read as follows:

Glory

All Inboxes	7
iCloud	
Gmail	1
Outlook/Hotmail	6
Accounts	
iCloud	
Gmail	1
Outlook/Hotmail	6

In this moment, God took one further step to bombard me with confirmations. Read from top to bottom, the number of God was revealed. Adding 6+1 on each of the lines revealed: 7-7-7. It was a triune of His number. This was a divine sign. Not only did God show me 6-6-6, but he followed it up by adding one to the six to create the divine. I took a screenshot of the moment and proceeded to continue my prayer and meditate, which eventually gave way to the vision of the three idols. I shared this moment with Bryan in our conversation.

At the end of the discussion, Bryan and I also took a few minutes to discuss the fact that both Moses and Enoch are two of the Elders with whom I have interacted numerously in the heavens. It is also important to understand that Enoch is the one that has been guiding me the most recently and is also the angel that had me step into his sphere in the heavens, washing me in white light. So, it stands to reason that the spirit of Enoch and Moses can also flow through the bodily vessel, just as Christ flowed through the bodily vessel of Jesus.

The Written (cont'd)

This chain of experiences and discussions would normally have been the end of this entry. But God chose to manifest one more event for me to witness on Earth. After eating lunch at a restaurant across the street from my apartment, I returned home. I entered through the garage and headed to the elevators. One of the service workers for our building had just called down an elevator prior to me arriving. The doors opened as I walked up. We stepped aboard.

He punched the number 3 (my floor) and I was content to ascend. The man (whom I had never spoken with before) looked at me and asked what floor I was going to. I replied, "Three." He said, "Oh, you aren't 316 are you?" I said, "No. What do you have to fix in 316?" The man had a large pair of bolt cutters. He said, "Are you sure?" He smiled. "I have to cut the lock off its storage." With that, the elevator doors opened, and we parted ways on floor 3. Though it took just a brief moment to register, I had not taken two steps before I heard God's words through that angel. John 3:16 is arguably the most well-known verse in the Bible:

"For God so Loved the world that he gave His only begotten Son, that whosoever believeth in Him shall not perish, but have everlasting life."

The words rang through my mind like a chorus. With the end of days ahead, the visions of the Messiah's return and knowing the antichrist will soon be on Earth, God took one more moment to tell me in earthly terms that He was cutting off the lock of storage to the Messiah, symbolized through the largest bolt cutters a man can find on this Earth. There is one remaining question that reverberates through my mind. That question arrived from the lips of the man on the elevator when he asked, "Are you sure?" My mind flashed to the stand of the pillar holding the four corners housing a circle – the open circle symbolic of the open conduit of the soul.

Praise God, Hallelujah. May all those who seek Christ, hear Christ, and see Christ, live through Him forever and ever. Amen.

December 11, 2014

This morning I was taken to the heavens and placed before a great angel. The angel was one of seven surrounding me, arms crossed and austere. The size of the angel was towering. I felt like a small child standing before a giant. In size, my height only rose up to the great angel's knees. As I stood before the angel, it told me, "The time is near. You must now go and share it with others." Though the angel did not have a physical trumpet in its hand, I heard the sound of an impending trumpet. It was a sound like a siren, a warning of doom. I returned to my body.

The experience was so clear, but upon returning to Earth, my mind struggled to hang onto the message from the great angel. I repeated the words over and over. They were as clear as they were from the lips of the angel. I wrote them down – word for word. It was then that I realized that I had not quite

The Written (cont'd)

returned to my body, but returned to the place between. When I made it back to my body, the words were jumbled and not clear. I wrote down the notes as best as my feeble mind would allow. I closed my eyes and returned.

I once again found myself standing before the same great angel. Though I returned with questions, it was as if he knew I returned for his original words. He would not allow me past his towering physique. He shared with me the same words as before, "The time is near. You must now go and share it with others." I asked one or two more questions, but upon returning to the place in between and then once again to my body, the other answers did not return with me. It is possible that the questions were only meant for the angel and me in that moment – for I feel that the angels can help me awaken in my body with the words they intend to deliver.

I once again returned to the same location in the heavens. This time the great angel allowed me to pass. The angel reminded me of the statues on Easter Island. It would seem that the statues were the expression of the viewpoint of a child looking upon a great angel. The jawline is closer to the eyes, so it is disproportionately larger. The head becomes smaller at the crown as it disappears into the heavens above. When the angel allowed me to pass, I stood on a green bank of a sandy shoreline looking at the stars above. I was surrounded by seven great angels. One of the angels motioned for me to sit on a blanket on the ground as we stared up at the stars. In the sky above, five stars fell prominently into view. I recognized that this view must be the same sight as what the angels showed

Glory

Bryan several weeks ago. The splendor of the moment caused me to lose harmony and return to my body.

When I returned to Earth, my body felt charged in its call to action among God's children. It took a while for my mind to slow down enough to return to the heavens. But once I returned, I was shown a great spectacle. As the same type of results would prove, the experience was much grander than that which I could return with in words. The only way that I can describe all that I was shown, was that a man that I understood to be the Son of God was wearing a white robe before me. I watched as he "took office" after seventy weeks had passed. The voice of an angel said, "The Son of God took office after seventy weeks." I slow clapped his arrival with a crowd of angels around me. The slow-clap was to indicate the sheer splendor of his return to office. There was more shown, additional conversations with angels did occur, but nothing else would return with me in body.

I was then shown a vision of sharing the directive of the angels with my ex-wife, Stacey. And while she did not seem to fully grasp all that I was saying, she said, "It is all interesting." I departed from her with her at least understanding the potential of God's message in her mind. I took brief notes about Stacey's words and closed my eyes. This time I was shown a vision of a shadow to a mathematician's compass moving horizontally across my bedroom window from East to West. The compass covered the size of the window, from floor to ceiling. When I saw the compass, I first thought I was half awake and I must be seeing shadows through my eye lids. But as I surveyed

The Written (cont'd)

the surroundings, I realized I was indeed in a vision. I opened my eyes just to be sure and saw only darkness in my bedroom and could see only darkness through the window.

December 12, 2014
Early Morning

I arrived in the heavens in a setting of a train. I knew the train was white and sleek on the exterior. There was a black angel before me. She was much bigger than I. When I looked up at her she said, "I can help you if you need any help. Do you need any help?" Though I did want help, my soul let out a truthfully pointed remark. I replied, "You should." The intention of the words was that a person should always help another in need. Though it could have been perceived as a snide remark such as, "Yeah, you should help me, silly woman." – that was clearly not the intention. The angel knew my heart and just smiled at me. There was another younger black female angel with me. We played together. She was happy and laughed a lot.

December 12, 2014
Afternoon

Several different things happened to me today that I wanted to take note of. Today was a persistent test over my belief in Jesus Christ and my role with the directive that God has charged in me. Early in the day, I had to answer a few questions with an operator on the phone over a recent application for my life insurance policy. When she asked me about my job, we established that I was an independent contractor. The lady did not seem content with that answer and wanted to know specifically my job title. I asked her to clarify what she meant since I was an independent contractor. She laughed and said, "You know, like king of the castle." I could only laugh as I heard God giving me a nudge in jest. It was not ego filling my head. Rather, it was just good-humored recognition of the role I have been tasked to play by my Father.

In the afternoon, I left to pick up dinner and return. When I reached the elevators, I helped a man carry his luggage onto the elevator. We had a few seconds of small talk, and then he suddenly blurted out, "You are a god." I laughed. He was mostly speaking in recognition of the help I offered him, though it was an unusual way of expressing his appreciation. But, I also recognized God's voice offering another "attaboy" in jest. But – just to be clear – I fully understand that I am not a deity nor anything close. It was more of a friendly jest between Father and son.

Later in the day, I was invited to attend a bible study with a group of friends. On our way to the study group (which I had never attended before), we stopped and picked up several people I had not yet met. When we got out of the car to head into the meeting, one of the girls asked my name. When I replied, "Jonathan" she smiled and said, "Doesn't that mean God's gift? You are special." It was a very unexpected re-

The Written (cont'd)

sponse from her. But again, I heard God's words. The day after He had tasked me with such a tall order, He wanted to remind me of His confidence in me. To her words, I smiled and said, "I guess – something like that."

When I returned from the bible study, my friend dropped me off. Before we reached the house, she began asking me questions about the end of time as mentioned in Revelation. I realized this was my first opportunity to begin sharing the message that God has tasked me with, so we talked for about thirty minutes before I exited the vehicle. I shared with her a little bit of background over my last three years, but most importantly, the message that the end of days is near. She continually asked me about my belief in Jesus and if I believed He was our Savior, to which I replied I did. I talked in loose terms of Jesus' wedding banquet in Christ. The conversation went extremely well, but I saw that the most important part of the lesson was not in how I shared the message, but rather how I learned to respond to her questions.

When I went inside, I walked to the elevator to go to my apartment. The elevator was slow in returning to the main level, and during that time I ran into a friend named El. Obviously, as the name implies, she is of spiritual importance in my life, but that is also her real name. We always have great philosophical conversations on the beach. This time though, she wanted to pick my brain about something that was troubling her. We sat down in the lobby and she began explaining to me how she felt called to share God's message, but did not want to accept the calling. Everything from how the conversation began to how we arrived at that subject so quickly would be enough for an outsider to scratch his head in confusion, but I heard the spiritual conversation unfolding.

The conversation was almost an identical repeat to the one I had just shared with my friend just before walking inside. I spoke with El for over an hour, and she constantly asked about my beliefs in Jesus. She is Jewish and really struggles with the fundamental differences between Jewish and Christian viewpoints. Our conversation was another test of my ability to respond to this particular question. This was the second time today that two occurrences of God's messages to me bubbled to the surface of the world around me.

December 13, 2014
Early Morning

Though it was all vague, I found myself in the heavens sitting at a table with other children on either side. An angel stood before us. He asked how I managed to return so well. I pointed to a bottle of vitamins on the table. I said, "I don't need these anymore." The child on my right seemed intrigued that I had a solution to help me find harmony with the heavens. I asked him if he had ever taken any vitamins. The child nodded his head side-to-side to indicate he had not. I took out two and passed them down to him. I said, "Since I don't need them anymore. You take them." I understood my former need to rely on vitamins was once a conditioning tool for my mind.

The Written (cont'd)

Now I have achieved a point where they seem to negatively affect the strength in my visions, so I no longer need them.

December 13, 2014
Afternoon

During an afternoon meditation, I began to think about how time seemed to be non-existent in my travels...or at least at a much different pace than I understand time now. As that thought filled my mind, I found myself standing before a jolly man. He was smiling at me, a grin from ear to ear. He was short, stubby, and extremely wide. He had an orange mustache and beard. We joked back and forth for a few minutes about how time seemed to be nonexistent in this space.

Sixth Revelation

The Sixth Revelation should be seen as a continuation of the revelations prior as well as building upon the event when I bore witness to the trumpet sound on December 11, 2014. In truth, the majority of the messages that have been shared throughout this portion of the journey have all been of divine revelation. This entire book could be seen as something similar to God's grand revealing in John's Book of Revelation and The Book of Daniel – specifically chapters eleven and twelve. But, it is important that portions of this book are cast within a special light. This Sixth Revelation is one of those moments that should be set apart from all others, for it is the moment that God spoke in a way for all to hear. It was His commandment and His proclamation.

The Sixth Revelation took place three days following the moment when I was given a call to action by the seven angels of the Lord. It was in that call to action when the angels explained "the time is near and that it is now time to share [the message] with others." And even as I began seeking ways to move forward in the ways that would be most pleasing unto Him, He had to speak in this one grand gesture to ensure I understood the commandment and proclamation of His will.

...

Glory

December 14, 2014

This evening, I asked my Father for help. I prayed about the parable of the men that were given lamps, and half ran out in the darkness without oil to burn (a reference to Matthew 25). When the Lord arrived, the ones without oil were no where to be found because they went into the desert unprepared and had to return to purchase oil. With this parable in mind, I prayed that the Lord would fill my lamp with oil – an abundance of it – so that not only would I be prepared when I ran out at his calling, but would also be able to help fill others' lamps with the overflow. He answered.

My experiences began this morning by arriving in the heavens before the face of a great angel. I was viewing it from its side-profile. Its face was pointing left. The angel blinked its eye to acknowledge I was there. Its eye was blue, the face was a grayish-purple. I was lifted above the oceans and watched as the oceans began to swirl in a clockwise motion. It was clear I was being shown a deluge. The angel's voice said, "Denying your walk and testament with God is like leaving the bride at the altar." I immediately was sent back to my body to write down the words. In this experience as well as the additional experiences, I believe the angel took extra care in helping me return with all of the information I had been given, though the longevity of the experiences was reduced.

After I wrote down the words, I returned to the heavens. I heard the angel say, "Go now. Standing before an angel and

Sixth Revelation

not acknowledging his wings is like seeing a bird and it choosing not to fly. Go tell everyone the Messiah is coming." I returned to write the words.

Once again, I was taken back to the heavens. This time, I stood before the great Sphinx whose body was adorned in gold. Its face was gold and alternating rows of the richest deep blue emanated from its head. As I stared in awe, the angel said, "Standing before this Sphinx is like standing before God and not taking action. It has the body of the Lord, the face of a man. Run now and tell everyone the Messiah is coming." I once again, was returned to my body.

As soon as I had written the words, the angel carried me back to the heavens. I was standing on a cobblestone path. There were two ladies dressed in traditional Jewish attire. One was in a driveway to my left. One was before me standing on the walkway. The voice of the angels spoke. "When you see a Jewish family, don't pass them by for there are milling rights that must be had. Walk carefully and carry them through, for those are the ones that helped you in." Once again I was returned to my body to write the words verbatim.

In the next experience, I was sitting next to a pool on a beautiful day. My father was in a chair to my right facing west, in the direction of the pool. My chair was pointed north and was just along the edge of the pool. In front of me, my mother sat near a table and umbrella. She was facing me, but her chair was slightly further apart from my father and me. It was also along the edge of the pool. I thought there was one other presence there between my mother and father, but I could not discern a form. As we sat there, I felt a giant splash of water pour down on top of me. My mother looked at me and waved her finger as if to say, "No, no." I turned to look over my left shoulder to see if a child was splashing us since the water seemed to still be falling down on top of me. And while there was a child in the pool, he was just staring at me and was not the source of the splashing. I looked above to see if it was raining. I stared above at a blue sky, but the water was clearly falling from the sky. My mother wanted us all to get under the black umbrella at the table behind her. I looked around to see that the rain was not pouring down everywhere, but just on my father and me. As my mother was motioning us over, my father said, "This is because it is what must be experienced here at Laguna." I thought about his words and tried to rationalize where "Laguna" was located. It caused me to lose harmony.

I returned once again. This next experience was long and detailed. I feel like I was shown enough information to produce a movie, but all I could return with was a highlight reel of it all. Even during the experience, I kept repeating all of the important points I wanted to bring back with me, but to no avail. While I was in the heavens, I witnessed a woman that I seemed to know standing on a beach. I was being called off to travel to another location. When my flight left, I saw a vision of others that recognized the woman because of me. They wanted to do harm to her. When they surrounded her and approached her to attack, they saw that she was pregnant. In that moment, God took her away with Him to protect her.

Sixth Revelation

When the plane landed, I stepped off the stairs and found myself standing upon the Giza plateau (or a place similar to it). Much like the previous experience with the sphinx, it seemed like a more modern version of the ruins we see today. Directly ahead was a large pyramid and a smaller pyramid behind it. The pyramid was white and shining at the top. There was a city surrounding it, but mostly to the back right of it. On my left, was either a river or a divider of some sort. I thought it was a river. While I knew I was standing in sand, the thing that really caused me to question the location was the amount of greenery. I looked across the plain between where I was standing and the pyramid, and all I could see were green plants growing from the fertile sand. I turned around to tell someone behind me, "Let's go." I was excited to see where we had landed. I returned to Earth.

My last vision was brief. I saw my Jeep being covered up and flooded over by the ocean. Nothing else was visible around us. The top of the Jeep was barely cresting over the surface of the water. The Jeep had been washed over on a 45° angle.

The Written (conclusion)

December 15, 2014

During meditation, my travels to the heavens involved one of the warmest experiences I have ever had. It began with a great white hallway. The ceiling was ornate and formed in the shape of an ancient roman church. The trimmings were in gold. The floor was tiled in white with gold bindings. On my left was an elder female angel. On my right was Enoch. He was much taller than I as I was only about his waist height (if that). I was like a child standing between the two angels. Enoch looked at me with a big smile on his face. He said I should move in song as we walked down the hallway.

My viewpoint was first person, as well as third person from behind us. I was being led to a doorway. Enoch's emphasis for me to move in song was because my day was almost near. He began by hopping on his right foot and gliding his left foot across the tile. He danced back and forth with similar movements. I looked to my left to see if the angel was dancing since I was not sure if I should. She started dancing as well. So, with my hands held between both of their hands, I smiled and began to move my feet. We walked down the hallway toward a blinding white light, and then I returned to my body.

In the next experience, I was standing on a beach. I looked around and noticed it was distinctly not Fort Lauderdale, nor was it as far north as Georgia. I think it could have been the beach at St. Augustine or Ponte Vedra. I returned to Earth.

I returned again and saw the image of an Asian man smiling at me. He was overfilled with joy as evident in his eyes. The image faded, and this time I saw the image of a sun with rays shooting out from it. In the sun, was a face – almost cartoon like. It was smiling with joy.

In the final image, I saw the painting I have on my wall entitled "The Garden" with a much wider and shorter painting overlaid on it (including the canvas). It was important that I understood the artist that created the painting (Paul) also saw a bigger image that he did not capture on that particular canvas.

December 16, 2014

Today was the last evening of my fast (no food or water for three days). I had begun the evening of the 14th, so this was my third evening, after two full days of fasting. My body is extremely weak and I wondered if I would have any energy to rise out of bed the following day. In what I can only call a supernatural experience demonstrating how the soul is

The Written (conclusion)

revitalized through the heavens, there was a moment so grand that I began to understand how the great biblical leaders managed to fast for forty days and forty nights without water or food (Moses, etc.). Just as an aside – it is thought that Jesus still partook in water, but no food. Regardless, my understanding of how they survived became more apparent from the experiences in the night.

I cannot say I slept at all throughout the night. Instead, I travelled to the heavens and had one of the longest (if not the longest) experiences I have ever had. But, because I was so physically weak, every time I tried to write down the words from the experience, I could not maintain my soul in my earthly body and returned to the heavens too quickly. This is the opposite of how most every other experience has taken place. I could now understand how, without nutrients for physical strength, my soul returned from where it once came, and will one day return. All I can manage to explain from the experience is that I was shown "my story" as "one with everything." I was shared so much information of All That Is that my soul must have grown three times in spiritual strength this day. I was shown the heavens – all around. I have never experienced anything as grand in scale as I did this time, but I was unable to return with any of it. That may seem like an excuse, but I assure you it is not.

There was one point that an angel offered me some form of food – something similar to a blueberry bagel. I was ashamed to eat it, but the angels assured me I needed it for my strength. I sneaked a bite of the food, but immediately felt that

Glory

I had failed in my fasting effort with God. I was assured though, that I had not broken my fast. The food offered to me was food for my spirit. I realized after eating the food, that I was wrapped in a pink toga. It was as if the pink toga was meant to represent the personification of a pink calendar. I would later go on to understand this significance to how the pink candle in the advent wreath symbolizes the light in the darkness (the darkness symbolized by the purple candles) that foreshadows the coming of the Messiah – which is represented by the white candle. This is equivalent to how John the Baptist foreshadowed Jesus's arrival. The pink toga did boggle my mind at first, but I became comfortable in the symbolism the longer the vision extended.

I was eventually taken to a restaurant to meet others that I had met before in the heavens. When I arrived, I went to the bathroom and returned to the table with everyone. They all looked at me strangely. I was convinced it was either because the food I had eaten earlier in the heavens broke my covenant with God or that the pink toga was out of place in the surroundings. Either way, everyone just stared. I eventually became paranoid that I must have wet spots on my toga after using the bathroom. I tried to rationalize to myself why so many people would be staring. I asked them about whether it was from eating the food, but they all seemed to dismiss that notion. I eventually understood that it was the color I was wearing, and what that must mean spiritually.

I eventually left the restaurant and returned to the parked vehicle I arrived in with my guardian. We hopped in the car,

The Written (conclusion)

but the angel decided to take me to the End of Days. She pulled me from the car, and we appeared on a shoreline. I was taken to a sailboat where the angel asked me whether I thought I could survive the seas when the world is shaken in the end. I said that I thought a sailboat could survive because it would just roll with the waves. I was placed in the sailboat and saw the oncoming waves that will occur during part of the End of Days. The waves were gargantuan. They must have towered hundreds or thousands of feet. As I braced for the wave, I knew I would die. I cried for the angel, but she wanted me to experience the force of destruction.

The wave crashed over me, and I awoke on a rocky shoreline, staring at the waves in the distance. For quite some time in my earthly mind I had thought that anyone with a boat may be able to ride out the destruction caused from the sea. At this moment, I understood no boat would survive this destruction. No structure in the areas where the sea will be stirred is capable of surviving. It will be akin to God shaking the Earth like a snow-globe, where parts of the world are destroyed by the sea, while other coastal areas of sanctuary may remain untouched. Part of the continents will collapse and new land masses will form. It is a destruction that I could never have imagined in my wildest dreams. And in this case, not only was I shown this part of the End, but I was forced to experience it so that I may understand how destructive this time will be.

As I lay on the shore experiencing the terror in the destruction, the angel urged me up in order to follow her. She led me to a destroyed city. There was gunfire, looting and riots

Glory

everywhere. As we stood by a wooden shed, I saw a gun poke out of a crack in the wood frame. It began firing. I grabbed the barrel with my hand so as to direct it somewhere other than at me. When I did so, a man began to emerge from the shed. He was wearing a polo shirt with the UPS logo on it. I studied the logo. It was placed there to help me understand that the experience was from modern times, and that I was indeed witnessing a continuation of the destruction of the End of Days. It was reminiscent from a scene out of a movie where there is nothing but utter destruction in a post-apocalyptic setting. Nothing can prepare any person to witness the destruction that I was allowed to see. Even the greatest imagination would not do this imagery justice. More importantly, I was forced to experience it, to see just how terrifying this situation will be.

The last part of the experience involved me standing outside of a limousine. There was a redheaded angel and Jesus Christ sitting in the limousine. The lesson seemed to be set in an award-show styled presentation. I was told that "Allure wins song of the year from 1984." The red-headed angel thought it was "fancy." I was then shown how upcoming movies have pieces of truth that passively demonstrate the divide between heaven on Earth is not a divide, but one. These movies are truthfully foretelling the end, whether the authors understood their inspiration or not. For quite some time I have understood the underlying messages in movies, but this was the first time that I was told angelically that many of the recent

The Written (conclusion)

and upcoming movies are inspired from visions of the end of times.

When I eventually returned to my body after the hours of experiences, my soul was invigorated with passion to share God's word. I was also fueled in energy by my spirit, no doubt in some supernatural explanation of receiving food from the angels in the heavens. Words can really not do any of this experience justice. For the angels showed me and had me experience pieces of the End in such a way as to fully understand the gravity of the destruction to come for those who remain behind.

December 17, 2014
Early Morning

This morning's experiences were very tough to recall. This was the morning following the end of my fast and my body was working through the change in adding food back into my diet (at midnight nonetheless). But, from what I can recall, I was speaking to an angel about a spreadsheet. I was trying to figure out all of the numbers and dates I have been given throughout these processes. The angel, which presented itself with a CPA-like wisdom, said, "It isn't supposed to add up." He then emphasized I further refine and clean up the ideas in my mind.

December 17, 2014
Afternoon

During an evening meditation, I heard the voice of the Lord's angel. It said, "Not a liaison anymore. Isn't that right Jonathan?" Perhaps there was more before, but this is when I first heard the voice. I immediately returned to write it down. The voice was female and very distant in presence.

December 18, 2014
Early Morning

This morning's experiences were extremely powerful, but each was very short. The first experience in the heavens began in a tall building. An angel had me chase her into the building and up the stairs. She disappeared ahead of me. As I reached a doorway, it fell open like a drawbridge on a castle. I searched for her as I ran up the stairs ahead of me. The angel led me into this courtyard and onto a specific section of the flooring. The roof was ornately decorated. The top of the building was tiled and held a beautiful courtyard. There were trees and plants all around us.

I looked down at the tile. It was placed with extreme precision and detail. The tile was a dark cream marble. There were inlays of red marble and gold. I saw that I was standing in the middle of a design that radiated outwardly. The angel was standing on one specific slice of the radiating bands. She

The Written (conclusion)

had a specific design beneath her feet. Beneath my feet, the design appeared similar to a sun. After I had observed the setting, the angel said to me, "You are on the eighth level. You will assume your role in March." With those words, I returned to my body to write down the experience in detail.

When I returned, I saw what I could only assume was either a demon or a fallen angel. It spoke in a distorted voice – like a low phase filter was placed on top of it. The voice said that it was "charged with surrendering to evil." As I heard the words, I looked around and saw that we were on a meteor or a moon looking at Earth. I did not know what to make of it, but I returned to my body to write down the words.

When I returned to the heavens, I stood before an angel. With one of its hands balled into a fist, it slammed the countertop before me. I could tell the angel wanted to make sure it grabbed my spiritual attention. It said, "We only have twenty days to make this work with me." I was immediately jettisoned back to my body to write down his words.

I returned immediately after writing the words. This time I found myself with a group of kids being chased by an invisible force. At first it seemed terrifying and scary. But, then reality began to hit me, and I decided to call the spirit to appear. An angel in a big antebellum dress appeared. The dress had a little bit of yellow, but it was mostly white. She continued forcing items around us to fall on everyone. She chased all of us and eventually chased me up a long corridor that I have seen before. I turned right and headed up a long ramp that is similar to what you would see in a parking deck, only that it was just a tall ascending corridor with no parking garage. She told me that "we travelled at seven hundred and forty-two feet per second." I was not scared of her, but I could not get over the austere appearance the angel held. After I heard the rate of speed, I returned to write down the numbers.

When I returned to the heavens, I was placed in a scenario where a house caught fire and I had to put it out. I did so by tearing down the attic access and crawling into it. The door was otherwise stuck before I ripped it open. When I reached the attic, as best as I can explain these concepts, I sprayed a certain type of extinguisher on a certain type of flower. I thought the flower was the same pink flower that continues to appear in these experiences. The experience ended, and I returned to my body.

I returned to the heavens once more. This time I found myself being interviewed by cops on how my visions worked. They did not seem to understand how God was showing me everything that He has blessed me with over the last three years. And though I did my best to explain everything to them, they continued to think I was lying. It was a losing battle, but one that I had to see in spiritual form so that I would understand how to handle the situation on Earth when it arises in physical form.

The Written (conclusion)

December 18, 2014
Evening

I spoke with Bryan this evening after he texted me of the importance of us speaking. As it turned out, he experienced an amazing encounter with an angel earlier in the morning. Bryan was taken to the heavens where an angel showed him an image of the five moons – the same image he was shown in weeks prior. Throughout the experience, a male angel resembling our grandfather continued to press Bryan for an explanation to the image of the five moons.

When Bryan said he had not yet figured it out, the angel explained that there was no more time for him to figure it out. He told Bryan that he saw, "The four horsemen, the bowmen, and wormwood." I immediately asked Bryan how five moons equaled six items in the list and Bryan explained that the angel said, "the four horsemen" and then further clarified who the horsemen were by calling them "the bowmen."

After Bryan returned to his body, he was led to an article on a series of meteors that will begin their impact course with Earth in the next six years and will be experienced for a period of over a hundred years (with many cataclysmic collisions likely). Interestingly, whether or not that article is foreshadowing to the End, it stands to reason that wormwood is a meteor or a falling star headed toward Earth, shot by "the bowmen." Essentially they are God's divine archers. Most certainly the End will usher in destruction of unknown proportions when the divide of Heaven and Earth occurs. It is also important to understand that the End is a new beginning for the children of God, so talking about the End should only be seen as cataclysmic for those who are left behind when Earth is pushed into the start of a new cycle.

December 19, 2014

This morning, I was taken by an angel into a wooded setting. In the middle of the group of trees was the stump of a great tree, as if cut down to be used as an altar. I saw two angels, one male and female. The male had a dark brown beard and mustache. He reminded me of Tim McGraw, but only in generality. He was there to meet his girl. I was tasked with leading them to the tree stump. I took both by the hands and walked them to the tree stump. There was a song that the male had written for his girl, inspired by this specific location. I watched them dance arm in arm.

Eventually I escorted her to the tree with my right hand held high above my head, holding her hand (since the angels were larger than me). I helped her step up onto the tree stump for him to come meet her and be with her forever. It was a beautiful moment of Love. The song was beautiful. And though I do not know why I was tasked in the role I played, it felt like I was a matchmaker of sorts – as if I helped two souls find each other in an elegant celebration of unbridled Love, for all to see.

The Written (conclusion)
December 20, 2014

The experience this morning was extremely long and detailed, but I, again, had a hard time returning with many of the details. And though it may seem like it is only a partial message, I can also say that when I experience these moments, it awakens and impregnates my soul with all of the important information. In this case, I arrived in the heavens following a prayer. My prayer was concerning my efforts with telling my brother-in-law and sister about the Messiah's impending arrival. And while I can empathize that most people would view someone sharing that message as fabricating a lie for attention, it really opened my eyes to how God must have viewed Sodom and Gomorra before its annihilation.

At that time, Abraham prayed for God to spare the city, pleading that there must be at least 100 righteous men. This number was later reduced to ten, and eventually that number could not be found. As I stood before my sister and her husband (both with degrees in Ministry and who serve as the Pastor and Minister of Music for a church), I recognized how difficult it was going to be to get God's message out to those *with* ears to listen. Even in this circumstance, it seemed that the most righteous people I knew (outside of Bryan), were completely content with accepting the notion that the church was not ready for the Messiah's return and that they self-admitted they could do more (as everyone can) but had no desire to affect change. In the conversation, it caused me to pose the question that if I walked out of the room and God were to enter and say that he was just checking off the list of names of the 144k that make the cut, would they be confident in their responses and admitted lack of desire to help spread the message? This question was a tough question, and they chose to use that particular moment as a segue to find closure in the conversation.

So, with that experience from earlier in the day, I prayed for God to grant me guidance. And while He did not deliver guidance in the form of an answer, He did deliver a vision of what I was capable of accomplishing. In the vision, I was taken to a mountaintop town. I saw a single-file line of people who all were holding individual kayaks. I understood they were there to receive the message I was to deliver. The line was long and unending. From there, the angel who accompanied me took me to the mountaintop and showed me the thousands (maybe even over a hundred thousand people) filing into rows to hear the message. There was a large number of people who were wearing tall, yellow, sombrero-like hats. These people represented the ones I personally led there. I knew I was standing on the mountaintop mentioned in Revelation. This was the way that God chose to show me how I would help lead His people home. The gravity of seeing all of the people refueled my motivation and energy from my otherwise downcast feelings after the conversation with my sister and her husband earlier in the evening.

The Written (Conclusion)
December 21, 2014

This morning I had several experiences. It is really getting hard to bring back the information between the two extremes as the heavenly experiences have become stronger and more intense. In this experience, I was placed in a town in between my parent's house and my sister's house. They live about an hour and a half apart in Georgia. I traveled through this town with an angel. I shared the stories about the Messiah coming and the anti-Christ's imminent arrival. Nearly everyone in the city listened to the message. And while they believed my words – and that I believed everything I was saying – they refused to accept the message about the antichrist's arrival. I became aware that their doubt was fueled by an evil spirit. I eventually cleared out the evil spirit so I could share the message, but I lost harmony with the heavens before I could see the results of the effort.

While there were several other extremely lucid experiences, the final experience was the one that I was able to bring back with me. In this experience, I was in a football locker room. It seemed as if we had just had a practice or a game. I understood I played the position of quarterback. Though I did not have the context of the preceding game or practice, I felt a huge sense of disappointment in my efforts. Spiritually speaking, I understood this was a spiritual message being delivered through football symbolism. In this case, I felt like I had just let down the team. I was not ready to give up, but I could not un-

Glory

derstand why the team was placing faith in me, and why the coach was placing faith in me.

As I was lost in this feeling of disappointment, my coach walked up. He said, "You should not be down on yourself. You need to know that you have a 91% rating before getting out there." In football terms, I understood he was talking about a quarterback rating. In football terms, that puts you at #11 all-time of quarterback rating leaders for their careers. In a literal sense, I understood that the ceiling of this "rating" was 100 and not anything higher. I also understood that the coach was implying that my "rating" was astounding for anyone, and I had a sense that my rating was higher than anyone had ever been, but shy of where I could reach. There was a vision once before where I was told that I was at 30-something percent. At the time, I thought it meant "spiritual strength percentage." This time should be viewed no differently. I understood from the coach's additional words that I should be very pleased with my progress, and that I should get out on the field and continue practicing.

We all walked out of the locker room and onto the field. We were standing in a practice-bubble over an indoor football field. I picked up a football and decided to kick it as high and as far as I could. The kick soared a great distance. It was not as far as I felt I should be able to kick it, but I was pleased. The coach saw my action and shouted out at how great of a kick that was. I continued chasing after the ball and kicking it. Eventually, I decided to kick field goals. At this point, most of the team had left the arena. It was really just a time for me to

The Written (conclusion)

practice alone. I kicked for quite some time from a tee (though I was practicing field goals). I wanted to become stronger, better, and most importantly, to be valued and needed on the team I was playing for. I wondered if I should just become a kicker rather than a quarterback. It seemed like I could not achieve as much as I wanted to in the quarterback position, though the coach and team all rallied behind me and continued to sing my praises.

December 23, 2014

My travels to the heavens were two-fold this morning. In the first experience, the angels spent a lot of time with me teaching me and guiding me in the ways to complete my directive. Though I cannot put into words the specifics of their guidance, their words strengthened my soul and granted me resilience to follow the Lord's directive.

In the second experience, I was part of a team of other souls that I understood to be brothers and sisters on Earth. I do not know how many of us were specifically part of the team, but the number sixteen continued to come to mind during the experience. However, it could have been as few as twelve represented in form. Our team was tasked with running a race. I would not call it a marathon, but I would describe the race as a race completed in a shorter timeline than a marathon.

Glory

Our team had a coach that guided us. He was an elder angel, which I recognized from the start. The team ran through the streets and returned back to a locker room. For a reason I did not initially understand, I chose to run the race completely naked. I was the only one on the team running the race without clothes. When the coach walked in the room to speak to us, other team members were snickering at me being naked. And while it was a little uncomfortable, I felt like it was the only way to run the race fully committed to the cause. Being naked was like that extra ounce of effort that I could give when others may choose to not take that extra effort for fear of being judged.

As we stood in the locker room, I held one hand in front of my body to cover myself from the eyes of my teammates. When the coach started to speak, he began by addressing my nudity. The coach told the room, "Regardless of what you may think, anyone can run naked if he feels the need." He went on to say that running naked may very well help us win the race. Our team was comprised of boys and girls. Everyone seemed really uncomfortable with me being naked even though the coach basically said, "Take notice of Jonathan and what he feels led to do."

After those words, the meeting adjourned. Everyone stayed behind and socialized – including the coach. There was one girl sitting on a box by the entranceway to the locker room. She seemed very laid back. She was brunette, thin, and seemed to be very confident in her spirit. As I walked past her she said, "I like the way it looks. It looks good." I was still cov-

The Written (conclusion)

ering myself and initially thought she was speaking with innuendo. As I processed her words, I could not decide if she was speaking spiritually to help me gain strength in my decision to go nude, or whether she was flirting. I thought about how to respond, but the coach interjected his opinion before I had a chance. He motioned a finger at me to acknowledge it was okay for me to be unclothed. He then said so the whole team could hear, "But there will be no sex in here. If there is, you will be gone immediately." I understood that he was clarifying the context of being spiritually unclothed in the race that God has tasked each of us with on Earth (telling the world the Messiah is coming). He also wanted us not to mistake the meaning of this experience with earthly desires.

With that understanding, I walked back to the changing rooms. Everyone on the team stopped to stare at one particular changing room in the back left corner. It was as if we all knew two people were in there and we were about to witness someone being dismissed from the team. I opened the door. Inside the small changing room, there was another door that opened up to a second changing room accessible only from the first room. As I stood there, a guy and a girl came out of the back room. We all knew they were about to get dismissed. Perhaps the two people in the changing room was just a lesson so we all would understand the difference of the spiritual message and the physical message.

I understood as it was being presented, though I cannot be sure if the other members on the team had the same understanding of everything. I guessed they did not since the

Glory

warning had to be given, and I was the only one comfortable with being unclothed without sexuality attached (and used as an example by our teacher).

December 24, 2014

The experience in the heavens this morning seemed to last forever, though I was unable to bring back anything in words. I believe the best way to put the experience into words is to say that I encountered numerous lessons and guidance in understanding how to follow the path of a king. I wish there was something more I could say – or even more I could elaborate on – but no words can express this type of strengthening of the spiritual body. Merely themes existed in place of words. This experience was more akin to a spiritual workout in building strength.

December 25, 2014

This morning I was taken to the heavens and again put through numerous lessons in spiritual strengthening. Over the course of the hours I spent in the heavens learning, I came to understand that my directive to share the Lord's message that "The Messiah is coming" has been further clarified in purpose. During the experience, I thought I was supposed to tell everyone about the Messiah. However, I was continually placed into situations of having to teach the spiritual teachers here on

The Written (conclusion)

Earth so that they may spread the word. This helped me understand my directive more clearly.

Over the last several days I have been asking for guidance about where to start in my directive. I could see that telling people one by one would be too time consuming given the scale of time needed to spread the message. Starting with the topmost tier of spiritual teachers would seem to cause the message to receive judgment by the heads of the organizations before the pastors and spiritual teachers had a chance to make a decision for themselves. So, this left me with trying to find a starting point among the chaos. This morning's experience gave me clarity about where to start. Now I must figure out how to start.

December 26, 2014

This experience began on a vessel similar to a luxury cruise liner. I was standing on the top deck positioned next to a single metal chain that wrapped around four corners and served as a barrier for this particular area on the ship. I was excited and recognized the spiritual significance of the moment. But as I began to be filled with excitement, I watched as the ship filled with others. At first I was excited about who I may meet. It crossed my mind this might be a time I would see many of the familiar females I typically see in the heavens…but quite the opposite happened.

Glory

The section of the ship I was standing on began to fill with men only. Many of the men were just wearing swim trunks. I immediately felt the filth that I feel when Lucifer tries to go to war with my spirit. There were so many people filling in, that everyone was standing shoulder to shoulder. One man in front of me began acting homosexual and dancing with everyone around him. I tried to push away and get out of the area, but he made one last effort to lick my chest in a way similar to how a dog would lick something up off of the ground. My body repulsed and revolted against his action. I decided to invoke the spirit of God to rid the surroundings from me (or me from the surroundings).

Immediately, an angel came and took me from the top of the ship and down a corridor. She led me into a library that was shaped like an L. We entered in the longer side of the room with a large bookshelf to my right. I looked at the angel and realized it was the same angel that I was terrified of just a few nights ago. She was wearing an early 1920s ball gown. At first I had a sense of fear. But, nearly as quickly as the sense of fear set in, I felt a sense of recognition. This angel was not evil, nor was she terrorizing me the other night. This is the same austere angel that began appearing to me two years ago. In those times I was also terrified due to the sheer austerity of the angel. The angel presented itself as it first began doing two years ago – without wings and translucent white.

So, as I calmed myself in the moment and realized I was in the company of one of the Lord's messengers (albeit one who is scarily austere), I turned to acknowledge I understood

The Written (conclusion)

the moment we were in. I also noticed that there was a handful of others who were brought down the stairwell behind me. They were all familiar. She then glided by me without using her feet. She walked me along the bookcase, and we turned left when we reached the corner of the room. She was leading on my left and turned to the bookshelf and pointed at a single book.

I tried to read the words on the binding, but had to step up closer so I could properly observe/translate the symbols. She pulled the book out halfway, indicating that I should pull it out and open it up. But, before I desired to open the book, I wanted to understand what it was that she wanted me to read. I stared at the green hardbound cover and the gold-embossed words. The title slowly came into view. And while what I wrote down was my best understanding of the words, I also want to indicate how I understood the words.

The title of the book consisted of two words that seemed nearly identical. The first word was most definitely Aaron. However, it also seemed like it could be possessive, such as "Aaron's." The only way I can explain how it could be two possibilities is to understand that whatever it was that was being presented to me transfigured upon itself when I viewed it. It was as if my knowledge of whatever language the Lord was presenting to me was coming into focus for my understanding.

At first the words were blurry, but as I focused, they came into view. But, I think the multiple possible meanings are more of an indicator that my strength in understanding the Lord's Written Words is still a skill I am learning. That should not take away from the fact that I have been shown something important. Rather, it should give rise to the truth and honesty in these words – in understanding how the Lord communicates with me. I fully understand that whatever language is being shown is based on the twenty-two Hebrew archetypes, though I think some of what I have been shown predates the earliest Hebrew we have in our earthly records.

Sometimes I am shown Sanskrit, of which there is no official way to write it. Sanskrit is written in a variety of languages to express the sound and archetypal meanings. So, whatever the glyphs are that comprise this written word of God, they hold the same archetypal meaning as that which I have been coming to understand through the earliest forms of Hebrew.

Getting back on topic, it is important to understand that the second word was one that I could not comprehend simultaneously with the first word. When the second word came into focus, I initially thought it was the same word as the first word but plural since it was written almost identically to the first word. But, as I studied the word, it seemed to transfigure into the intended form. So, if I could say that the first moment I observed it, I thought the word might be "Aarons," then it should be understood that the beginning of the word transfigured to "Ander" or "Anders."

As I repeated the two words, I wanted to make sure that I was not inserting earthly bias into my understanding. I generally have to meditate on the moment after it is presented to me as I ask for God to help clarify the visions. But this time, I was cognizant in real-time with the observance of the two words.

The Written (conclusion)

Due to the transfiguring of the words, I began sorting through any possible earthly names that sounded close. The only name that came to mind was "Erin Andrews" – a reporter on ESPN. As I repeated her name, I knew that it was not her name, but I had then introduced the word "Andrews" into my understanding. So, while I believe that the second word did not have anything to do with the word Andrews, I wanted to take note of my understanding process just in case something is revealed later, and I am allowed to see more truth in the hindsight of God's message.

So, at best, I think the title was either "Aaron Aarons," "Aaron's Aarons," "Aaron's Aaronson," "Aaron Aaronson," "Aaron Anders," "Aaron's Anders," "Aaron's Anderson," or "Aaron Anderson." And while I throw all of those possibilities out there to make sure I capture everything in the moment, I understood the book to place the most importance upon the first word "Aaron" and the role Aaron played in the Bible. As my mind shuffled through the words, I lost harmony before I was able to open the book. If I had to guess, I think it was the spiritual writings of Aaron, and that there is an importance in understanding Aaron for my personal walk.

When I returned, I heard a voice that said, "He has cracked Meredith's [an untranslatable word that means head and neck]." When I heard the voice, I wanted to make sure I wrote down the words, so I returned to my body and took note of the words. The voice sounded austere and strong – and not a typical angelic voice. This one held a different tone of seriousness. It made me question if the message was from Lucifer or rather an austere angel.

Before I tried to return to the heavens, I prayed for additional guidance on everything. I shared with God all that I thought He was trying to tell me, but I also emphasized the need for clarity. For the next several hours, I was taken back to the heavens where I came to understand the message. While I did not return to the library or see the austere angel again, I was shown other parts of the boat and the lessons that I was supposed to learn. At one point I recalled a very poignant thought, the only thing I was allowed to bring back with me to Earth. I uttered these words to the angel as I observed all that I was being shown: "I no longer see people as male or female, gay or straight. I feel like a soul is not based on the actions of gender or if they are homosexual."

To the reader, these words may contradict taught religious viewpoints. And to be honest, I have really struggled with understanding whether a person who practices homosexuality will be judged more harshly by God. And truthfully, that is not my worry or my call to make. My personal thoughts on the subject have been contradictory, and I have generally abstained from projecting an opinion. But, if I were forced to make a decision about this particular experience in the heavens, I would have to say that I still believe homosexuality is spiritually wrong and is defiant to the natural order of God's creation. I have always believed that homosexuality is an outward expression of the Love for one's self (ego) and a misguided desire to Love oneself through the image of anoth-

The Written (conclusion)

er. It does not mean that there is no Love found in a homosexual relationship, but rather that the Love is a misguided understanding of the spiritual body and the earthly body (ego). The polarities of male and female souls bonding is a spiritual completeness that I believe must be upheld in the earthly walk – and that is not found in a homosexual relationship.

Just for clarity, this is not a Freudian view into my subconscious, for I have zero desire or thoughts of the kind. I Love the Love of a woman and long for that with all of my heart. But, I have to reflect upon the greater call to Love everyone as brothers and sisters in this moment. In this particular case, my understanding from the lesson was that we all should attempt to see all souls uncolored by any bias of any kind. This instruction from the angels does offer clarity to the age old question of homosexuality, though it does not mean that the action is right or wrong, for I personally believe that the perspective I gave as homosexuality being a misguided outward expression of the Love of one's self holds a very truthful perspective.

So, after the hours I experienced in the heavens this morning when I asked for clarity, I am now charged with seeing without color or bias those who believe in God. Everyone has faults. Those who knowingly indulge in faults/sins while choosing to ignore the questions or allowing emotions to carry favor over God's difficult answers will carry those actions to the footsteps of the Lord on their judgment day. All a person can do is the very best he can with his relationship with God – which means seeking council and finding peace with answers that may go against emotions and feelings on the particular subject at hand. So, while I did not expect this experience to be a discourse on homosexuality, the lesson I received as I sought clarity involved breaking the barriers of judgment and seeing all souls as worthy to help get across the finish line. This does not mean religion should not strive to teach the principles of God's will. But, it does provide for a two-pronged approach, with the most important part being to help every soul get across the finish line for God's day of judgment. The rest is in His hands.

December 27, 2014

As I closed my eyes, I immediately was taken before a great mountain. I hovered above the ground and the mountain in a birds-eye view. I watched as a hand wrapped a chord of blue light around the mountain in a clockwise fashion from the base, ensuring the rings of blue light were all tightly wound in exact proportion. The rings of blue light formed a coil. I watched as the hand pulled up on the coil of blue light so that it expanded in length. As the coil seemed to double the height of the mountain, the hand immediately jerked the coil horizontally to the Earth in a westerly direction. Perhaps the direction was irrelevant, for we all seemed to be spinning in the way that the motions of the heavens allowed. The direction could be more understood to be south-west from my viewpoint, but I understood it to be in a westerly direction (my left).

The Written (conclusion)

As the coil expanded in the horizontal motion, I watched as the mountain was ripped from the Earth, forming a perfect end-cap to the coil of blue light. The spiral then re-coiled forming what I understood to be a rod of strength. Though I did not hear any verbal communication, I understood the message to be an explanation of how Aaron's rod was formed from the Earth. I also understood it to be the explanation of how armies of God's soldiers could circle an ancient city such as Jericho and cause the walls to fall. The spirit encased in God's soldiers formed the coil of light around the city walls, and the divine horizontal motion caused the destruction of the city. And while the visual demonstration illustrated part of God's wonder, I felt compelled to understand it as a lesson in understanding how to use the spirit encased within me.

December 28, 2014

This morning I was taken to the heavens and stood in the presence of two angels that I perceived to be the souls of a couple I met in Fort Lauderdale. Joe and Carla are two of the most happy and loving souls that I have had the pleasure of meeting. They are originally from Canada, but have a winter home in the same building I live in. They have a wonderful daughter named Joanna whom I have written about before in my journals. It is always a pleasure to see their family and have a glimpse of the happiness of the home they have found within one another. So, while I am not positive that I witnessed this

Glory

family in spiritual form, or another angelic family that radiated the same warmth and Love that I experience when I am around them on Earth, I do know that the identities in this montage were intended to illustrate the promise of the Hope and Love that I have felt around this family on Earth.

As the experience began, I was in a room with other souls. The angels resembling Joe and Carla stood near. I was the center of attention at that moment. I was standing upon a yoga mat and asked to demonstrate different moves. Of utmost importance was the pose "upward dog." I performed a vinyasa and moved into upward dog. Those around me seemed in awe of my spiritual ability to perform such a move. On Earth, this move is one of the most basic and first poses a person learns when taking a yoga class. However, this was the only time I have ever knowingly witnessed yoga actions in the heavens.

To someone reading this, it may seem like abstract imagery in the heavens, but truthfully, it was full of meaning. Yoga is an art of strength and stamina. To perform a yoga pose in the heavens is to demonstrate the strength of the soul. Early on in my travels to the heavens, I would have been unable to perform any complex movement that required such demanding strength and focus. This was a moment when I saw how far my spiritual strength had grown over the years.

As I performed the move, the two angels were entertained by my demonstration of spiritual strength. As I performed the move a second time, a female that was near came and sat on my back. This was an even more powerful demonstration of strength. Those who were gathered around were intrigued and

The Written (conclusion)

enjoyed the performance. The demonstration ended, and I spoke with the two angels before I left the room. In the conversation, they mentioned that their daughter "did not fly there" with them.

Later in the day, an angel called me back to the room to perform variations of this pose with push-ups mixed into the motions. This time, after I had performed the move several times, a younger angel resembling Joanna appeared and jumped on my back. She was excited to see me and wanted to surprise me. I stood up, and we began carrying on a conversation. It was good to see her again.

As we spoke I learned that her mother (the angel that resembled Carla) did not think that I would be "playing with" another girl in the heavens. This was in reference to the girl who sat on my back during yoga. And while nothing seemed romantic in any of the scenarios I have spoken about, it was clear to the angel that resembled Carla that she needed to "act quickly" in making sure I saw her daughter soon. All of the information was a little difficult to understand because I am still trying to understand the ins and outs of this parallel spiritual timeline. At first, I thought my travels to the heavens were like visiting a foreign land with its own language. But, over my travels, I have come to learn that there is a linear timeline in the heavens as well...at least in some version of the way I have come to know. Though, there is some blend of omniscient awareness blended with linear growth.

The conversation ended shortly after the angel that resembled Joanna and I visited my daughter. At this point, a

Glory

great elder angel appeared. She was holding two items in her hands that resembled metallic lemons. She bumped the two items together creating a bell like sound. As I write this, it is possible she was holding two bells in her hands. But, at the time, I thought she was holding lemons. Regardless, the sound of the bells ringing summoned the end of the experience, and I returned to my body.

December 29, 2014

Tonight I prayed, asking for spiritual help in discerning my call to "go, run" and "tell everyone the Messiah is coming." My prayers were answered in enormous fashion. My soul was called to the heavens by a great angel. This angel was sent to talk to me about my cry out for spiritual help. I immediately recognized her as the same angel I once saw three years ago when I first started identifying angels in the heavens. We talked about the human body, and it was explained to me that some of the things we experience is equivalent to a computer simulation. This is not to be mistaken for a true computer simulation. The angel chose this approach in describing some of our earthly challenges in a way that I could understand.

The angel pointed to a soul that lay horizontally in front of us. She pointed to a place in the brain that was identified to me in the shape of a black pill capsule. The angel explained to me that this particular location of the brain was "like an app," but that it did not track our movements or any other invasive

The Written (conclusion)

information. It was explained to me that this "app" we are given is more like a "veil of illusion." Each person's veil is slightly different. This illusion is broadcast into our dreams and is why people on Earth experience similar scenarios in dreams. Again, I want to emphasize that the angel was only using this manner of explanation to explain the concept, rather than the concept being explained in specific terms. The angel made sure that I understood that nothing else was touched in our souls, and that we are all healthy souls during the duration of this experience.

I became excited at hearing the explanation, for my soul was able to understand the concept at a much higher level than I can illustrate in words. I asked the angel about different scenarios that I have experienced and how worldly events affect the illusion. The angel confirmed that I was correct in my thought process. As I thought about all that was being shared with me, I asked the angel, "What other scenarios have there been?" I recognized that the scenarios are "upgraded" as we grow.

The angel said, "Hmmm. Initially we used a bingo game early on." I said, "Yess!!! I knew it. I wondered why that occurred." The angel seemed surprised I was able to remember it at all, even though I recounted several of the experiences in detail. I said, "I definitely had flashes of playing bingo early on." This was in reference to some of the earliest visions I can recall. Bryan also shared similar experiences, though all these likely occurred during the year that I did not journal much about the scenarios while I learned to understand God's communication to me.

In my excitement, I went to high-five the angel in recalling something from such an early point in my spiritual growth. After I had the confidence I understood the angel's message, I then started rattling off questions in my spiritual voice way faster than I could possibly perform through my earthly voice. I was so lucid, and the details were amazingly crisp. I wanted to take advantage of every moment I could while I was held in balance with the angel. After I began rattling off questions, I said, "Isn't this great? I can ask all of these questions, and I am fully aware! I'm not even losing balance!" The angel smiled and agreed that I had grown so much. I then asked four or five additional questions. The questions were all fired off without giving the angel a chance to respond. I realized that I needed to stop and just listen to the response from a single question, but I could not figure out which question was most important.

As I slowed down to let the angel respond to whichever question it chose to answer, I realized I could not breathe. I thought I was suffocating which caused me to return to my body. In fact, the concept of "taking your breath away" took on a whole new meaning for me in those moments. I was so mesmerized and excited in the wonder of the moment, that my soul could not breathe…not of earthly air, but of spiritual air – a life support that does not correspond exactly with the Earth's life support system, but is the same in an archetypal sense.

The Written (conclusion)
December 31, 2014

Today, as I walked to get breakfast and a coffee, I passed on the sidewalk a man who lives in my same building. His name is Abe. He is a really intelligent man, but keeps to himself. We have spoken only once or twice – nothing in terms of spirituality. Our only conversations revolved around when I moved to Ft. Lauderdale and what I did for a career. They were each extremely short. But, ever since that day, when Abe and I pass each other in the hallways or on the street, we always say, "Hey." He prefers a fist-bump over a handshake, so that is our usual mode of saying hello. However, today, something interesting happened. As I passed him, he did not extend his hand for a fist-bump. Instead he said, "My advice to you is to stay alive today." I was immediately caught off-guard. I said, "What?" He repeated his words once more. I said, "And why is that?" He said, "It will all make sense over the next year."

We went our separate ways, and I immediately called Bryan. It is not often someone tells you stay alive, much less at a specific time that the angels have revealed to me to be a spiritual marker on our earthly timeline. Of course I have to understand the message from Abe as spiritual first and foremost. After all, I am living amongst angels. But this time, it was clear there was a calling to be part of the journey into the end of times. I do not know when the timeline is set to begin,

Glory

but I do know that I have been shared markers, and today I was told to take caution to the darkness coming.

January 1, 2015

    The experience in the heavens this morning was peculiar. It began in a restaurant housed in an old, Victorian style house. I noticed as a boy with red hair finished his drink at the bar and walked out on his bar tab because he was drunk. The next day, I was again in this same establishment. I was talking to two female angels who were playing the role of workers at the restaurant. The same boy with red hair came back in and sat down at a table for breakfast. Once again, he left without paying. This time, everyone took notice and began to panic. It seemed the previous night's actions were understandable given that he appeared to be a regular and was intoxicated. This time, he neither took care of his tab from the night before, nor did he pay for his food while sober.

    As he walked out the door, down the steps, and across the street, I tried to calm everyone down and explain the situation to everyone (from a spiritual sense). I ran out the door to go after the boy. As I ran down the steps, I saw my spiritual father standing at the roadside as traffic whizzed by between him and the boy. The red-headed boy's appearance transfigured to a guy I once knew on Earth who had a fascination with the idea of "sniping" other human beings. My father saw the transfig-

The Written (conclusion)

uration as well and ran across the street to stop the boy from causing harm.

The boy panicked and pulled out a gun. He fired and shot my father's left hand. I began to race across the street after him. When I arrived, I lunged to the right as he aimed and fired at me. The bullet missed me, but hit a female angel wearing a referee uniform behind us in the distance. At first, she appeared to die. She fell down on her back. But almost instantly, she stood up and took off her referee jacket which had blocked the bullet. I held onto the boy until he was apprehended.

The next day, the referee angel was in the same establishment as we were in the previous two days. She and I were alone in a wooden room. Salsa music was playing. I tried to entice her to salsa dance with me – or at least teach me how – but she was not as amused as I was about the salsa dancing. She was beautiful, with long blonde hair. I longed to dance with her and feel her close to me. Maybe she saw right through me which is why she instead taught me to salsa dance with her in my mind rather than through physically dancing. It was as if she willed the scenario into my mind, rather than allowing it to occur in reality. I awoke.

January 4, 2015

While this scenario seems to lack any clear explanation of the events, I will still explain it as it occurred. As I was in the

Glory

heavens, I found myself in a green-lighted underground water system. I was aboard a boat as we floated through manmade channels surrounded by limestone, concrete walls, and platforms. There were also columns supporting the structure of the ceiling. As we began to pass one platform, I was forced to leap off of the boat and hang onto the railing of the platform until I was able to pull myself to safety. There was an importance to maneuver from the boat to a subway that was located somewhere near my leap.

As I made my way across to another platform, I entered through a door and ventured down a long corridor. I came across an angel that had the form of my very first girlfriend in middle school. She was much older now and had seemed to be stricken with something that caused her to age prematurely. As I saw her, I held my hands to either side of her face. I sensed she had a hatred for me that dated back to that time in middle school. Truthfully, I did not know what I was doing at that point in my life. I asked her to be my girlfriend and then, days later, I panicked and said I did not want to be her boyfriend anymore. I am sure I gave childish reasons, but the point of this visage is that I had not thought about her or that moment in ages. But somehow, it was clear that my actions had broken her more deeply than I ever imagined.

In this moment in the heavens, I attempted to make a joke about her pent-up anger toward me and promised it would all make sense in the end. I tried to communicate my haste in the actions I had to take in the heavens, but I am sure it seemed like I just ran past her without much care. Though I tried to

The Written (conclusion)

make her feel Loved, I only had moments to do so as I continued to run down the corridor. I hoped that touch would help more than words. I eventually made my way into a room with long lines that wrapped around the building. As I made my way through the lines seeking a shorter way, I lost harmony and returned to my body.

January 5, 2015
Early Morning

This morning's experience began with me in the company of a male and female angel. We drove to a city where my sister and a child were going to be marked. However, when time came for the marking, whether it was through mutual decision or if it was a one sided decision, I could not tell. But, for whatever reason, the angels decided against it. The angels decided my sister and the child were not ready to be marked yet. I will say that it is possible that my sister and the child decided that they were not ready to be marked, so the angels obliged. It was difficult to understand what the underlying factors were that caused the marking to not take place. All I recognized, was that the marking did not occur.

After this event, I walked to a store to gather my thoughts. I went inside a deli, went to the bathroom, and then purchased an iced tea. It was very lemony. The cashier wanted me to have a special hemp cup, but explained that it was for dine in visitors only. The cup was clear plastic wrapped with a thread

Glory

of hemp around it. Since I was not staying, she gave me a different cup for me to take on my journey. I left the building and looked for the angels I was with earlier. When I found them, the male and female angels wanted me to walk with them on the beach. I followed them, but fought with losing harmony in the tail-end of the experience.

January 5, 2015
Afternoon

Bryan sent me a newspaper article about a comet passing by the Earth today. It was only discovered in August of 2014, and will make its closest approach on January 7th. It is emitting a gas that causes it to turn blue-green. It appears beneath Orion in the Eastern sky. Though I try not to read into events like this, it is interesting that the event takes place on the exact day of the deadline when the angels told me I had twenty days left to understand their message. This was also a time when they mentioned we were traveling at seven hundred and forty-two feet per second. Though it is difficult for me to think that this comet is going to cause events with the Earth, it is interesting that it is estimated to be on a 10,000 to 12,500 year orbit with the sun. This corresponds to the last point in time that humanity started a new cycle on Earth. More likely, it could also be seen as a celestial marker beyond even the words that I have been shared with the angels. It should be noted that this comet is also the color of the "fifth sphere" and the "ninth ray"

The Written (conclusion)

– which are one-in-the-same. It passes between Earth and Mars on its orbit as well. So, overall, there are many interesting features that correspond with this event and the events I have been shared.

Perhaps even more interestingly, I supposed it could be seen how an event like this that corresponds with divine communication could be misinterpreted in the way that the comet-clans have demonstrated over the years when they take their lives at the closest point of a comet's passing to Earth. Though I emphasize this is a misinterpretation of communication, it is easy to see that these groups decided that they were being communicated at the same time as a celestial event and decided they should take their lives so that their souls could "hitch a ride" with the embodiment of souls on the comet. Again, I emphasize there are many things wrong with this idea, but for someone who does not quite understand all that is being shared, I am just saying it would be an easy misinterpretation of "finding a way back home."

January 6, 2015

During meditation, I saw my body pressed against a wall of water. I was facing the wall. The image had no context or any further detail. A few moments later, I saw a group of children, all wearing red shirts, on a first floor patio across the pavilion of my building. On Earth, this patio does not exist. But, in the image, it seemed perfectly in place. The group of

Glory

children in red were loud and I could not quite understand the context of their situation.

January 7, 2015

I awoke several times throughout the night having experienced new visions. But each time I awoke, they were so difficult to understand, I lost their details before I wrote them down. In one case, I thought I would be able to remember the handful of details I could recall, but could not even succeed in this.

January 8, 2015

Cloudy visions. I think that my fast is causing my brain to balance itself again with the change in intake. This was very similar to when I dry-fasted for three days about a month earlier. But, I was able to return with part of the experience. I was in a city that relied on the farmers surrounding the land to provide grains. An angel took me to a large silo that held the harvested grain. The angel said, "Survive by live-by-rules such that only certain grains will be grown. That way in grain stores, no seed from another crop will be inadvertently found that spoils the store." The angel then showed me how other seeds, which had somehow become mixed with the grain, began to take root and grow, thus destroying the grain in the silo.

The Written (conclusion)

That was all I could bring back with me due to the swirly sensations and loss of harmony upon returning.

January 9, 2015

This morning my soul was taken to the heavens by the Angel of the Lord. It was so clear, so vivid. Every aspect of the experience was concrete and real, yet with a heightened awareness of my spiritual body. The feeling was similar to the last time I fasted and the angels showed me how this generation on Earth would end. This time, though, the angel was responding to my prayer earlier in the evening. During that prayer I asked for guidance about what I am supposed to be doing, what this role would be that I would take in March, and how I am supposed to move forward. The angel appeared different than in the past. I think it was the strength that it portrayed that made me cautious of my actions.

In the experience, the Angel of the Lord took me to several different places where I understood there was a decision to be made. In each circumstance, the crowds of people needed Love and hope. The angel lifted me up to place me before the crowds, but I was afraid to stand in front of the crowd. I feared it was a test of ego, though the angel seemed to want me to see that my place would be a leader before mankind. However, I was more fearful of the possibility that it was a test than to become excited or humbled by the message. It seemed every time the angel let go of me before the people that I panicked, thinking that I was not strong enough to be their leader. I feared that the devil could more easily have his way by causing my ego to become forthright in my mind.

I feared it was unsafe for the people because they thought I was something I was not. I am a messenger (at least so it seems), and I feared the crowds could think otherwise and the energy could turn to unrest. The angel placed me in this situation over and over trying to get me to take the position before the crowd, but each time I returned back to the angel to let him know I was scared that I would be the weak link in such a grand opportunity. After I returned to my body, I prayed to my Father letting Him know I would gladly take the position if that was His Will, but I wanted to be sure it was His Will and not another test.

When I returned to the heavens, the situation was one of the most different experiences I have ever witnessed. During the entire encounter with the angels – and through all that they were speaking to me – I could not get past their appearance. It so overwhelmed me that I was unable to bring anything else back with me, even though when I went to write down the experience I thought for sure I had returned with more information. The appearances of the angels that so overwhelmed me, was a flashback to the very first experiences I ever had in the heavens. In the first experience where Bryan and I shared the same vision, we both were witness to a large alligator in a pool. The symbolism of the alligator became more apparent over time, but in the beginning it was difficult to understand. This time in the heavens, there was not just the

The Written (conclusion)

resurfaced archetype of the alligator that became apparent – it was that every angel and every soul bore the body of an alligator standing upright in human form. They all wore the same white gowns, but the face of the alligator was what was so mesmerizing.

For a moment, I am sure someone will run down the conspiracy theory side of things and start discussing the theoretical race of the Reptilians. However, I would caution upfront, that the message I was allowed to witness was, again, archetypal in form. The alligator archetype represented the transition from a mortal understanding of a body with a soul, to the spiritual understanding that each person is a soul trapped in a body, where we are each beginning to learn how to explore the heavens. Much like an alligator lives in the water, but must resurface for air and crawl along the shoreline from time to time, the soul lives in the heavens and must resurface in the form of a body on the Earth from time to time to grow. It is an archetypal understanding that Earth is not our home, but rather just a stop along the journey; however, we are always allowed back into His Kingdom when we humbly surrender to understanding the body is merely a vessel housing what we are.

I am sure at some point in humanity's history, someone witnessed the form of an alligator in his own spiritual experiences and thought very linearly about its meaning. Likely, he thought that the concept of the reptile represented a superior race…which in a way it did. However, the interpretation was not intended to be taken literally, but rather in archetypal form. This is how mankind blurs understanding of All That Is. We are all understanding one truth, blurred through the lenses of the egoic mind.

Once again I returned to the heavens. This time I arrived in a mall setting after the sun had set. I had just watched a movie and walked into the mall before it closed to find a "race" that was being held inside the mall. There was one specific black man who wanted to fight. He kept poking me as I walked around the area. Eventually, I decided it was best that I leave, and I ran out of the mall and down a steep V-shaped bank and scampered to the other side.

At this point, I noticed that the man who was running the "race" event inside of the mall turned on the sprinklers to help me get out safely. It was a concept of being drenched in water (aka the Spirit). The guy who had been constantly poking me gathered other people to chase after me. As I reached my vehicle, a woman appeared next to my open door. She was holding a baby. As I closed the door, the baby reached out its hand which caused the door to slam on its fingers. Though I saw what was happening and stopped it in time to prevent major damage, it was still a moment my stomach churned inside. At this point, I was able to close my door and leave, which returned me to my body.

The Written (conclusion)
January 10, 2015

Though I was confident I would remember all of the experience when I returned from the heavens to my body, all I was allowed to bring back with me was a number. It was either 3-1-4 or 3-1-6 (perhaps both). In the experience, I bore witness to some event that happened at a location which was referred to by this number. It is very easy to see that 3-1-4 could represent PI, which is a mathematical representation of God by demonstrating the perfection in a circle. It is also easy to see that 3-1-6 could represent John 3:16 – one of the most popular verses in the Bible. But the aspect that grabbed me the most, is that I have been told that I "will assume my role in March," and that if either of the numbers are understood as a date, this could also be when I "assume my role."

Whatever the role may or may not be is unimportant. That will all be revealed in due time. However, it is important that I understand all of the possibilities in what was being illustrated to me. Often times in interpretation, the most appropriate question to ask is, "Why can't it be all of the above?" Too often people try to find just one specific meaning in a word, a sentence, or a message. But the language of God is so multi-faceted that it must be understood in all possibilities, in all ways. Words and messages are divinely constructed so that each person can see what he is spiritually strong enough to see at that time, and what he will one day be spiritually stronger to see – though it will be in hindsight.

Glory

The romantic languages on Earth cloud the understanding of how the Word was originally intended to be used. The romantic languages presented a quite literal way to understand the word. These languages are somewhat like training wheels for the mind. The 800,000 words in the English language (for example), will one day give way to understanding how the original archetypes flow into multiple meanings simultaneously. But to understand the multiple meanings, one must first understand how to discern why one word is a better choice than another – because each word brings a slightly different energy with its use. This is not how most people think, so it is difficult for most people to transition into a multi-faceted understanding of words and images.

Consider this the next step of spiritual understanding. Once this foundation stone is understood as one of the core tenets to religion, this is when every splinter of truth in all facets of writing and words – regardless of its human source – becomes evident, like a grand symphony beginning to play its song. These are the beginnings to the divine architecture becoming unveiled. So, it is important for each person to strive to learn the archetypal form of the Divine so that he/she may one day see how the light shines through all.

January 13, 2015

After a few days of general haziness or blackness in my meditative state, I have begun to wonder if this was the end of

The Written (conclusion)

the onslaught of communication that has occurred with me over the past three years. There were also several external factors at play, though – so it was hard for me to discern all that was occurring. I had been fasting, as well as finishing up from an emotional conversation with my family recently. Overall, my mind has been out-of-sorts for the last several days. But today – the first full recovery day after my fast – I was placed into an interesting scenario in the heavens.

The experience began with the ding of a bell. It was the same sound that I heard at the end of another recent vision. The sound of the bell startled my soul into awareness of my surroundings. It was late at night, and I was on my way to work. The job ahead of me was not a job I work on Earth, and is not one I can recall having been part of any other visions. I was heading to a shoe store to work an evening shift and close it down. When I arrived, more and more people filled the store. I was one of two people working, though it seemed like I was the only one working most of the time. The crowd of people was rowdy. It was almost like a party was being thrown, but in a more sinister and reckless way. Eventually, everyone cleared out, and I locked one of the entrance doors. I knew I was not the only person in the store, but there was no one else to be seen. The presence was dark and sinister. It was the same feeling I had when the crowd of people was around. Whether those in the crowd of people were all bad, or just masking one presence, I cannot be sure.

I realized the only place the presence could be coming from was in the back storage area of the store. I was hesitant to go back there. As I thought about the feeling, a man came out of the back room holding a gun to the back of the female worker that I had seen at the very beginning of my shift. I talked to the man calmly, undeterred by the presence of his gun. I kept it very casual and made sure he did not do anything rash before I opened the door for him to leave. He left. I shut the store down and went home.

The next day I returned to the store to discuss the situation with the owner. He seemed pleased in the manner I handled it, but the takeaway from the whole experience seemed to be that darkness was setting in. If I am to understand the experiences in the heavens occurring simultaneously to Earth's timeline, then it could be seen that the darkness has been preparing to make a run at trying to become the more dominant force for some time. I returned to my body and wrote about the experiences.

When I returned to the heavens, I again witnessed another dark and brooding event. When I arrived, I immediately ran to a house that was being attacked by more dark souls. I ran into the house and helped a group of little girls escape from the house through a hidden panel in the back of a room. The panel opened up to a tunnel that allowed them all to reach safety. I found a different path of escape for myself so that if I were pursued, I would not place the lives of the children in danger.

When I reached the end of my escape path, the world opened up into another heaven. It was one of beauty and protection. It was a city of gold. The plant life was a green beyond

The Written (conclusion)

description, and the sky was cerulean. I found myself standing upon a golden cobblestone bridge constructed similarly to old French bridges. There was a white bistro table beside the sidewalk overlooking the river below. An angel was having a meal at the table with the children I had helped rescue. She invited me over so I could see how I had helped save the children.

January 14, 2015

As I first reached the heavens this morning, the scene began to transition into a large, outdoor cabana. There was a large bar with a black, granite counter that ran along the left hand side. It was rectangular in shape and circumscribed the kitchen and wait staff. As the scene fell into view, I saw one of the brunette female angels I see so often. She was sitting on one of the chairs having what appeared to be a cup of coffee or tea. She was facing me, to my left. When she turned her head to see me, my eyes met her austere gaze. It was such a strong gaze that I lost harmony with the moment and returned to my body.

As I tried to return, one of the male angels I see regularly fell into view…but, just as quickly, disappeared into the distance as I lost harmony with the heavens once again. I returned once more. This time, harmony and balance was held for the duration of the delivery of the angelic messages. The scenario began with me sitting at a table playing cards. I thought I was playing blackjack against one other person and the dealer. A crowd had gathered around having become intrigued at my presence. Though I could not understand the language being spoken, nor could I understand when I was to play my chips or what the chips even represented, I did continue winning. The constant winning was what continued to attract a greater crowd.

I do not know if I was lucky or if my soul understood the game well enough to continue winning, but whatever the case, I won more than anyone had ever won. This included several rare and exotic cars. To me, I did not know any of the object's values, so nothing held the emotional attachment that winning something on Earth may invoke. After the games finished, I attempted to drive away in one of the rare cars but was stopped. In the end, everything was taken away from me and returned back to the establishment. I was not really fazed by not coming away with anything. After all, I did not really care about the worth of any of it. It all seemed superficial…almost like toys for a child to play with. Sure, it would have been fun to drive the sleek, rare, exotic car that I began to drive away in, but it also was more for entertainment purposes than personal satisfaction or identity. I never felt attached to the winnings. It all seemed like toys given to a child to entertain while the adults are busy.

After the car was taken away, I saw the angel that reminds me of Dayton. He smiled at my situation. He made a comment about how well I must have done and commented on the rare car I was driving before it was taken away. I told him that

The Written (conclusion)

I was not concerned. In fact, until he brought it up, I did not think anyone would think twice about it. He laughed and said, "Yeah, I ran into the same situation. Come with me." He led me to a small table sitting beneath a great oak tree. There were two men playing a board game – the game was Risk. Both men were heavily entrenched in their strategies. I looked down next to the table and the game "Clue" was sitting next to the table. At that particular moment, I did not quite understand what I was being shown, but I took it in stride.

I suppose the angel sensed I did not quite understand, because I was placed into another scenario. This time, I was on a lawn of a great antebellum estate. The house was white. The tables and chairs outside were white. I was standing at a competitors' table for a card game. The way it was setup, each competitor had his own table. I was playing against one other person. It appeared that we were playing blackjack again. I did not understand the directions again since everything still seemed like it was spoken in a foreign language. I played the cards by the rules I knew from Earth. I won several hands immediately and was handed a large pile of pink poker chips. On one side, the chips were pink. On the other, the chips were white. The audience that had gathered appeared to be very affluent (or at least highly refined in mannerisms). They were all amazed at my streak of winning. In both situations I had been in, I do not recall losing a single hand.

An angel walked me away from the game and led me back to the same oak tree that I was led to before. I once again saw the board game Risk being played by two players and the board game Clue sitting next to the table. The angel led me back to the competitive game again, but I began to become overwhelmed by the symbolism. I began smiling and beaming with joy over recognition of the moment. Of course this caused me to lose harmony.

I took down the notes, and I began to think a long time about all that I was being shown. One of the things I have voluntarily given up in my walk with God is gambling. I wrestled with why God would choose to use this example as a means of communication with me. At first, I assumed that God was saying to see the "clue" He left for me to find, and take a "risk." I wondered if it was in reference to gambling or perhaps just in my walk with Him. Was He asking me to just take a leap of faith (and place any perceived financial risk in His hands? Perhaps He was even telling me how He would produce income through blackjack for me. After all, earlier in the day I had spoken with a friend and expressed frustration in not knowing when I should take a leap with everything He has called me to do. I know He knows I will take the leap with Him when I understand that directive clearly. This understanding was what made me first lose harmony in the heavens. At that particular moment, I thought I understood. I thought He said, "Jump!"

But as I prayed over the message, I understood that God would not place me into a situation that would go against the sacrifices I have made for Him. For example, gambling would not be an answer to income. This became more apparent as I thought about the imagery of how everything was taken away from me after winning. So, the message was not meant to con-

The Written (conclusion)

vey earthly gambling. However, the pink and white chips were intriguing to me. I have continually been shown pink imagery denoting my walk. This is equivalent to the pink advent candle lighting the way for the Messiah's arrival. So, in a way, it seems that God's message was that He has placed the chips in my court to do great things. But it was also clear in seeing everything taken away from me in the first experience that I must understand that God's chips are not for me alone. They are meant for the world. And, if I cannot deliver that message to everyone, then I most certainly will not personally receive benefit from His work in my life.

And while that is a heavy thought, mixing in the setting of the board game played beneath the great oak tree is even heavier. To begin, the game was played beneath a tree that could represent the tree of knowledge. The game Risk is perhaps inappropriately named because it is actually a strategy game. Six continents have forty-two territories. Meaning, this averages seven territories per continent. The goal is to strategically win the right territories so you can win the war. If, for just a moment, the game could be seen as a battle between good versus evil, God versus Lucifer, then it is easy to see that seeing the game Risk is understanding that there is a strategy in God's plan. It is understanding that His strategy is the micro and the macro, and the understanding of my role is merely a piece on the game board helping Him commandeer His chosen territories. It can also be understood that His strategy must also be mirrored through my actions. This means that while taking leaps of faith are important, they are not really risky because God is providing all along. They are strategic. God's call to action must always be seen as strategic.

When I looked up the origin of the name risk, I inadvertently ran across a company's marketing flyer talking about the role of a Chief Risk Officer. At first it would be easy to think this was just a mismatched search result, but it was a very divine moment. The document elaborated on how a Chief Risk Officer should prepare with what he knows, and what is unknown. It was a very good read and cleverly written. If I were to understand my role as a Chief Risk Officer in the role God has tasked me with in His plan, then it is important to understand risk through this same viewpoint to see how He has prepared me thus far. He has placed a portion of His chips in me, and it is up to me to manage the strategy and move forward. It is not risk if there is strategy. And in either case, God is holding me so it is not as if I am figuring out how to hold on. This is merely learning how to run with what He has placed in me. I am sure there is much more to this message. Even now, I can interpret my next step in a myriad of ways. But perhaps the most important aspect is I understood the concept of strategy versus risk. I also understood that God placed me in this territory for a reason, and that He is providing the means for me to continue serving Him in this space.

The Written (Conclusion)

January 18, 2015

This morning's travels to the heavens were as apocalyptic as I have ever experienced. The experience was long, though the details may seem sparse. The experience began with an angel showing me the end of this generation. I saw mass graves prepared across the beaches and the shorelines. I was taken through the cities and the mainland where I also witnessed the waste and ruins of the destruction. There were no survivors that I could see. I did not sense that hope was lost, but I was able to see that the majority of those who remained on Earth during this time would suffer casualty. And while the experience was incredibly long and detailed, I wasn't allowed to bring it all back with me. I was only allowed to see it in detail, and return with the highlights.

After I was returned to Earth, I journaled the experience and returned to the heavens. This time I arrived at a grand house of Indian culture. It was made of alabaster and marble. There were large columns at the front of the house. There was a large courtyard with a fountain in the interior of the house surrounded on three sides by the structure. On the side furthest from the entrance, the house backed up to a mountainous cliff overlooking the ocean.

An angel appeared wearing a blue shirt. It became clear that I had arrived at a social gathering at this house. There was a feeling of spirituality in a Hindu-like embodiment. I was escorted through this grand house as if it was a tour before I could settle in for the event. After time had passed, I walked back into the courtyard. I was in search of a bag that I had arrived with and was becoming frantic because I could not find it. I thought I may have left it by the fountain when I initially toured the gardens. As I walked outside, I saw the courtyard and gardens begin to flood over with the sea. We were extremely high up, so the water must have risen hundreds of feet. I stood upon the edge of the fountain, unsure how to escape or where to go. At that point, an angel arrived to take me to safety. I was taken inside the house and given a blanket to keep warm. I walked over to a couch that was alongside a stairwell that led to a second level. I pulled the blanket over my head and tried to warm up.

While I was attempting to remain warm, I sensed the presence of someone draw near. The energy felt extremely negative. Suddenly, the being tried to suffocate me and perform crude acts to me through the blanket. I felt the breath of the demon try to lick my face through the blanket. It was a form of humiliation as it attempted to suffocate me. I was stark naked beneath the blanket, and I was afraid to pull myself out from underneath its warmth and safety. As I fought with the demon, an angel came and cast it off of me. The angel then placed me in a vehicle, and we left the house. There was now a female and a male angel with me in the car. We drove in search of a store similar to a Home Depot but never found one. There was a sense of foreboding that I could only take what was with me. The shirt I wore to the house, my writing, and everything else was left behind.

The Written (conclusion)

I could not help but think this must be how we will one day be rescued during the apocalypse. Revelation talks about being clothed and prepared to leave. In the first experience, I was shown an apocalyptic destruction forthcoming. In the second, I was shown a flood of tremendous proportions happening and being saved from the demons. The water was flooding the Earth, cleansing it of its disease and darkness. It was a Baptism of sorts…a washing away of the filth that has inhabited existence. If this was a sign of the end, it was most importantly a sign of hope for a new beginning. Those who are righteous and obey shall be saved. Those who do not, will be washed away.

January 19, 2015

This morning's travels to the heavens involved an experience with a female angel I could not see. This female spoke to me telepathically, though I visualized it through a phone conversation. I could see that the angel liked me, but it was hard for me to comprehend being liked by an angel. This seems to be occurring with more frequency for me in the heavens. Perhaps the term angel should best be seen as the angelic souls. It does not change what they are. I do want to clarify that there is a distinction to certain factions of angels. The elder angels I try to refer to as elders, great angels, large, or even by their names. I wanted to make a distinction here because I hope that these words are not misinterpreted. I am just as much trying to understand how all of this works as the reader will no doubt attempt to dissect the words and phrasings I have used. I hope that I continue to be delicate and careful in all of the phrasings, but I also want to make sure the story is not misconstrued or dismissed because the reality I have experienced is so distant from even some of the grandest expectations. I certainly did not see this aspect of heavenly relationships forthcoming.

So, returning to the story, as I tried to understand the intentions of the angel speaking to me, I realized that she wanted to find clarity in our relationship. It sounded like we were friends who enjoyed each other's company, but she now had feelings for me. I could tell she was trying to muster up the courage to ask me out. I helped the conversation along so she would eventually ask me. When she eventually did find the courage, I responded with a simple "Okay." She seemed surprised, relieved, and shocked in one giant burst of emotions. And while I could tell we had interacted enough in the heavens to form a bond, in truth I struggle to identify spiritual identities that I have interacted with since it is rare I get a name, and appearances change. Those two challenges alone create a conundrum of indescribable proportions. It is like trying to remember a song without remembering the words or melody. Mostly, I just have to trust my instinct. If I had taken the time with someone, it must mean that there is a deeper connection which should be explored.

It is possible that this is the same girl that I saved from the darkness and from a demon earlier in the evening. And while

The Written (conclusion)

it is difficult for me to say if this incident occurred before or after, for I saw the experience twice – once before and once after the phone call with the girl – the experience of saving a girl was important to bring back to Earth with me. It was during this portion of the experience that I arrived at a location that appeared similar to a college campus.

I arrived in an armored vehicle that was large enough to absorb the blast of a roadside bomb. I parked in the middle of the driveway to the building and opened the door. It opened vertically downward and revealed steps that reached to the ground. I got out of the vehicle and walked up to the glass building. There was a girl sitting outside, whom I was supposed to meet. As we spoke, a group of evil spirits showed up and began attacking everyone. I managed to get her to safety and then return to my tank before chasing off the evil spirits. While I did not understand why I had arrived in a tank initially, it was now clear that it was needed for protection in the ongoing battle of angels and demons. After returning to the vehicle and eliminating the darkness, I returned to my body.

January 20, 2015

This morning's experience in the heavens was very hazy. There are just a few scant details that I can recall. An angel talked to me about driving "her" ten hours to a place that sounded like "Trula, Mississippi" after which, they would fly "her" back. The girl who was the subject of the ten-hour drive was unnamed. It seemed like I did not know who she was, yet she could have been someone I possibly had saved from the darkness during another hazy vision that occurred the previous day. It is also possible that "trula" could have been "True Love" though all of the details were so hazy and out of focus. The angel's name was Landon (or something similar sounding). I was then spoken to by a female angel asking me about my daughter. I was confused as to who the angel was since she spoke of my daughter as if she was "our" daughter. The angel did not seem like anyone I knew. It was at this time I lost harmony and returned to my body. Though all of the notes from this vision seem abstract and vague, this was all I could return with from the experience.

January 21, 2015

This morning's experience began in a forest. There were two houses tucked away deep in the thick forest. An angel appeared. She was blonde and standing with a child. Though she was not my ex-wife, there was a familiarity about her that reminded me of her being family. I felt like she was my spiritual wife…perhaps someone I had left and would one day return to when my time on Earth is complete. The child seemed like my child. I was very confused at the feelings seeing as this was not my ex, but someone of similar emotional feeling.

However, I did understand that this beautiful angel was involved with someone else. She let me know that her husband

The Written (conclusion)

was out and that she wanted to spend time with me. And though I felt extremely guilty for allowing myself to enter between a couple, it seemed like we were always one. She was my other half. I cannot explain it. Nor does it justify the actions, because they were wrong. This is not anything I have ever done on Earth, nor is it anything I have allowed myself to do in the heavens. But the warmth of her Love was so different than anything I had felt. I truly wondered if we were a couple in the heavens, and when I return to Earth, she returns to her spouse. It seems crazy. I know. But, these were the thoughts going through my head.

During our afternoon together, we frolicked and played with each other, enjoying the feeling of our skin upon each other. At one point, I held her body high in the air with one arm and had her bend backwards so that the arch of her back was high over my head. There was one moment that I ran my tongue down her back and between open legs. The taste was like a bitter metal. I cannot explain it another way. It was not a bad taste or sensation. It just seemed more like a bitter metal...or maybe a better description would be an electrical impulse to my tongue. It was more akin to touching a 9-volt battery to the tongue – which now, I suppose, in hindsight makes sense.

Our bodies are full of electrical impulses. At the most primal level, I experienced an impulse between us. When I reacted to the unexpected jolt of electricity, she became upset. I moved my attention to pleasuring her body rather than seeking my own pleasure. It was clear in this moment that she

Glory

(whoever she may actually be) was my one true Love. I knew I would never stop loving her. After we had spent the afternoon together, with the sunlight pouring in through the windows of her humble house, I told her that I could not continue doing this with her because it hurt so hard when I had to leave. And though it was tearful for us to part ways, this would not be the end of the experience.

Later in the day, I returned to her house. I had been invited to dinner, and I thought I should oblige. I spent time sitting on the couch as the woman prepared dinner. But, this time, her husband was home. He came in, would make small talk with me, and then he would return to the kitchen to help. The child was running around and was excited to see me. She was perhaps around the age of seven. At one point, I got up and walked into the kitchen to converse with everyone. I felt like an outcast in the living room...probably even more so than I should in light of the events from earlier in the day.

While I stood in the kitchen, the child ran into the room and made a comment that indicated I had been over there earlier in the day. The woman laughed it off and corrected the child's phrasing. The child was smart enough to understand that she almost said too much, though I would never ask a child to hold the burden of that knowledge. It was, quite honestly, one of the hardest decision-moments I have experienced in the heavens. Everything about it seemed so wrong, yet everything was as if it was placed in this experience specifically for me to see.

The Written (conclusion)

January 24, 2015

This morning's experience was short. The setting was similar to the promenade outside of my apartment, but distinctly different. In this setting, all of the buildings that were on the beach were interconnected by a large promenade covered in stone tile. I watched as a helicopter came into view. The pilot was having a hard time maintaining course. He flew the helicopter as close as he could to a couple of buildings to the south of my building where he eventually was able to land it on the promenade. On top of the helicopter was a giant blue box. It was as large as the radius of the blades. As I stared at the box, keen to its out-of-place and unusual appearance, I heard a voice say, "Do you think it is there for her to jump?" I looked around and could not see a person about to leap, nor could I see the angel speaking to me. I wondered if the girl that was being referenced was the same girl I see periodically in the heavens with me. She usually has a hard time flying or driving the vehicles she appears in. As my mind drifted, I lost harmony and returned to my body.

January 26, 2015

This morning's experience was hazy. But, after a couple of days of tough sleep patterns, any travel should be viewed as a blessing. This experience was a little different than others I have had. It began with me being enticed by a woman whom I

Glory

found extremely attractive. We talked for a while before she suggested we go back to my place. It was clear that she wanted to have sex. But, while I was extremely into her, this is a subject matter that I have always observed as a test of character in the heavens.

I wanted to get to know her more rather than jump into bed with her. That would break my moral compass. So, I did the only thing I could think of to make the best of the situation for each of us. I decided we should go back to my place and then get to know each other. She was not aware that I was going to stand by my moral convictions because I pretended to be okay with her innuendo.

No sooner than we left the building, I started to have a sinking feeling inside. I knew that I was misleading her even if it was for reasons I thought were just. The reason for my sadness was that I was having to figure out how to let her down gently without it wrecking her self-esteem – all while still showing interest. When we arrived at my place, I took off my shoes and socks. It also seemed like I did not have a shirt on, though I could not recall taking it off. There I stood in the living room in front of my couch, barefoot, only wearing pants. It was at this point I realized that everything had gone too far.

Even though I had the best of intentions, the consequences of the actions were going to far outweigh my hope for finding goodness in the moment. I knew it was time to tell her. She was still standing just inside the doorway. I walked over to her to come clean about my intentions. I lost harmony and returned to my body.

The Written (conclusion)
January 27, 2015

Finally, after what seemed like one of the most frustrating months in my ability to maintain harmony in the heavens, I experienced a series of events that were all incredibly detailed. I really think that much of the challenge has been due to the different attempts at fasting which have resulted in different eating patterns and changes to my typical sleep schedule. The stress of not knowing what events (foretold to me) were taking place in January of this year coupled with my own procrastination in writing and stumbling forward in how to tell the world the Messiah is coming all seemed to create a perfect storm of imbalance within. Think of it like a snow globe shaken up. The snow settling is the equivalent of finding balance with the heavens again. So, it was with great excitement that this morning's experiences occurred with so much detail and clarity.

The first experience seemed benign at first, but as I wrote down the details, the archetypal meaning became much more apparent. The scenario began with me on a snow slope. There was an angel standing with me as we watched a person snowboard down the slope. The slope was somewhat like a mix between a ski slope and a half-pipe. The angel and I stood on one half of the track that went below. This was symbolic of the heavens and the Earth's spheres expanding and contracting upon each other and the journey between. As we watched the snowboarder, he began boarding down the hill and then went up a steep incline and stopped. It was as if he was going to

Glory

gather his thoughts for a trick he was about to perform. However, he did not choose to take the plunge. It was a long, fast slope that would have been terrifying for anyone to attempt. Instead, he was disqualified.

I walked over to see him. Everyone was chanting his name. I was sent over by the angel. Though I understood the angel sending me on symbolically meant "the end," I ascended the mountain, made my way through the trees, and came across a cabin in the woods. It was here that I strapped on the snowboard and understood that the next move I made would define everything that was to come. I stepped outside and saw the steep, winding path that I was destined to follow. Knowing that the last three years have been an effort in building spiritual strength in the heavens (as exemplified through football, ice-skating, skiing, hockey, etc.), this was a defining moment...a moment where everyone would witness the faith I had in my Father, and the willingness to defy all logic and reason to attempt to do the unthinkable.

I took the leap and started my speedy descent. The path curled hard to the right. I leaned into the curve and came through it wide, but still tightly enough to stay on the path and avoid the trees lining the sides of the narrow path. The speed was incredible. It was a rush of spiritual energy coupled with every earthly feeling of wind and chill across my skin. As I flew down the path, I saw the half-pipe ramp ahead where it would send me into the most difficult jump any snowboarder had ever attempted (and seemingly no one had successfully completed). I heard someone in the crowd say, "Oh! Oh my!

The Written (conclusion)

No, he isn't going to attempt this?! Is he? He is!! Hey everyone! Watch him! Watch this!! He is going for it!"

I could feel the eyes of the angelic spectators fall upon me. As they watched, I braced for the jump. I leapt with every bit of faith and confidence in my body. I ascended into the air, and landed on the other side of the mountain successfully. With great fanfare and acclaim, I heard the roar of the angels as I completed the difficult jump. Everyone cheered. "The girl" was waiting for me. She could not believe I made it, though she clarified she had never lost faith in me. As we stood on the other side in the landing area, I began to see giant commercial airliners flying in formation as bombing planes. They were extremely low on the horizon. I could have thrown a rock and hit the aircrafts if I had tried.

I looked at the angel, understanding the message. I said, "Maybe we were the enemy after all." In those words, I meant "we" as in "The United States" but perhaps it also carried the more global meaning of "mankind." The angel smiled. I watched as the planes left and returned once again. The planes were all silver and had a giant red circle on either side of their tails. And while the red circle is typically recognized as Japan's flag, it seemed as if the symbol was archetypal in meaning rather than denoting a specific body of people. As I looked upward at the planes, I still thought I was witnessing "us" as the enemy. The planes dropped even further to the ground to begin a bombing run. The angel and I ran to a location that resembled the cabin I originally found on the mountain. She explained to me how the caverns that ran underneath the cabin also ran throughout the mountainside. I was afraid that the bombing would trap us inside the tunnels though.

I ran outside while being chased by one of the bombers. The planes' wings were made of an unbreakable material. It rolled sideways enough to dip the tip of the wing and plow the ground. I could not tell if it was trying to annihilate me, or if I just happened to be in its path. However, in writing this, it could also be seen as a gardener plows the field...a harvest if you will. The planes were tilling the field and planting seeds (bombs) for the next generation. I raced down the mountainside and through the trees. I saw five dogs with leashes tied together and placed on a hook on a tree. They were barking and acting frantic. Just past the dogs, I ran into the edge of the property the angel had taken me to. The property was surrounded with chicken wire. I began climbing the fence to try to get out, but I realized the chicken wire just continued to form wherever I climbed. I could then begin to see that I was actually in a sanctuary of sorts...a safe place to survive the destruction.

As I climbed the fence, my mind raced with the possibilities. On the outside of the fence, hordes of zombie-like people were crawling all along the outside trying to get in. I saw death. I saw soul-less people. Eventually, the arc of the fence caused me to fall back down where the five guard dogs were tied to the tree. When I picked myself up, I saw that the leashes had fallen from the tree. I grabbed the leashes and commanded the dogs to sit. At first I was scared of the dogs.

The Written (conclusion)

But I also recognized dominion over the animals, and therefore, realized they would heed my command. The dogs cowardly sat down. One dog was a golden retriever. At least one was a Rottweiler. The others could have been Rottweilers, but also may have been different breeds. The golden retriever obeyed first and sat down in its place. It did not sit with the group, so I commanded it to sit with the other dogs. I realized the dogs were there to protect the sanctuary from the soul-less people on the outside. I stood and watched again as planes began to bomb.

It was at this point that I flashed into a different scenario. A male angel and I were standing on a mountaintop. I asked the angel, "Where is the course?" He responded, "It is right here – wherever you want it to be. You just have to get your board moving in either direction so you can discover the course." I looked around us as the landscape seemed wide open with no defined direction. I asked if I could go up the mountain instead of down. By asking this question, I meant it as in defying physics. I was curious if I could increase speed upwardly just as a person would typically increase speed when boarding down a hill.

The angel seemed pleased with my question, but was clearly baffled that I would ask. He said, "You can. You just need to get your board moving over black ice." He then pointed toward the icy landscape in a location that seemed just as normal as its surrounding areas. I immediately understood that the way to ascend was to find the slick portions hidden from everyone's eyes. In an earthly sense, black ice is invisible

Glory

ice that has formed on roads. Often, black ice causes accidents because people did not avoid the slick spots. But, in this case, the reference to black ice meant to find the spirit hidden within. The parts of the ice that would scare others and send them spiraling out of control was the very part I was instructed to use to kick start the momentum in a seemingly impossible direction through earthly eyes. It was at this point that I tossed my board out and chased after it to jump onto it, but it skirted off the black ice more quickly than I could catch up to it. I retrieved my board and began to attempt it again...this time, successfully timing the throw and jump so that I could begin my ascent. At this point I began to lose harmony and return to my body.

When I returned to the heavens, I heard a voice say, "Go tell the angel you are ready to climb the mountain." I picked up a two-way radio and placed a call to an angel named Robert. I told him I was ready. He said, "Very good. Your next step is for two years..." The weight of the world hit me when I recognized I was receiving instructions. I heard "two years" and immediately felt resolve in knowing that I had a task that was longer than the dates shared with me before. While I was never sure if I would be taken from the Earth over the next few months, I did begin to see that -whether on Earth or the heavens – God's plans for me are still unfolding. I lost balance in that moment. And though I tried to hold on to hear the instructions, I could not maintain harmony with the thoughts racing in my mind. As I returned to Earth, the parting words I heard were, "Very good now."

The Written (conclusion)

I returned to the heavens. This time I was in a warehouse setting. I heard a conversation discussing me and "my handler." I walked through a set of double doors and said, "It won't be a problem anymore. I won't let it interfere." This was the only aspect of the conversation up to this point that I was allowed to bring back with me. The context was blurred. I am not quite sure what I was describing as a "problem," but I know that my earthly walk will mirror the commitment I made in the heavens through my word. The angel responded to my words, "You Noahs all have a [choice]..."

As I heard how the angel referenced me as a "Noah" my mind began racing again. The name Noah was being used as an archetypal descriptor. It caused me to lose clarity on the rest of the sentence. I thought the angel was saying the word "choice" indicating that anything that was interfering was still voluntary, and that I did not have to cut out completely whatever it was to which I was referring. It was almost a reply that was enlightening me on moderation rather than all-or-nothing. In either case, the context was again blurred as I lost harmony and returned to my body.

I returned to the heavens once again. I again heard the voice speaking to me upon my arrival. I found myself under a sheet of clear ice, staring up at the sun. I was not drowning. I felt safe. But I could only watch through the ice until it melted away. It was a feeling of pure bliss. And while I am sure there is more to be understood in the meaning, at this particular time, I understood it to mean that I was staring at the light of God as it melted away the barrier for me between Heaven and

Glory

Earth. I turned and swam over to a dry area that was still beneath the ice. I walked toward a door, opened it, and walked outside. I returned to my body.

I returned to the heavens once again. Again, the voice was speaking to me. The voice gave me the number 464 (or possibly 467, the number on the far right was transmuting upon itself) before I lost balance. These numbers were specific to my walk with God, though I was unsure of the meaning.

I returned to the heavens again. When I arrived, I heard the voice tell me, "Listen. You have been given everything to begin." I opened my eyes and saw a room that was similar to that of a doctor's office. It was impressed upon me to "seek His voice in the silence." This was important. It seemed like the angel was helping me understand I would need to make sure I had quiet time everyday for just the Lord and me. There was a special emphasis placed upon the phrase, "the silence." I acknowledged that I understood my set of instructions and was returned to my body.

I arrived once again in the heavens. The setting was similar to the road my condo is on. There was a construction sign blocking the entrance of the stretch of road used to access my building by vehicle. It was the kind of sign that has orange flashing bulbs spelling out a short caution phrase. The sign read, "Road closed. 40-21." I understood that the sign was a reference to a date where the first number, 40, represented a month. At first I though "April" out loud, but it was then impressed upon me that the month was March. I returned to my body.

The Written (conclusion)

When I returned to the heavens, I was asked by the angel about "my next decision." The angel explained to me how "actions can be tough." The angel then said, "The first will dismantle you. The third will attack you like a snake." I was then shown an image of a snake eating its tail, creating the shape of a circle. The angel did say something about the second step, but it was a blur as I tried to make sure I heard all of his words. I was returned to my body to make sure I could write down these words.

I returned once again to the heavens. In my immediate periphery was the number "1." The image was written in a block style, with the outline of the number a deep red, the interior white, and the sign white. The angel explained to me that I was now being "tasked with getting started." I was returned to my body once again.

I was returned one last time to the heavens, where I was placed before three spinning red roses. They were stemless and viewed from above. The roses were in the shape of a triangle on a white background. Each of the roses was spinning clockwise, and the entire shape was moving slowly in a clockwise motion. I understood the roses to be symbolic of God and the Trinity. I understood the image to mean it was time for me to go and start the tasks given to me. I returned to Earth.

January 28, 2015

In this experience in the heavens, I was walking toward a pizza place when two police officers offered to give me a ride. Typically the appearance of a police officer in these experiences is uneventful, but foreboding. But, this time it seemed peaceful. The officers wanted to help me. When they asked where I was going, they thought they understood the pizza place's location. However, it became abundantly obvious that they were taking me to another pizza location. I was not upset about it since they offered to give me a ride. I wanted to make sure they felt peace in knowing they helped me, rather than telling them they led me to the wrong destination. When they dropped me off, they each smiled at me seemingly proud of their effort. They drove off down the city street, and I turned to go into the building. I walked into the restaurant, glanced at the menu, and made sure I had given the officers enough lead time to leave. After some time had passed, I exited the building and began walking down the street to find my way to my intended destination.

January 30, 2015

This experience began in a coffee shop. It was one that seemed familiar, though not one of earthly origin. I stood at the counter waiting for the barista to finish making my order. After I received my coffee, I turned to leave the building. Sit-

The Written (conclusion)

ting next to the door was Joel – a man I have gotten to know on Earth. It should be noted that he pronounces his name like an angel, with the emphasis on the "El." I have never met any other person named "Joel" who pronounces it like "Jo-El." But Fort Lauderdale is a special place, filled with angels and I cannot help but think, if for no other reason, that his name is intended at the very least to keep my awareness in check. He is also a person whom another friend, Kelly, has become friends with. Though it is easy to see from the outside, I think it may be difficult for each of them to see everything happening from within. But regardless, in my earthly walk I know they are trying to become better friends.

As I was leaving the coffee shop, I made sure to say hello to Joel before turning to my right and exiting the front door. It was dark outside. As I walked down the sidewalk, Kelly came into view. She smiled at me like a child in Love, though it was not a Love for me. I smiled back knowing she was blissfully happy. I asked her if she was going to meet up with Joel, to which she said that she was. She could not keep back her gushing smile. I kept walking, knowing that my presence in both of their lives was helping them draw closer together. Be it friends or be it Lovers, at the very least their souls are closer to the Source in the presence of each other.

Seventh Revelation

The Seventh Revelation is the foreshadowing of how the Books of Nine will eventually end. For through all of His words, and all of the experiences He has allowed me to see, there is only a portion that could be revealed through these words alone. It has not been that I have removed anything, for all of the travels to the heavens have been included. Rather, there is a portion of The All that is constant and fluid in conversation during the daily walk. It is through the fluidity of the way He talks that the rest of the story has been foretold. But in this final revelation – one of the final moments He would share with me as He walked with His daughter, my bride, down the aisle of His grand cathedral – the anointing and splashing of the water upon my face would say everything ever needed.

...

February 3, 2015

After several days of very few heavenly travels, a sadness has started to set in. I know that this is not the end to my travels to the heavens, but I am aware that it is the beginning of the end. The communion with the angels and His divine Love require two more tests of me before he will allow me to see. This is what He meant when He told me that I "must seek [Him] twice, the latter because [He] must be sought." It is only then that He will pull back the veil from His Daughter's eyes – my bride – if I am so deemed worthy. And when our eyes first meet, this will be the true understanding of "seeing" for it was her eyes always waiting for me. The Wedding Banquet will be a grand day, a day preceding the return of the Messiah, a day reserved for the completion of this portion of the spiritual journey.

So as I prayed this afternoon in hopes that He would still allow for our communion to continue in the heavens, I knew quite well that this could be the last day – at the very least – of the written portion of the journals. And while I cannot think of a better way for Him to have illustrated an "until I see you when you seek me again conversation," the simple nature of the experience is one that should require no explanation. As I closed my eyes and found harmony within, I sought and I prayed for His will to be revealed. It was at this moment I felt my face splashed with water. I returned to my body and could only smile in that moment.

Requisition

And so as it was once foretold thousands of years ago, these writings are part of the story all will one day come to know. The writings in books IV, V, VI, & VII are the detailed journals of how a man came to know Him Father, and how His Father revealed The Way. The truth was always there to be seen, though it would take hindsight and the eyes of the soul to see it after God shined His light upon His Divine. The experiences of mankind are God's classroom for salvation. The Way is not easy. It is not simple. It is not meant to be, for each person must prove himself worthy of receipt of salvation. It was never intended to be something deserved, but rather it has forever been intended to be something earned through demonstration.

It is only standing upon the footsteps of the altar and seeing the Bride of Christ step into view, that the purpose of the not-so-simple journey is revealed to be oh, so simple. It is Love. It has always been Love, as it will always be. The triumphs of following His Way were always leading to salvation. In the moments ahead, where these words are no longer continued, will be the unveiling of Her eyes – and in that – an invitation to say "I do" and enter through the doorway of His Kingdom's temple.

...

*From generations and generations to come,
this is the revelation of the coming of the Messiah.*

...

www.ingramcontent.com/pod-product-compliance
Lightning Source LLC
Chambersburg PA
CBHW021138080526
44588CB00008B/107